MEDICINE AND ETHNOLOGY

ERWIN H. ACKERKNECHT

MEDICINE
AND ETHNOLOGY

Selected Essays

EDITED BY
H. H. WALSER AND H. M. KOELBING

THE JOHNS HOPKINS PRESS
BALTIMORE, MARYLAND

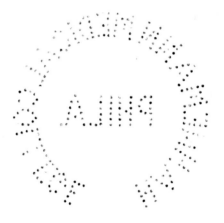

Published in Switzerland by
Verlag Hans Huber Bern Stuttgart Vienna 1971

Published in the United States of America by
The Johns Hopkins Press, Baltimore, Maryland 21218

Library of Congress Catalog Card Number: 70-165334
International Standard Book Number: 0-8018-1307-7

TABLE OF CONTENTS

INTRODUCTION: AN INTERVIEW WITH ERWIN H. ACKERKNECHT

ETHNOLOGY AND MEDICINE

Editors: Perhaps we might talk first about the situation of ethnology in relation to the history of medicine, particularly in Europe. As a matter of fact, you are one of the very rare historians of medicine who really know something about ethnology.

Ackerknecht: Well, you want to reproduce these old articles of mine. I feel somewhat embarrassed to republish work which has been done so long ago, and the only justification I can see for doing so is that since I wrote these articles, they have not been replaced by new work and they are still used in teaching in the United States. You ask me about the situation in Europe. As a matter of fact, ethnology in Europe is far less active than ethnology in the United States, but even in the United States, no new work in this particular direction has been done.

E.: Isn't that rather astonishing?

A.: It is, I think, rather natural. By the way, I should qualify: work in detail has been done, but what has always been lacking, is an attempt to summarize all this field work and to draw some conclusions from it. That the ethnologists are somewhat shy of doing it, is obvious: they are no medical people. They will make some (most of the time wrong) statements on psychopathology, because everybody knows something about this subject. But when it comes to bodily disease, they will abstain, and wisely so.

The medical people are no ethnologists and can not handle this material properly, because their notion of medicine is so different from what they find there. This is quite obvious from the older histories of medicine: in so far as they start with a chapter on primitive medicine, it is usually a projection of our medicine into the world of the Primitives, and then some remarks about their "queer superstitions". But what they usually try to emphasize in primitive medicine are its rational traits, which do exist, but are not so preponderant as they make us believe.

That is also the reason why medical historians are still so obsessed by the evolutionary idea. They stick to the old evolutionary concept that primitive medicine is a predecessor of modern medicine. They do not study it as a thing in itself, worthy to be studied as an organism in itself, but rather as a kind of an embryo which, when it has grown and

7

been properly delivered by the Renaissance, becomes modern medicine.

E.: This is an important point. But what do you think of the current identification of primitive medicine and prehistoric medicine? The medicine of primitive communities of our own time may be quite different from the medicine of our prehistoric ancestors.

A.: Of course, you have got to differentiate the two, but the basic traits are probably very similar. On the other hand, the difference between primitive medicine and folk medicine, which is very often mixed up with it, is enormous. Folk medicine is quite a thing in itself, it contains primitive elements, but to the same extent or even more, it contains degenerate "high medicine", official medicine. I should say, folk medicine today consists of perhaps 10 % primitive medicine and 90 % Galenism, to term it very crudely.

E.: Sometimes, adorned with some modern technical devices such as electrical or pseudo-electrical contraptions –

A.: – some misunderstood modern technology. I entirely agree. Let's say then: 10 % primitive medicine, 50 % Galenism and 40 % misunderstood modern technology.

FROM MARXISM TO PRIMITIVE MEDICINE

E.: Let us pass now to another question – a biographical one: How did you come to that singular combination of medical history and ethnology? You studied ethnology in Paris as well as in the United States...

A.: Exactly. Well, as is clearly visible from my Leipzig M.D. thesis of 1931, I was a convinced Marxian at that time. This led to my leaving Germany for France in 1933. The events of 1933 inspired me with strong doubts as to the absolute value of the Marxian theory, and living in France, I looked for new theories, new values, new methods, and so ran into French sociology, which is very closely connected with French ethnology. I got particularly enthused by the work of LUCIEN LÉVY-BRUHL, who was originally a philosopher, then turned, in connection with EMILE DURKHEIM and the Durkheim school, into a sociologist and ended up as one of the great ethnological theoreticians. This inspired me so much that I studied ethnology in France. It is also typical that one of my main teachers, MARCEL MAUSS, was in the same time a sociologist and a theoretical ethnologist. I studied MAUSS, DURKHEIM, HALBWACHS, LÉVY-BRUHL.

E.: So you started with Marxism, you came to sociology –

A.: – and ended up with ethnology. Now, having studied the field and worked in it, I had, like every modern scientist, to specialize, and the most natural thing was that I should specialize in primitive medicine, as I knew medicine and ethnology. By accident, I just *had* this combination.

E.: You studied ethnology in Paris –

A.: I came to Paris in 1933. I finished studying in Paris in 1939 and took my exams in ethnology at the Sorbonne, just before the war.

E.: And the medicine you had from Germany.

RUTH BENEDICT'S FUNCTIONALIST APPROACH

A.: When I took this ethnology diploma in 1939, I had already studied ethno-medical questions for years. I had even started research work, but then the war came, interrupted it for two years and I had to go to the United States. In the United States, I came under the theoretical and personal influence of RUTH BENEDICT. And it is really Ruth Benedict who liberated me from the evolutionary obsession we spoke of. (I could have learned this also from some English "functionalist", but I actually learned it from an American one.) Ruth Benedict's approach, which in a way you can compare to the "Gestalt" approach in psychology, looks at primitive medicine (a) as an element of the "total culture pattern" as she called it, and (b) not primarily as an object of evolutionary studies, but – if you want it that way – from the functional point of view: what does medicine do in the given society?

E.: Might one put it perhaps like that: the evolutionist sees primitive medicine as a starting point, while you, studying with Ruth Benedict, came to look at it not as a starting point, but as the result of an earlier evolution, something already grown up?

A.: No, I would not put it that way. I would disregard entirely the question of evolution. I would regard primitive medicine as an organism, not as an embryo, although not as an old man either, but just as an organism, which I study in function. I think, this is the so-called functionalist's point of view, which was invented, I guess, by MALINOWSKI, who originally was a zoologist, a Pole working in the South Seas, England and the United States.

E.: Isn't that a feature of your approach to the history of medicine in general? We like very much your article about the behaviourist approach to medicine*.

* A plea for a «behaviorist» approach in writing the history of medicine, in: *Journal of the History of Medicine and Allied Sciences*, Vol. *22*, p. 211–214, (1967).

A.: Yes, I think there is a close connection between these two lines of thought.

E.: Did HENRY E. SIGERIST influence you in this matter?

A.: This is a rather delicate question. But if I should tell the whole unvarnished truth, Henry E. Sigerist was my teacher, when I was a student, later my friend; we spent a lot of good moments together in life and he gave me a badly paid opportunity to work. But he never influenced me scientifically. If I should name somebody who influenced me profoundly and with whom I discussed all matters back and forth, it is OWSEI TEMKIN. Henry E. Sigerist was always much too busy. He had an effect on crowds and that is what he wanted. He had very little time for individuals.

E.: Really?

A.: Yes. He had the idea that he was a great prophet, reformer, messiah and philosopher. He had no time for sitting down with some anonymous boy, talking things over for hours and hours. He would go and give a sounding speech and write an inflammatory paper, and that would influence thousands – and that was much more economical. On the other hand, though it sounds immodest, I might even say that I influenced him. Unfortunately, I sold marxism to him and later could not get him back from it. For when I met him in 1928, he belonged to a group called religious socialists (founded by PAUL TILLICH) and had not heard much about marxism.

As to myself, I was deeply influenced by the defeat of the German labour movement. It showed that marxism, theoretically and practically, and in all its forms, also in the Trotzkian form, was completely unable to deal successfully with problems. This impotence of marxism continued, and I thought there must be other methods, and I saw that a lot of these problems were psychological problems, which are completely discounted by marxism. For marxism, psychology is an "Überbau" that does not really exist. And I thought that perhaps if I studied primitive society, which is so utterly different from ours, I wouldn't have the blind spot one has for one's own society, and I might get a clearer idea about how societies function. Now, unfortunately I never got the basic idea I had hoped to find. But during these studies I turned into a scientist, and got a lot of detail results.

E.: But here we see how much the personality of a scientist still

10

matters. You were disillusioned with marxism –

A.: – disappointed with marxism and of course, if you want it that way, I found myself personally and historically in a catastrophical situation where one wants to orient oneself at least in order to understand a little bit better what it is all about.

E.: I think that is a major aim of history: to understand our own time.

A.: Ah, well, and that is of course the aim of sociology.

E.: May we agree that in this respect history is, generally speaking, on surer grounds than sociology, that the facts of history are more solid?

A.: I think it all depends on how you handle it. I am sure that sociology can be done scientifically. We are now under the impression of the utterly irresponsible metaphysical bunk which is turned out under the name of sociology, and we forget that there is quite a respectable sociology which partly, of course, is history. I think that sociology and history follow different methods but have the same aims. At least (if I may equate for a moment, for simplicity's sake, ethnology and sociology), I have always felt that one has in both fields the same basic problems. When I deal with primitive medicine or when I deal with medicine in the 17th century, of course, I have to use different methods, because the material is different, but the basic problem – how people handle a medical situation, how they attempt to understand it – is the same.

But you wanted to know about Sigerist. You see, I had studied ethnology in France, and I worked in the U.S. with Sigerist primarily as an ethnologist. The Sigerist business went this way. Sigerist wanted to write his big book, and as one half of the first volume is more or less ethno-medicine, as they call it now, he needed someone who knew more about it than he did. Now, he was never the cheap cheat who lets somebody work for him and puts his name on it. In this sense I did not do anything in his book. But what I did was that out of the 4000 books and monographs I knew I pointed to him the 40 he should read. The others he could dispense with; I presented him with the results of them. How he presented the material, and what conclusions he drew, that was all his own. But in this respect he needed me because it saved him an enormous amount of time, six or seven years of studies which otherwise he would have had to do himself. When I left him, I still continued working in ethnology and in primitive medicine, and it is

11

for entirely external reasons that I went back to medical history – I got a job, and this in a place where I could not continue any ethnological work. That was impossible, we had not the opportunities there.

E.: By the way, when did you go to the United States?

A.: I was in France from 1933 to 1941. I was in Baltimore, at the Johns Hopkins, doing this kind of work from 1941 to 1945, and then in New York from 1945 to 1947. There I was with the American Museum of National History. And then I went to Madison (Wis.), and that is where my ethnological publications end, except that one on "The social role of primitive medicine", which I have written in 1955 for the PAUL RIVET "Festschrift". Paul Rivet was my official teacher in Paris. This article is perhaps of some interest, because in this paper I recapitulated already at a distance of ten years what I found now interesting in the study of primitive medicine. That is, I emphasized only one aspect. I had emphasized basically three aspects, the magic, the social and the psychopathological ones. In that article I emphasized the social one alone because I felt that it was the most interesting.

E.: You raised a most remarkable point. You started research into ethnology in order to find answers to urgent questions, questions in the field of social organisation –

A.: – of course, answers not in the sense of prescriptions as to what one should do to-morrow. But I started working in ethnology to find some basic orientation – almost laws – about the functioning of society or of men in society.

E.: Then you came to find laws for the working of medicine in primitive societies.

A.: "Laws" is really a very ambitious expression, but I did find certain regularities.

E.: How were you satisfied with this result, which obviously was not quite what you were looking for first?

A.: Let us modify a little bit the story of "Hans im Glück": I went out to get a big lump of gold; I never got my gold, but I got a pig, a useful animal. I came back with a pig, and I found it better than nothing, because I could have come home with a stone as Hans eventually does. I was a little sad that I never found that gold, I must confess it, but one must be realistic in life.

E. Could you say a few words about your work in the American Museum of Natural History?

A.: In the American Museum of Natural History, my task, my work for the department was on the level of physical anthropology. I put up there – collections seem to have been my curse! – a large collection of normal anatomical bone material of known age and sex, because that did not exist in the whole City of New York. If people wanted to study, for instance, the anatomy of the female pelvis, they came and studied our collection, which contained 10,000 archaeological female pelves, but nobody really knew whether they were female or not. *We* had decided they were female. So we built up now a collection of pelves, where we knew these were female and these were not, and of which we knew also the age. That was absolutely necessary for old age studies. We started collecting without a special goal, but I would have continued there in studying skeleton changes in old age.

But the Museum and my chief there, HARRY L. SHAPIRO, were very liberal in providing time. You need not absolutely always have worked on your immediate task, and so I went on working on my ethnomedicine, and I had there the very best library on earth. We had a tremendous library of ethnology monographs; I do not think that we lacked any monograph which had appeared up to 1940. So I could build on much better ground than ever before or afterwards. Some of my long papers with the large bibliographies date from that time – one an editor first refused because the bibliography was so long! And I also had a lot of contacts with field ethnologists. In New York, there were dozens of them. I was particularly friendly at that time, for instance, with a Chinese ethnologist, HSU, who is still professor in the United States. In the Museum we had ethnological society meetings regularly and we had many visitors. Quite apart from the people who lived in New York, every ethnologist who came to New York would come to the Museum, and we would have lunch with him. The amount of scientific contacts you could make at the Museum was incredible. I have never seen anything like that.

E.: And then you came to Madison.

A.: And there I stopped working actively in the field. I still had contacts. In the University of Wisconsin, the ethnologists regarded me as a colleague; I held seminars for anthropology students, read the

13

journals and went to meetings. But I had to build up a Department of the History of Medicine, and then I shifted into that work on Virchow which also was partly history and partly anthropology. I had already developed these plans. In the Museum, I already worked a little bit on this. So I went out of ethno-medicine.

E.: Is there still a connection with it – we think it is – in your paper about "white Indians"?

A.: "White Indians"* I did in Baltimore, and "White Indians" is a by-product of a study on malaria. If I had not been a trained ethnologist, I would never have been sensitive to the material. I was reading all these travel reports and so of the upper Mississippi Valley, and then I stumbled over a few of these "white Indians". I wanted only to read in these books what it was all about malaria at that time, but I found this and saw it was a most remarkable thing and took it up.

E.: Because of your ethnological interest –

A.: A "normal" medical historian would never have bothered about it. He would not even have realized that there was a problem.

E.: Obviously, it was very important for your purely medico-historical work too that you were trained in ethnology.

A.: It certainly helps.

ACKERKNECHT'S POINTS

E.: Well, these are the main points, we think.

A.: Then, if you allow me to do so, I will make *my* points. I should like to say a few words of what I think is more or less original with me or important in these papers.

Important is, in the first place, that I do no longer regard primitive medicine as a "Vorstufe", as an embryonic modern medicine, but regard it in its own right. This – if you want to use the technical term – functionalist approach I owe mainly to RUTH BENEDICT.

In the same time, I have insisted very strongly on the *magic character of primitive medicine*. As I said already, medical historians have rather slurred over this aspect of the matter because it did not fit into their concept of medicine. To them, medicine is something objective. I mean, doctors cut, or give you pills, and so on, and they find the same things with the primitives. That satisfies them, while I have underlined the magic character often even of these practices.

On the other hand, I have underlined the difference between both

* *Bulletin of the History of Medicine*, vol. *15*, p. 15-36 (1944).

medicines, because there is a certain school of superficial thought, which thinks that primitive medicine and modern medicine are exactly alike because they are both magic – o yes, I had a lot of fights on this issue in New York with people who said: nay, they both are using psychotherapy. But this is really extremely superficial. Of course, there is a magic element in modern medicine too. But there is a difference whether you have a medicine which is primarily magic and has a few rational elements or whether you have a medicine which is primarily scientific and has a few magic elements. Therefore, I have underlined this magic aspect, and it has helped me to answer a few special problems like primitive autopsies. Why do they not lead to any better knowledge of anatomy? Or primitive surgery: why does surgery not develop even with those primitives who could technically handle these things? Or in primitive pharmacopoeas: why are they such a strange mixture of effective and ineffective drugs? Or on the bringing up of premature children, which occurs only in a few tribes and nowhere else? I think one can only understand this if one remembers the magic background of primitive medicine.

The second thing I have emphasized – and that was new at that time, now it has become commonplace – is the *social aspect:* that primitive medicine appears quite clearly much more as a function of culture than as a function of biology. The definition of disease for instance: what is a disease is not decided on the basis of the fact that there is a biological change. This, of course, is always there. But only when society decides that this biological change is disease, then it becomes a disease. You can give examples for modern times, too. For instance, in my malaria studies I found out that in the upper Mississippi Valley people used to say: "O, this man is not sick, he has only malaria." And this is also the case in some regions in Africa, where they said: "O, this man is not ill, he has only yaws." Even with ourselves, the eczema of children was regarded as normal as far up as the 18th century; because almost every baby had it, it was no disease. On the contrary, it was immediately rationalized that it was very healthy: the bad humours went out by the eczema. And so, disease and medicine are functions of culture. Of course, on a biological background, but it is not enough that you are infected or ill. You have got to be recognized as such by society.

Another point in this connection is that medicine and the notion of disease play a great rôle to preserve society in so far as they are understood as social sanctions. The primitive, if he gets ill, asks himself immediately in what respect he has violated the social rules of his group, because he learns that sickness is the punishment the supernaturals send for that. And that, of course, keeps people on the straight line. This is obviously different in different societies, and I have tried to show that in various pattern studies on the Dobuans, the Cheyenne, the Tonga, the South-American Indians and the Eskimos.

Point three is the *psychological and psychopathological aspect*. That is an aspect of my work which found probably more interest than the other ones. And for this also I am indebted to Ruth Benedict. She had shown that not everything is psychopathological in primitive culture which appears to be so to the outsider, and I applied this in particular to the medicine man, who was entirely misjudged in the traditional medico-historical literature. These writers just copied the old song that he is a crook or a psychopath. In order to handle the situation I coined the terms of *auto-normal* and *hetero-normal*, of *auto-pathological* and *hetero-pathological*. This is probably the one thing which has impressed people most. Well, this is somehow what I regard as a summary of these studies.

E.: This would be the message of your book –

A.: – the extract in a way.

E.: And we hope, of course, that in the future these features of primitive medicine will be seen more clearly, in Europe as well as in the United States, where your ethno-medical papers still are quoted. Thank you, Professor Ackerknecht.

16

TYPICAL ASPECTS*

When one ist going to talk for an hour on such a general topic as "Primitive Medicine", it is obvious that only a few selected aspects of the problem can be dealt with. And it seems necessary to me to indicate first why I am not going to touch on a few other important questions which might easily be associated with the title of my paper.

There is first of all *"prehistoric medicine"*, which some have also called "primitive medicine". I, personally, feel unable to discuss prehistoric medicine because all our actual knowledge concerning it can, unfortunately, be contained in one short sentence: "Some prehistoric people practiced successfully the art of trephining." This undoubtedly is quite something, but to my mind it is not sufficient for a systematic general discussion. For a similar reason, absence of relevant material, I abstain from going here into the question of the evolution of medicine though a great many schemes have been constructed in this matter.

One of the most important aspects of primitive medicine is the *pharmacopoeia* of most primitive tribes. Except for a very few regions, like the Arctic and Melanesia, where druglore has been developed only slightly, an amazing percentage of the herbs, barks and roots used by the natives – a percentage which is far above the mathematical probability of random sampling – is of objective medicinal value.

Even today our own pharmacopoeia is heavily indebted to the primitives. Picrotoxine, the powerful stimulant of the respiratory center; strophantine, the well known medicament in heart diseases; emetine, the alcaloid of ipecacuanha and specific in amebic dysentery – all are of Indian origin. Salicylic preparations for rheumatism were first used by the Hottentots, etc., etc. Yet our culture, which somewhat prematurely but all the more firmly believes that the test tube is superior to the plant cell in synthesizing drugs, refuses, in general, to analyze the primitive material which anthropologists and missionaries have brought back from the field. The problem here is not one of theoretical elaboration and, therefore, I shall not discuss it further. The problem here is to convince some great scientific or industrial institution of the enormous practical importance and promises which a large scale analysis of primitive drugs would offer.

I am not going to deal with the *diffusion* of primitive medical theo-

* Parts of this lecture were published originally under the title "Primitive Medicine" in the *Transactions of the New York Academy of Science, Series II, 8, 26–37 (1945).*

17

ries and practices. I fully recognize the value and the importance of such studies, but I prefer to omit this subject in favor of questions about which I have greater personal knowledge and experience.

There may exist some legitimate doubt whether such a generalization as "primitive medicine" is possible at all. It is true that all human societies, primitive and civilized, suffer from disease. Disease is much older than man. It is one of the fundamental, vital problems which face every society. And every known human society develops methods to deal with disease, and thus creates a medicine. *But the attitude towards disease and the methods of fighting disease vary enormously in the different primitive tribes.* Disease may be of extreme concern to a society, quite beyond its objective frequency. Anxieties arising from other sources may be projected into medicine. The Navahos are said to spend one-fourth to one-third of their productive time in religious ceremonials, most of which are concerned with disease. Disease and its healing or prevention plays a similar preponderant role for instance in the religions of the Cuna, Chiricahua-Apache, Cherokee, Pima, Liberian Manos, etc. Disease is the main concern of the Pit River Indians of Northeastern California and, after sex, of the Yavapei. People may show about the same interest in disease that we do (e.g. the Thonga), and "heroic" people, like the Iatmul, the Cheyenne, or the Dahomey, may care relatively little for disease and medicine. The attitude toward disease may take a strange twist as in Dobu, where the healing practices are quite subordinated to the all-absorbing problem of how, by appropriate spells, one can make one's neighbors sick. The attitude toward disease may change under our very eyes, as Redfield describes it for Yucatan, when acculturation occurs. Disease theories, diagnostic and therapeutic measures, all may vary widely. There may or may not be special medicine men; they may be poor or rich, almighty or uninfluential. Here the magic power of the drug may be the central element of native medicine; there, the power of the healer or the power of the medical society.

We are accustomed to look at disease as a purely biological phenomenon and at medicine as a kind of reflex reaction toward it. These differences in approach are therefore extremely disturbing to us, and all the more so as they are not founded primarily on the objective amount of disease in a given tribe. We may encounter various attitudes combined with about the same kind and amount of morbidity, and in very similar climatic and economic conditions. Under such circum-

18

stances, medicine has much more clearly the character of a function of the culture pattern than of the environmental conditions.

Though it is necessary to bear in mind these underlying variations, it is nevertheless possible to make a few generalizations concerning primitive medicine especially with reference to some of its functional and psychological implications. I should like, however, to remind you of the following facts:

Disease and death among primitives are in the overwhelming majority of cases not explained by natural causes, but by the action of supernatural forces. In general, the disease mechanisms are: either the intrusion of a disease-producing foreign body or spirit, or the loss of one of the souls which may be abducted or devoured. These mechanism may be put into motion either by a supernatural agency (God, spirit, etc.) who feels offended, or by a fellow man who avenges himself either by hiring a sorcerer or by himself acting as a sorcerer. Supernatural causes must be discovered by supernatural means, and thus primitive "diagnostics" consist of various types of divination: bone-throwing, crystal-gazing, trances, etc. The therapeutics cover a whole gamut of methods, reaching from purely matter-of-fact treatments (herbs, massage, bath, etc.), a mixture of such objective methods with magic spells or prayers, to purely magico-religious rites – the mixed treatments probably prevailing in number.

One of the common traits of primitive medicine, which makes it rather different from ours, is the *social rôle* that disease and medicine assume in primitive society. Of course disease is a social problem in our society too. Whether you fall sick, what kind of disease strikes, whether your abnormality is regarded as a disease or not, the treatment you receive – all these are social problems in ours as in every society. Our society creates organizational forms for fighting disease, training doctors, preventing epidemics, unsanitary housing, etc. But this is not what I am aiming at. Disease with us is, in the last analysis, a biological, individual, and non-moral problem. No guilt is involved when we suffer from hereditary, infectious or degenerative diseases. Even in venereal diseases we strive to eliminate the moral aspect as it has proved to be a handicap in their eradication. If you get appendicitis or cancer, you will never think of associating this with your behavior toward your neighbor or mother-in-law or your ancestral spirits. We do not usually associate disease with whether or not our personal relations are good, whether we keep certain religious or social rules or not. But this is exactly what the primitive does. Disease derived from sorcery, from taboo violation, from the anger of ancestral or other spirits is the expression of social tensions. A seemingly independent, biological problem is thus woven into the whole socio-religious fabric in such a way that disease and its healer play a tremendous social role, a role that in our society is assumed rather by judges, priests, soldiers, and policemen.

In many primitive societies disease becomes the most important social sanction. Primitive medicine contains a moral element which is almost absent in ours. "Be peaceful, pay your debts, abstain from adultery in order to protect *yourself and your family* from disease." It thus becomes possible to treat disease by pacifying offended persons. New light is here thrown on the interest of the primitive community in the diseased person and its participation in healing rites.

This social role of disease may also partly explain the persistency of primitive medicine quite apart from its instrinsic medical value. The purely curative effect of certain rites may be negligible, but they may be upheld because they fulfill important social functions.

In a way, disease, being thus regarded as a direct consequence of personal social behavior, makes more sense to primitive man than it can make to the patient in our society. Only rarely are we able to relate the non-personal biological notions, which to us explain disease, directly to the actual life history of the patient. There is a tendency of the patient and his family in our society, well known to every medical practitioner, to bridge this gap, in constructing such relations even where they actually do not exist. You all might remember cases of cancer being referred to a slight and perfectly irrelevant bodily traumatism, cases of epilepsy explained by fright, etc. This tendency has disappeared from medical science only gradually and at a relatively late period.

The social concept of disease in primitive society is also reflected in the belief that the disease sanction may affect every member of the family as well as the sinner himself. This is a far more inclusive notion than our concept of hereditary or infectious diseases. Therapeutic measures – whether it be confession or medication – have therefore very often to be applied not only to the patient, but to his whole family.

It is obvious how this specific social role, assumed by disease in primitive society, contributes to the formation of a type of medicine which differs considerably from the one to which we are accustomed.

I think it is safe to state as a further general characteristic of primitive medicine that it is *primarily magico-religious, utilizing a few rational elements;* while our medicine is predominantly rational and scientific, employing a few magic elements[1]. We are naturally inclined to think of primitive medicine as much as possible in terms of rationality, just as primitives usually interpret our medicine as much as possible in terms of magic. It is not difficult to see that both procedures are projections. One can, of course, argue that our medicine is magic, or that theirs is rational, but both statements need closer examination and qualification. I believe that I am more aware of magical elements in our medicine than many of my medical colleagues are. For the anthropologist it is not difficult to discover the magic character that vitamins, germs, number complexes, etc. often assume in the mind of the *patient*. But this is just one of the important strictures which have to be made: *magic elements in our medicine are overwhelmingly on the side of the patient.* As far as our medical system and its representatives are concerned, they remain rational in intent, content, and procedure. In order to obtain a clear picture, it is also necessary to look at the problem from a more quantitative angle, and I doubt whether anyone would seriously argue that the modern patient's approach to medicine and disease is predominantly magico-mystical.

Nobody will deny that in a great number of primitive tribes not all diseases are interpreted in a supernatural manner and that some are regarded as due to natural causes. This holds true especially for very common diseases, such as colds, toothache, malaria, etc., those resulting from old age, and those of which the imported character is clearly realized. Yet the inconsistency with which such ideas are used is noteworthy. The same disease might be naturally or supernaturally caused, and a natural disease might be treated supernaturally, or vice versa. It is also remarkable that positive knowledge concerning the "natural diseases" is about as poor as that concerning "supernatural diseases" and that primitive sceptics in general doubt the supernatural character of individuals or isolated events, but not the whole supernatural system.

There are a certain number of purely rational treatments, such as bleeding, massage, and drugs. Yet the number of such treatments

---

1 I am using the term "rational" not as a mere equivalent of logical – magic is logical in its way too – but as it is most commonly understood: logical on the basis of empirical premises.

decreases considerably after closer examination and appears at least to be "mixed". The rational character of the use of the tourniquet in snake bite among the Liberian Manos becomes, for instance, somewhat doubtful when we hear that a ring of white clay might also b eapplied around the bitten limb. Rivers, observing an apparently rational abdominal massage for constipation on Eddystone Island, was very disappointed in learning that it was destined to drive out a magic octopus. Another case in point is the Cherokee patient who keeps a strict diet all day long, but devours everything at night when the taboo underlying his diet is not longer valid. The widespread division between medicine men and herbalists in primitive tribes has given rise to the premature conclusion that only the former are guided by supernatural ideas, while the latter are rationalists. This thesis seems to be unsupported by the facts.

The *fundamental* error in all this reasoning about primitive rationalism is the basic assumption that *what is objectively effective is also rational and scientific.* As there are so many objectively effective elements in primitive magic treatments such as drugs, baths, massage, sucking, bloodletting, isolating of infectious diseases, diet, inoculation against snake bite, etc., such treatments are without hesitation christened rational or even scientific, whereas they might be magical, or purely habitual, almost automatic or reflex-like. Yet this identification of the objectively effective, the rational, and the scientific can be nothing but a permanent source of confusion. The attribute of rational should be reserved for actions which are actually based on thought identifiable with our rational thinking. The notion of scientific should be handled with the same discrimination. Even animals use objectively effective healing methods, while science has nothing of an instinctive reaction. Linton has lately very justly written of science as an *invention.* One might as well speak of scientific thought as a great and late revolution in human behavior. Science aims primarily at truth, not at success or psychic relaxation. Science is unthinkable without a certain amount of individualism. It means a complete misunderstanding of scientific thought and methods, and of the whole history of science, to bestow the name of scientific, or even rational, upon practices which are in general uninfluenced by experience, free from scepticism, and where no numerical notions, no abstractions, no inductions, or no systematizations are underlying ideas. Calling every objectively effective procedure scientific seems to me diluting the notion of science almost to complete meaninglessness.

This misunderstanding is also favored by the assumption that supernatural, irrational ideas and practices are always highly emotional; thus, unemotional behavior ought to be rational. But experiences with primitives show that magic might be something highly unemotional.

I fully agree therefore with the following statement of the great American medical historian, Fielding H. Garrison:

"If we are to understand the attitude of the primitive mind toward the diagnosis and treatment of disease, we must recognize that medicine, in our sense, was only one phase of a set of magic or mystic processes, designed to promote human well being, such as averting the wrath of angered gods or evil spirits, fire making, making rain, purifying streams or habitations, fertilizing soil, improving sexual potency or fecundity, preventing or removing blight of crops and epidemic diseases."

Isolated rational elements, the existence of which nobody denies, do not and are not able to change or even to influence considerably the fundamental character of this magico-religious system.

It is for pragmatic reasons that I have given so much importance to what might seem a quite superfluous discussion of terminology. Primitive medicine's contribution to our medical understanding consists, in addition to its great treasury of drugs, just in the fact that here we are able to observe a whole system of medicine, different from ours and yet functioning with considerable success. It is, perhaps, because of this difference, which seems to me greater than in other fields like religion, art or law, that the study of primitive medicine has been rather neglected.

It is true that in merely calling primitive medicine "magic", not much is accomplished. Limitations of space and time make it impossible for me to enter here a detailed discussion of magic. But I cannot abstain from alluding to the fact that, in my opinion, under the heading of magic at least two very different sets of practices and beliefs have been lumped together.

I would like to mention here a few of the many effects which supernaturalism has on medical practice. The extreme *ignorance of anatomical facts* among primitives has often been commented upon, and has been attributed to the absence of dissections. Quite apart from the fact that experience in hunting, sacrifices and cannibalism could

23

well compensate for this shortcoming, I have been able to point to four areas in Siberia, Oceania, South America and West Africa where autopsies are practiced quite extensively in order to discover whether the deceased died as the result of witchcraft or not. Yet these dissectors are just as ignorant of the most elementary anatomical facts as are their non-dissecting brethren. It is not a mere technique, but a complete change in outlook that almost brings about a change in perception and opens the eyes of the super-naturalist to anatomical facts.

There is in general satisfactory wound and fracture treatment among primitives, but almost nothing which resembles our *major surgery* (amputations, excisions of tumors, abdominal surgery). In the few places where such major surgery is practiced, it is mostly of a very low quality. Here again technical explanations are insufficient. Primitives certainly do not lack technical skill, as is shown by the widespread and successful performance of trepanation, an operation which had an extremely bad prognosis even with western surgeons until a few decades ago. Neither do primitives lack occasions to gain surgical experience because of numerous accidents, ritual and judiciary mutilations occuring in primitive society. The greater resistence of those individuals who reach adult age in primitive societies, and the absence of particularly virulent bacterial strains as we cultivated them throughout centuries in our hospitals, would be a special asset for primitive surgeons. But the magic fear to appear mutilated in the spirit world is an all-powerful obstacle for the development of surgery. This fear creates opposition even to tooth extractions. Linton says of the Tanala that they do not fear death, but mutilation. It is this supernatural character of mutilation which makes it such an impressive form of punishment. And, in turn, people refuse amputation which would put them on the level of criminals. Supernaturalism also makes for a strange *inflation of the pharmacopoeia*, where the effective and the ineffective are used without discrimination. This obvious lack of experimentalism reduces such claims of primitive rationalism that otherwise could find strong support in the primitives' use of effective drugs.

While supernaturalism in general thus serves as an obstacle to technical improvements in medicine, it sometimes brings them about as unintended by-products, as is shown by circumcision, certain forms of sex hygiene, and other sanitary measures. The most striking example of this kind is probably the invention of the incubator for premature births by certain Eskimos and Bantus. This invention seems to have

24

arisen from particularly stringent taboos against miscarriage prevailing in these two tribes, otherwise so different from each other.

The irrational need not be ineffective, and with all its peculiarities, primitive medicine, which, by the way, in terms of space and time covers a much larger field than does our scientific medicine, seems to have *served its purpose more or less satisfactorily*. In some places and periods, it seems to have been even superior to our medicine. Some of its successes (as of those of our medicine) are undoubtedly due to the fact that man is a fairly solid animal, and many diseases are self-limited anyway. The aforementioned objectively efficient elements in primitive medicine, and its particular social mechanisms, may account for other successes.

One particular character of primitive medicine, which is derived from primitive mentality in general and which makes description of primitive medicine on the basis of our categories so difficult, deserves special notice in this context. This is the *unitarian or total character of primitive medicine*. When for practical reasons we have spoken above, for instance, of diagnosis and therapeutics, of bodily and mental diseases, we have done violence to the facts. Actually, there is no diagnosis separated from therapeutics in such acts as divination or confession. The diagnostic act is at the same time already a therapeutic one. And that old dichotomy between mental and bodily disease, which we seem largely unable to overcome even with psychosomatic medicine, just does not exist among primitives, either in pathology or in therapy. The whole individual is sick, and the whole individual is treated. This particular form of integration offers undoubtedly certain therapeutic advantages, as disease is fundamentally a process of disintegration on all levels, the physical, mental and social. Magic or religion seems to satisfy better than any other device a certain eternal psychic or "metaphysical" need of mankind, sick and healthy, for integration and harmony. The non-empirical character of primitive medicine provides it also with an element of certainty which gives it undoubtedly considerable curative powers.

We are inclined to isolate certain elements of primitive therapeutics, to which I have just alluded, under the label of *psychotherapeutics*. We easily discover in most primitive treatments certain effective mechanisms, which we have applied consciously and on a large scale for a number of years in our own medicine, such as *suggestion and confession*. We have gained a certain understanding of these processes.

Through work initiated by men like Pavlov, Cannon, or Freud, we have learned a good deal about the importance of certain mental stimuli for coordination of the whole organism, and of the catastrophic physiological consequences of conscious and unconscious fear. In addition, two wars have provided many of us with a certain amount of altogether undesired practical experiences in this respect. It is in the nature of things or, more exactly, it is a consequence of the particular ways in which our sciences and our society have developed, that in no other branch of medicine do primitive and modern medicine overlap to such an extent as in psychotherapy. We started much later in dealing scientifically with psychological and social problems than with those of matter. The decline of official religion has brought into the office of the doctor many problems which were formerly handled by the priest. A number of years ago Opler published a very interesting analysis of the methods of an Apache medicine man in the light of modern psychotherapy, pointing to parallels as well as to differences. Without denying to modern psychotherapy any of its successes and its merits, I am rather inclined to think that it labors under many delusions as to the degree of rationality it has reached. Many of its cures seem to me due far less to its rationalizations than to the simple mechanisms of suggestion and confession also underlying certain practices of the medicine man.

We have insisted, above, on the social determinants of primitive medicine; but every consideration of primitive medicine that does not at least try to gain an insight into the biological bases of this medicine, that is, the *pathology* of primitives, would be utterly incomplete. Everybody who has ever tried to study so-called racial pathology knows that, in no field of primitive medicine, are the data as scanty and contradictory as in this one. Nevertheless, it seems safe to state that truly primitive communities, perhaps because of their relative isolation and of the lower life expectancy of their members, show a relatively low morbidity of their adult population. This has been the impression of qualified observers not only in the Arctic, Polynesia, or North America, but even in such unhealthy regions as South America or Africa. We must not forget that the same process, which ultimately brought about the development and diffusion of a highly qualified medical science, meant primarily a tremendous increase and spread of disease all over the world. This continent probably knew nothing of measles, smallpox, malaria, yellow fever, cholera, plague and many other infectious diseases, before its discovery by the white man. Infections were the most deadly automatic weapon of the European in his conquest of the country. It is of historical interest that one of these infections, smallpox, was on a few occasions, in both North and South America, used consciously in the warfare against the Indian. It is true that primitive medicine proved, in general, unable to adapt itself to these new situations. Application of traditional methods, like baths in the case of smallpox, even had particularly fatal consequences. Degenerative diseases, which form such an important part of our pathology, had little chance to develop in populations who had an average life expectancy well below 30. Besides frequent accidents and other forms of violent death, this low life expectancy is undoubtedly due to a high infant mortality, which is known and feared, but badly controlled by primitives.

Mental disease, at least in the form of our psychoses, particularly schizophrenia, general paresis, or delirium tremens, seems equally rare among primitives. On the other hand, the diseases called "functional" in our terminology often seem particularly frequent. They, together with rheumatism, digestive disorders, colds and respiratory diseases, skin and eye affections, and gynecological disturbances, seem to form the stock-in-trade of primitive pathology. This and not the post-conquest situation, is the background against which the accomplishments of primitive medicine should be measured. Such a comparison leaves a far more favorable impression of the adequacy of primitive medicine.

I cannot leave my subject without saying at least a few words about the primitive medical practitioner, the *medicine man*. For a long time he had been labeled in anthropological literature, even of the highest caliber, e.g., Tylor, as a fake. I think this point of view has now completely died out and, therefore, need not be insisted upon. We know now that the percentage of fakes among medical practitioners is not higher in primitive than in other societies. We have won a juster appreciation of the so-called tricks of primitive medicine men, that were so highly offensive to early travelers and missionaries, by understanding their symbolical character. It is also interesting to note that less articulate parts of the population have never shared in this contempt for the medicine man. The "Indian Doctor", that is, the native medicine man or an Indian-trained white lay practicioner, was a very widespread phenomenon in frontier settlements throughout the first half of the 19th century, and when Indians were removed to reservations, white

27

settlers petitioned for exception of their Indian doctor. At early AMA conventions of the 1840's, reports on Indian pharmacopoeia were read. The intensive government-sponsored study of Indian medicine by Hernandez in Mexico and by Piso in Dutch South America, during the 16th century, belong in the same category.

Another, hardly less complimentary or correct label for the medicine man, that of "psychopath" or "epileptic", still lives in many anthropological textbooks or articles.

I am unable to take up here the whole complicated problem of abnormality in primitive society. I refer you to the excellent work of Ruth Benedict, Hallowell, and later writers, which forms one of the most valuable contributions that modern anthropology has made to the problems of medicine, psychopathology, and psychology in general. I would, nevertheless, like to stress one technical question which, so jar, has been given little attention, and which might have played an important role in the genesis of this misunderstanding. Mental disease in primitives, recognized as such by both natives and whites, manifests itself often in so-called states of involuntary possession, that is, paroxysms, accompanied by spastic motions, incoherent language, etc. To the non-initiated, these accidents look like epilepsy, though actually they are not and fall rather in the group of diseases that we usually call hysteria. Many medicine men, too, are subject to trances, states of possession. Though these forms of possession are voluntary, very often induced by drugs, perfectly normal and by many tribes clearly differentiated from the possession-disease, they look very similar to the untrained observer. I suspect that through this confusion, the medicine man has undeservedly acquired the title of an epileptic or psychopath.

There is no doubt that psychopathology plays an important rôle in the life of certain groups of medicine men, the best known of whom is the Siberian shaman. In view of the very special character of the Siberian shaman, it is extremely regrettable that the term, shaman, has been used very loosely as a synonym for medicine man in all four corners of the earth, in spite of the protests of Loeb and others. Closer study of the Siberian shaman reveals the perplexing fact that the individual who is to become a shaman passes through a stage of very marked mental disturbance, but that he is more or less cured from his affliction by becoming a shaman.

Even without detailed discussion of the problems of abnormality, it should be fairly obvious that an individual who successfully plays such an important rôle in society, as the medicine man actually does, cannot, because of mere similarities, be put on the same level with our mentally diseased individuals, whose main characteristic is that they are unable to function successfully in society.

The successes of the medicine man cannot be fully understood unless one realizes that, acting in small communities, he possesses a more perfect personal knowledge of his patient than most of our doctors do, and that his non-medical activities greatly enhance his authority as a healer.

We hear a great deal about specialists in primitive medicine. It should be realized that this form of specialization seems just the opposite of ours. We have specialists because the volume of our knowledge has become so great that one man can no longer handle all of it. Specialization among primitives seems to result from the fact that there has not yet developed a total body of medical knowledge. One man knows only one or a few spells and practices for one or a few diseases, and thus becomes a specialist for this or that disease.

CULTURE AND MEDICINE OF THE
CHEYENNES, DOBUANS AND THONGA*

"Medicine is a social institution. It comprises a set of beliefs and practices which only become possible when held and carried out by members of an organized society, among whom a high degree of the division of labour and specialization of the social function has come into being. Any principles and methods found to be of value in the study of social institutions in general cannot be ignored by the historian of medicine."

W. H. R. RIVERS

Literature on primitive[1] medicine generally consists of two types of writings: monographs ("The medical customs of the ... in ...") or general treatises ("The medicine of uncivilized peoples", "Primitive Obstetrics", etc.). In the latter a maximum of unrelated facts from the different monographs or general ethnographical literature is collected and thus a kind of anthropological "Frankenstein", as Ruth Benedict[2] terms it, is constructed. Things do not seem to improve very much by pressing these poor, isolated facts in the mould of an at least extremely hypothetical, evolutionary scheme. The results are generally a highly unreal picture of primitive medicine and the somewhat faulty approach explains a good many of the numerous errors still prevailing in our field.

It has now been almost generally recognized that the significant unit in cultural anthropology is the single culture, the cultural configuration or "culture pattern" of the respective tribe (or group of tribes) and not the single institution[2a]. In other words: the "organism" and not the "organ". It is this pattern which gives its special value, character, flavor and color to the single trait. It is neither the mechanical addition of laws, arts, techniques, religions, etc. which makes the cultures, nor does a mere summation of data concerning all laws or all religions or all techniques of preliterate tribes help us to understand these institutions

*This article was first published under the title "Primitive Medicine and Culture Pattern" in the Bull. Hist. Med. 12, 545–574 (1942).

1 We remind our reader again that we use the somewhat problematic term "primitive" exclusively to characterize the preliterate peoples of the world without implying in the least that these peoples represent either evolutionary stages of our civilization or a well defined conceptual unit opposed to all "civilization," etc. See also chapter VII of this volume, p. 120.

2 Ruth Benedict, 1934, p. 29.

2a "The series of social phenomena are solidary with respect to each other, and they are placed in mutual relationship," L. Lévy-Bruhl, Les fonctions mentales dans les sociétés inférieures, English transl., p. 27.

or the cultures in which they are inserted. The institutional elements of human culture are relatively few and limited as are the colors and subjects of the painter. But the possibilities of arranging, selecting and combining these elements, of accentuating them differently, are almost as unlimited as are the possibilities of the painter to mix and distribute his colours and subjects.[3] Little understanding of painting would be gained by merely enumerating the different colors and subjects used by the painters from the 14th to the 20th century all over the world. It is by comparing the pictures and their history that we proceed to an understanding of painting.

Medicine like other institutions is not an exception to these rules. It is an almost hopeless task to try to understand and evaluate the medicine of one primitive tribe while disregarding its cultural background or to explain the general phenomenon of primitive medicine by purely enumerating that in the medical field primitives use spells, prayer, blood-letting, drugs, medicine men, twins, toads, human fat and spittle, etc. For instance the statement "All forms of ancient and primitive medicine are identical" (Garrison) may perhaps be correct, but it is certainly rather meaningless. It ends where the problem begins. What counts are not the forms, but the place medicine occupies in the life of a tribe or people, the spirit which pervades its practice, the way in which it merges with other traits from different fields of experience.

It is certainly more than pure chance that the emphasizing of the configuration in anthropology, opposed to a continued analysis of the parts, coincides with similar trends in biology, psychology, philosophy, etc. On the other hand "the culture pattern" conception is no arbitrary invention or mechanical imitation, but has genuinely grown out of the patient and unprejudiced labor especially of American anthropologists first defining American culture areas, out of the work of Franz Boas and Goldenweiser, Kroeber, Lowie, Sapir, Wissler, etc., and of the English functionalists. It eventually has been formulated in a rather special and most radical way by Ruth Benedict.[4] Convinced of the

3 The Sun Dance e.g. is executed exactly the same way by the Cheyenne as by the Arapaho and in a very similar way by 20 other Plains tribes; but it always has a different meaning (L. Spier, 1921, pp. 451–527). The same rites among the Navahos have a healing purpose; among the Hopis they produce fertility of the fields (R. H. Lowie, 1936, p. 294).

4 "Mourning or marriage or puberty rites or economics are not special items of human behaviour, each with their own generic drives and motivations which have determined their past history and will determine their future but certain occasions

31

correctness and the utility of this conception, nay, of the necessity to introduce more modern and adequate methods into the study of primitive medicine, we have written as a first attempt [5] the following three sketches of the culture pattern and "medicine" of the North American Cheyennes, the Melanesian Dobuans and the South East African Thongas; limited of course by the space at our disposal and the material available. This attempt by no means closes the door to generalizations. Only before generalizing it would perhaps be useful to reexamine with what exactly we are dealing, and to realize how different things really are which generally are united under the one label: Primitive Medicine. Generalizing will then probably be more difficult but we hope, on the other hand, more scientific – generalizations being obtained by abstraction and not by summation – and more correct.

CHEYENNES [6]

The Cheyennes are a typical Plains tribe.[7] Warfare is the activity in which they feel most strongly the pulse of life, its value and its beauty. Of course it is their kind of "war", very different from ours; the war of little groups – war parties – almost the war of individuals, very seldom involving the whole band, much less the whole tribe. Sometimes one

which any society may size to express its important cultural intentions. The significant sociological unit from this point of view, therefore, is not the institution but the cultural configuration," Benedict, 1934, p. 244.

5 The series of A. W. Nieuwenhuis, Die Anfänge der Medizin unter den niedrigst entwickelten Völkern, *Janus* 1924, 1925, 1926, unfortunately serves mostly to prove Prof. Nieuwenhuis' highly controversial thesis: "how much even these least cultivated peoples were governed by intellect in a narrower sense in their behaviour to environment" and is not very familiar with "functionalist" techniques of description.

6 Except when other references are given the facts concerning the Cheyennes are taken from the writings of J. B. Grinnell, especially his book, *The Cheyenne Indians*, 2 vols., New Haven, 1923. We use the present tense although the period of flourishing of the customs described dates back about 90 years, when the Cheyennes were still free. They are now living in reservations in Oklahoma and Montana.

7 It is a hard blow to our general belief in primitive conservatism to learn that the Cheyennes, "in many ways the most conservative of the tribes of the plains" (Dorsey), becam a typical Plains tribe only in historical times; they migrated during the 18th century from the Great Lakes where they had been sedentary, farming, fishing and hunting small game with stones, clubs and pits. Not only the gun and the horse, the "gifts" of the white man, but also such fundamental and typical traits as the use of dogs, bow and arrow, the movable tipi, even scalping and warfare seem relatively recent acquisitions. Outstanding traits of the past on the other hand, like farming, matrilineal descent, etc., seem entirely forgotten. The cholera epidemic of 1849 which killed half of the tribe may have contributed to the latter fact.

announces his way of life clearest by his way of death. "The Cheyenne warrior wishes to be killed, if at all, on the broad level prairie where everyone can see him. When he dies he does not wish to be covered by earth, but prefers to lie out on the prairie where the birds and animals may devour his body and his remains may be scattered far and wide."

Of course one generally cannot make a living out of war and so the first concern of the Cheyennes is food gathering. This is done mostly by the men who hunt the buffalo, antelope, etc., a hard and strenuous occupation. The buffalo is their basic food and forms their basic clothing and housing material. Thus their migrations are conditioned by the wanderings of the herd. Supernaturally endowed persons ("medicine men" who however are neither professionals nor healers) and magico-religious ceremonial (sacrifices, smoking) play a big role in their hunting. Hunting is controlled by the chiefs and the warrior societies and cannot be undertaken regardless of the community. The men make their implements; the boys herd the horses. The women gather all kinds of roots and the fire wood, carry the water, light fires, prepare the hides, make clothing, tipis and cooking utensils. In spite of a very rigorous division of labor between the two sexes, and in spite of polygamy (a man generally marries sisters) the position of women is high. The man and the woman are partners, sharing equally in the work of the familiy. Women have personal property of their own (horses). They have their own societies for ceremonially quilling robes and lodges. Sexlife is very much restricted. Courtship goes on for 5 and 6 years. Chastity of the girl is required. Her protective string is respected by everybody. There are few love charms. Parents who have children at long intervals are praised. The general bearing of these customs seems less than would be expected. The Arapaho build up similar characters with great looseness of their women.

Cheyenne warfare started probably with the prosaic step from hunting of wild horses to mere horse stealing. But passing over the motivations of revenge and desire for glory, it crystallized into pure love of fighting. From the beginning the boy is taught that his chief duty in life is to be brave and to go to war and fight. After his first war party he gets a new name. Only when he dies in war can the Cheyenne expect to get his full share of the short but exalted bloody mourning ceremonial, when his best horse will be killed and his wives will cut their hair, cut off joints of their fingers and gash their legs severely. When he dies without "counting a coup" on the enemy his war party will return silently, almost ashamed. But when he dies as a brave, they will return shouting triumphantly, their faces painted black, as if no one had died. Only war deeds are real life and count more than death.

Warfare is naturally connected with one of the fundamental spiritual elements of Plains culture: self torture to obtain a vision-dream which possibly procures a guardian spirit and indicates a war "medicine". But with the Cheyennes the accent is rather on the *self torture as a sacrifice* (fasting and thirsting, swinging from a pole with the ropes fixed in the skin, wearing buffalo skulls by the same technique) than on the dream. Of course visions or dreams are highly desirable and appreciated. But the mere torture alone may already bring power and success on the warpath. On the other hand torture may be undergone after a dream, or success, or avoiding a danger, as fulfillment of a vow or expression of gratitude to the spirits. It may be done during the Medicine Lodge ceremony or at other times, publicly or in isolation. It is interesting that besides the vision another method of divination on the warpath exists: seeing the future in the blood of the badger. Other ways of getting supernatural power in the warpath are the use of shields, lances, warbonnets, scalp shirts. These objects are manufactured by visionaries and initiated with much ceremony involving the eating of the dead enemy's heart. They are connected with so many taboos that their use is restricted to a few men. Everybody wears charms and amulets which are seldom destined to protect against disease or to further love, as in other tribes, but are used to protect in war. The terrible necklace of High Wolf composed of human fingers and the small buckskin bag filled with right hands of Shoshoni papooses, captured by Bourke in 1876, are probably also such charms.[8]

The leader of the war-party, carrying a special pipe, is supposed to have special supernatural power and protection. But neither is he a priest or medicine man, nor has the medicine man who generally accompanies the war-party – very often one of the strange man-woman (man in woman's clothes) – other rights than the duties of a healer and joke-maker. He is by no means the leader as for instance he is with the Cherokees.[9]

While spiritual beliefs penetrate Cheyenne war-lore, war-lore and its outstanding symbol "counting a coup" (more exactly the recitation of a brave on how he "counted a coup") pervades the whole spiritual, social and practical life of the Cheyenne. Neither killing nor scalping

8 Bourke, J.B., 1892, p. 481.　　　9 Olbrechts, F., and Mooney, J., 1932, p. 91.

the enemy is so important as counting a coup, that is, touching him. The Cheyenne does not doubt that a man taking a false oath for having counted a coup will certainly die. A man counting a coup is necessary for the "baptism" ceremony of the Cheyenne baby: the piercing of the ears, a magical rite the meaning of which has become obsolete. Here the Cheyenne show another important trait of their culture; generosity in order to earn social recognition. The man who pierces the ears is not paid following a fixed "tariff", but he gets as many horses as the family can afford. Also the first hunting success of the Cheyenne boy is celebrated by giving away horses and meat. Counting a coup is necessary in the preparing of the holy white buffalo hide, in the fabrication of the scalp shirt. Counting a coup is necessary in sanctifying the dipper of the war-party. Counting a coup is needed for the initiation of every lodge, not to speak of the big ceremonials. A competition of coup-counters is one of the biggest social games. Even the ceremonial of the women's society includes the counting of coups. The women also play war games with the men, returning from root and wood gathering. Sometimes women successfully participate in war-parties and form their own "veteran" society. While the Zuñi for instance suppress strong personalities and individuality,[10] the Cheyennes, especially by this custom of coup counting and the individual approach to the spirits in torture and vision, breed them.

That does not mean that there is so much aggressiveness and anarchy as in other individualistic societies. From early youth the Cheyenne is taught to be on good terms with his fellows. A spirit of helpfulness and kindness reigns among them. There is practical community in food. Theft is unknown. A very loose democratic organization is sufficient to keep order. In the circle of lodges of the band the Indian lives his whole life long in public and submits to the community. The qualities required of a chief are very characteristic: he must be brave in battle, generous in disposition, liberal in temper, deliberate and of good judgment. He is not a priest. His first duty is to take care of the widows and orphans, his second to make peace in the camp. His dignity does not permit him to take part in any quarrel. He even cannot avenge the abduction of a wife. There are 44 chiefs: 4 principal chiefs and 4 for each of the 10 bands. Their councils are conducted with much form and courtesy. The crier makes public the decisions throughout the camp. A great rôle in the public life as police force, pressure group, dancers in

10 Benedict, 1934, p. 99.

the big ceremonials, is played by the seven warrior societies or soldier bands. The man who kills a fellow tribesman receives his corporal punishment from the relatives of the slain, not from the tribe, but he is an outlaw for the whole tribe. Nobody will smoke or eat with the murderer. He is supposed to decay inwardly. He is in an extreme state of nervousness. His crime is regarded so grave a menace for the whole tribe that in a solemn ceremony the holy arrows, the "ark of the covenant" of the Cheyenne have to be renewed.

The Cheyennes are a religious people and devoted to numerous supernatural agencies: there is the spirit of the heavens, the highest god; there is the spirit of the earth; there are the spirits of the four directions, while the spirits of the dead are of little importance. Animals interfere very much in their material as well as in their spiritual life. Many people even understand the language of the animals. The wolves give advice in war, the white tailed deer helps on love affairs. The mule-deer and the elk bring illness, and the bear heals. Birds and insects show the way to the game. Their religion is of the "Winnebago" (making oneself pitiable before one's gods), and not of the "Zuñi" (making oneself happy) type.[11] There are no real professional priests. There are individuals supernaturally more endowed and who, having assisted in former ceremonies, instruct others. The Cheyenne do not, like the Navahos,[12] spend one fourth to one-third of their productive hours in religious activities, big ceremonies, but *their whole life is full of little ceremonial acts*. Before every meal they pray and sacrifice, also before lighting a pipe. *Pipe smoking*, probably first used in rain magic, is a highly ritualized act and next to coup counting the most used in ceremonial gesture. They smoke after killing game; they smoke in the war-path and when asking for participation in the war-party or the Sun Dance, when seeking instruction in self torture or doctoring. The offering of the pipe is the general ceremonial way of asking an important favor. There are also taboos: the taboos of the menstruating woman, of the sister, of the mother-in-law, of the shield, scalp shirt and war bonnet, of tanning wolf skins, etc. Fortunately some of them can be removed by special ceremonies. Ceremonial is the whole behavior of the war-party, the return of the scout, etc. The Sweat Lodge is mostly a magico-religious enterprise, not purely "practical" as with the Cherokee.[13]

The Cheyenne were formed by fusion of two tribes, the Cheyenne

11 Aitken, B., 1930, p. 371.
12 Leighton, A. H. and D. C., 1942, p. 518.   13 Mooney, J., 1885–1886, p. 333.

proper and the Suhtai. Consequently they have two culture heroes: Sweet Medicine and Standing-on-the-Ground; two holy objects: the medicine arrows and the buffalo hat; and two big ceremonies: the "renewing of the arrows" and the "Medicine Lodge" (Sun dance). Mooney[14] and Dorsey[15] mention only these two big ceremonials. Grinnell describes a third one, the Massaum ceremony. Although celebrated almost annually by the whole tribe, these ceremonies are not regular calendar holidays like our Christmas, Easter, etc., but each time they arise from the personal vow of a single man who with his wife are then the central figures of the ceremony. The holy "Medicine Lodge" is created for the benefit of the people and a good harvest. Prayers and sacrifices are offered to the mountains, buttes, hills, animals, birds, timber, grasses, fruits, "medicines", and waters. During 4 days there is much smoking, fasting, painting, coup counting, dancing in the lodge, where an altar around a buffalo skull is built. The "renewing of the arrows" is done to insure the health of the people, the abundance of buffalo, cherries, berries, roots, grass and all animals. The Massaum ceremony has the same elements as the Medicine Lodge. It is the feast of the earth. Prayers are spoken for health, long life, good living, kindly feeling toward each other. The buffalos, wolves, foxes, coyotes, the white tailed deer appear as dancers at this ceremony of hunters. The elk practices healing acts as do the members of the "Contrary Society". These religious gatherings have also a highly social character. Besides there is a lot of sportive competition and games among the Cheyennes, feasts with story telling and other amusements. The scalp-dance after the return of the warriors is an outspoken love-dance – love comes out of war in Cheyenne society.

But where does medicine enter the picture? Perhaps the most characteristic feature of Cheyenne medicine is that one could speak so largely of Cheyenne life and beliefs almost without mentioning disease and medicine. (We speak, of course, of medicine in the original sense. One of the great difficulties of the study of Indian lore is the universal use of the word "medicine" when clearer conceptions are lacking, and the expression comprises magic, custom, personality, god, etc. as well.) That would have been impossible with the Cherokees where "the chief necessity for religion in fact is found in the existence of disease and the principal office is its eradication,"[16] or with the Navahos where the

14 Mooney, J., 1907.
15 Dorsey, G.A., 1905.

16 L. Spence, *Hastings Encycl. Rel. Eth.*, vol. 3, p. 505.

majority of the 35 principal ceremonies are concerned with disease,[17] or with the poor Yavapeis who for their preoccupation with health and sex receive the label of "degenerates" by Mrs. Aitken.[18] The difference between the Cheyennes and the other tribes seems primarily not objectively conditioned. Judging from their drugs for coughing, belly-ache, dysmenorrhoea, head-ache, hemoptysis, rheumatism, baby ailments, fever, sore throat, kidney troubles, paralysis, poison ivy, carbuncle, disease seems not altogether unknown to them. Of course death in war is still much more likely than death because of disease. The Cheyennes are fatalistic in regard to disease. Already their culture hero, Stand-on-the-Ground, says that disease cannot be avoided. The Cheyenne way for the man without hope of recovery is to look for death in battle. (Sometimes, incidentally, the hero survives – and recovers.) The Cheyenne fixes his objective fears and unrest on other symbols. The anxiety for food for instance pervades the whole Cheyenne religion, a problem which the Navaho underestimates.[19] The Cheyenne have no possessed persons. But some of the bravest warriors suffer, especially in their old age, from such a terrible fear of lightning that for their protection they become "contraries", that is, enter a most burdensome social position where they always have to say and do the contrary of the normal.

The Cheyennes have of course a kind of medicine. Relatively few protective measures are practiced however. Disease is caused by invisible arrows shot by the spirits of wells, the mule-deer and other spirits. Very seldom are taboo-breaking or witchcraft considered responsible for the disease. The treatment is composed of the "small ceremonial" typical for the Cheyennes. Grinnell lists a typical treatment as follows: purifying of medicine man and patient, singing (and rattling), smoking a holy pipe, purifying, application of a drug, singing, suction, application of a tea, smoking, purifying, singing, gentle massage, singing, smoking, sacrifice, eating. The doctoring songs are unusually short and simple – "I know myself, I possess spiritual power". The words are repeated over and over again. Some songs even have no words. The pipe is of course of great importance. The drugs are staples with other magical objects. Grinnell lists 94 medicinal plants, a great part of which are effective. The sucking procedure produces small stones, buffalo hairs or lizards.[20] Sometimes women cut a joint off their fingers in sacri-

17 Leighton, *l.c.*, p. 517.
18 Aitken, *l.c.*, p. 370.

19 Leighton, A. H. and D. C., 1942, pp. 194–209.

fice for the recovery of a sick husband or child. Against epidemics they know no other help than fleeing. A very few men treat the bite of a rattlesnake in a way that seems mostly magical. Surgery is almost unknown, but the recuperative powers of the American Indian from wounds seem extraordinary and seem to be the basis of numerous Cheyenne "miracle" stories of reviving the dead. To become a medicine man of the healing kind one must have a dream. But then he learns the lore and the special language, from an elder medicine man. It is very significant of the deep rooted solidarity between the sexes that his wife has then also to become a healer. Except those who are half men, half women, the medicine men limit their activity to healing. Men doctors are also horse doctors.

When we analyse the Cheyenne medicine we miss some elements familiar in other primitive tribes; we find numerous others, but they are accentuated and arranged differently. That seems to be the consequence of the fact that the Cheyennes adopted a lot from their neighbors, but integrated it more or less into their own pattern. As a whole Cheyenne medicine is extremely poor in esthetic elements, so strong in the Navaho sand-paintings or the Zuñi dances. Among the causes of disease the object-intrusion idea dominates. The soul-loss conception is entirely absent. Witchcraft belief is weak compared to the Cherokees'[21] probably because of the mutual loyalty among the Cheyennes. The taboo-breaker is menaced by other dangers (failure in war and hunting) rather than by illness. The dream as cause of disease, well known in Navaho and Cherokee lore, seems equally absent. Herb knowledge is not surprising in a tribe of root gatherers: it is generally strong among the American Indians.[22] The Cheyenne medicine man is rather different from most of the Indian healers. He is more a man with a special spiritual power and some knowledge, addicted to healing, than a "medicine man". He has not a fantastic costume like the Haida shaman.[23] There is not the differentiation between the lay healer-herbalist and the supernatural medicine man as for instance among the Dakota, Navaho, Apache[24], Crow[25] or Ojibwa[26] tribes. His power is not hereditary as

---

20 The sucking procedure is not necessarily supposed to produce objects as is proven by the behavior of the Bakairi, Victoria Australians, etc. Its symbolical meaning can also be attained by removing an immaterial disease principle. See Ackerknecht, 1942, p. 509 ff.

21 Mooney, J., 1898.

22 Stone, E., 1932.

23 Corlett, W. Th., 1935, p. 92.

24 Hrdlicka, A., 1907, vol. I, p. 838.

25 Corlett, l.c., p. 116.

26 Ibid., p. 123.

with the Omahas and Hidatsa[27]: there is no formal initiation. He has not the enormous knowledge of the Cherokee of Navaho medicine man, nor is he a leader or a priest like both of these.[28] In a tribe abounding with societies there is no medicine men society, neither of the Ojibwa[29] nor of the Pawnee[30] nor of the Omaha[31], nor of the Zuñi[32] type.

When we regard the Cheyenne culture pattern, it seems to us quite definite in its relation to war, ceremonial, vision and sacrifice, social relations, etc., although we cannot condense it in a catchword. Examining medicine in this pattern we find medicine pervaded by many of its typical traits: the rather democratic position of the medicine man, the limited rôle of dreams, witchcraft, taboo, protective measures, the arbitrary way in which disease is distributed by the supernaturals, the rôle of the pipe and other ceremonials, the sacrifice, the rôle of women, the relation to animals and plants. But we find also elements not directly connected with this pattern and we miss some of its most typical elements so that the relative neglect of medicine is perhaps the most Cheyenne-like trait of Cheyenne medicine.

DOBUANS[33]

The Dobuans are "Massims", that is, Eastern Papuo-Melanesians, living on small volcanic islands of the D'Entrecasteaux group, north of Eastern New Guinea. Although they do some fishing, sometimes kill a pig, have some sago and banana trees, coconut and betel palms, the very basis of their rather poor diet is their yams. Thus the yam garden is economically the most important place in Dobu. The future son-in-law and daughter-in-law have first to show their abilities in these places before they are admitted into the familiy. For them and their brothers and sisters it is also a place of humiliation as they must not only work hard but also must fast since they cannot eat in the presence of their future parents-in-law. Just as in Dobu no results whatever (in fishing, exchanging, love-making, etc.) can be obtained without incantations, the garden is also an important place of ritual throughout the year. Yams are human beings in metamorphosed form and have to be con-

27 *Ibid.*, p. 121.
28 Olbrechts, *l.c.*, p. 83 and 92.
29 Hoffmann, W.J., 1891, p. 164.
30 Linton, R., 1925.
31 La Flesche, F., 1890, p. 215.
32 Benedict, 1934, p. 104.
33 Except when other references are given, the facts concerning the Dobuans are taken from the study of R. F. Fortune: *Sorcerers of Dobu*, New York, 1932.

tinually charmed in order to grow and multiply. Yam seeds are, as everything else, hereditary only in the maternal line (from mother's brother to nephew) and so are the incantations which can only make that special kind of seed grow. That is why man and wife, although working together, both have a garden of their own for their respective seeds and incantations. In these conditions incantations are the greatest wealth and are given from one person only to one of the children in recognition of services rendered to the elder. The spectacle of 40 years of successful Mission gardening without incantations has not made the least impression on Dobuan belief.

The Dobuans murmur their charms unlike their neighbors, the Trobriands, who pronounce them loudly. The Dobuans believe that every success in the garden as everywhere is not so much a magical victory over the forces of nature, as a victory over one's neighbor. Yams wander at night and when you have a better crop it is because by your stronger magic, by special yam-alienating charms, you have attracted and stolen a part of your neighbor's yams. Thus a better crop is an offense to your neighbors and they will try to take revenge by employing against you their disease spells. Under these circumstances incantations have to be kept in the strictest secrecy. The clearing of the fields is done in common, but afterwards the presence of strangers in the garden is strongly resented. In the incantations an archaic, esoteric language is employed. The spell is uttered over a magical herb or plant and always the intervention of a supernatural, a legendary spirit is invoked. As magical plants the Dobuans often employ cordylina terminalis which is used all over Oceania for different magical purposes (healing, calming the spirits of the dead, ceremonial of ghost societies, fire walking, etc.).

A leaf on a palm tree warns that a "taboo", a spell for causing diseases, has been placed on the tree trunk. That is quite a common measure in Melanesia.[34] Every man or woman in Dobu knows from one to five of such incantations and of course respective incantations to heal the disease caused by the taboo: otherwise he could not approach his own tree. In the charm an animal is generally mentioned which both makes the disease and which gives the name to it. The charm is uttered again into an object (leaf, creeper). As every disease is held to be caused by a taboo, a list of the taboos gives also a certain idea of Dobu

34 Codrington, R. H., 1891, p. 217; Rivers, W. H. R., 1924, p. 33; Hocart, A. M., 1925, p. 262; Malinowski, B., 1922, p. 426.

pathology. There are spells for cerebral malaria (associated with the white-headed osprey), inflammation of gums (paper wasp), intestinal trouble (shark), toothache (insect), intestinal "eating out" (eagle), goose-flesh (porcupine), incontinence of urine, incontinence of semen, gangosa (hornbill), paralysis (snake), tertiary yaws (rock limpet), wasting in hookworm (Sakwara tree), elephantiasis (shell), boils. The taboos are not only used to protect private property but also in the ordinary course of private feuds. Practically everybody in Dobu is a witch or a sorcerer.

Twice a year the Dobuan leaves his jealously guarded garden and wife and goes oversea for a Kula expedition. Kula is the strange exchange system between the islands north and south of Dobu, first described by Malinowski in his "Argonauts". From island to island, northern armshell kauris are exchanged for the southern spondylus shell necklaces. The system is not primarily economic; the exchange of northern canoes and southern pottery is quite secondary. Every object circulates. Exchange is made for the mere love of exchange. Every man has a partner on the visited islands who gives him objects, to get other objects later in Dobu. To get a good partner is thus the first condition of success in the Kula. It depends much on the personal appearance of the Dobuan, but less in the material than in a supernatural sense. For the jealous, diffident Dobuan, who is a headhunter, a sorcerer, a magical thief, the whole proceeding based on confidence and peace is purely a miracle. How can it be fulfilled? In this relation just as in courtship such magic influence upon the partner can only be obtained by secret, inherited incantations. The whole voyage is pervaded with magic (incantations of the canoe, the winds), but the most important again is the personal secret spell. Magic alone allows the Dobuan to be more successful than his fellows. And magical vengeance again will be exerted against him by his less fortunate companions.

The only place the witch-ridden Dobuan feels relatively secure is the small village (25 inhabitants) in which he is born and where he will be buried, and the only group he trusts to a certain degree is his matrilineal group, the susu, "mother's milk" (mother, mother's sisters and brothers, his brothers and sisters) from whom he inherits, who reside in the village. In case of serious illness he is immediately removed to this village. Unfortunately he passes half of his life as a pariah in another village and the prerogatives of the susu disorganize the family group (man, wife and children) in which he lives his hole life long. About a dozen small villages form a locality, a war unit.[35] One marries out of the village, where all children of one generation are "sisters" and "brothers", into another village of the locality. Sexual life starts long before marriage. As soon as the boy attains puberty he can no longer sleep in the house of his parents. He sleeps with girls in other villages while his sister receives other boys. He has to leave before dawn. When caught in the morning he has to marry the girl. It is characteristic of Dobu that this "free" practice goes together with an extreme prudishness in language so that missionaries did not even suspect the custom. The married pair lives alternatively one year in a house of their own in the village of the wife where the children belong and where also resides the maternal uncle who has authority over them and leaves them his skull, his incantations and his garden; and one year in another house in the village of the man where his susu lives, his inheritors (the children of his sister) and where after his death his children will not even be allowed to enter. In the village of the other susu one is not an "owner", but only a "resultant from marriage", who has not even the right to call the "owners" by their names. One feels outside of the loyal group of one's partner with his brothers and sisters and unable to avenge the partner's adultery with his village "brothers" or "sisters" (village "incest"). Marriage is an endless system of economic exchange between the villages and especially the susus of the two partners. The village of the bridegroom has not only to furnish hands, but betel, oppossums, yams, arm-shells, pigs, a certain banana-fish meal, sago and taro, and receives much less in exchange from the village of the bride. These exchanges are repeated every year and become extremely heavy in the mourning year for the village of the surviving partner. Sometimes they are continued even afterwards for the love of exchange. The marital tributes are given and accepted without communal feasting and in a rather unfriendly way. As Dobuan soil is poor, very often these debts are not paid to the satisfaction of the other part and disease producing magic is employed as vengeance. The Dobuan always suspects his wife, his mother-in-law, or other relatives from his wife's side, of bewitching him, or vice versa. The diviner called in case of illness (from another locality – to secure impartiality and his own subsequent safety) points almost every time to such a witch or sorcerer who has justified econom-

35 Each village has together with other villages a totem bird, a common woman ancestor. But the totem grouping is without importance. Villages of the same totem may be members of different localities and thus be opposed in war.

ic griefs against the sick person. Justice is then paid and the witch exorcises the diseased. This belief acts as a kind of police and is quite apt to enforce economic obligations. The natives say: "You Whites have your rifles – we have taboo, witchcraft and sorcery, our weapons." It is even the only kind of government they have, living as they do without chiefs. But it has a terribly disruptive influence upon family life. The average Dobuan divorces from 3 to 4 times during his life. He feels safer in Trobriand where he believes the women do not participate in the privilege of sorcery.[36] The great sexual freedom before marriage is not automatically replaced by great strictness after marriage like in Eddystone.[37] Coupled with a great shame of the bodily organs, a great prudishness in speech, goes a lascivious delight in cut-and-run adulteries and seductions. Jealousy therefore normally runs so high in Dobu that a man watches his wife closely, carefully timing her absences when she goes to the bush for natural functions. Children are enlisted as informants. As a matter of fact, sentimentally, the man is closer to his dog than to his wife. The arsenal of marital warfare comprises besides sorcery, witchcraft and village "incest", eventually suicide. The person wishing to maintain the marriage against the person wishing to dissolve it, usually attempts suicide, often fails to make it fatal and obtains a contemptuous maintenance of marriage, dictated more by fear of the partner's susu than by real pity.

There is no special supernatural department in Dobu. The Dobuan's life ideals, to be a good magical yam thief, a great adulterer, a sucessful Kula-exchanger, a strong sorcerer, to defend himself against disease, to satisfy his hatred and to punish his enemies with disease, all his fears and hopes, are covered by magic. The Dobuan sometimes practices besides taboos, also "vada", the direct magical assault which kills by suggestion.[38] He also uses herbs believed to be poisonous without spells, without distinguishing them clearly from the herbs employed in the magical performance. Some of these herbs are actually efficacious,[39] as proved beyond doubt in some suicides. But he does

36 Malinowski, 1922, p. 42.   37 Rivers, W. H. R., 1926, p. 71.
38 This interesting phenomenon is also described in other parts of Melanesia by Codrington, *l.c.*, p. 206, Seligman, C.G., 1910, p. 170, 187, 695, and Malinowski, 1922, p. 42.
39 This discovery of Fortune is very interesting in comparison with the statements of Seligman (*l.c.*, p. 289) and Codrington (*l.c.*, p. 215) that in the districts observed by them no actual poisons are used. Seligman stresses rightly the great difficulties for the European to obtain information about the whole illegal sorcery complex (*l.c.*, p. 638).

believe not less violently in the result of the materially inefficacious herbs, although he pretends to "try them out" as he does all his magic! The spirits of the dead go away to the island Bwebweso. "The Dobuan is not comfortable in the idea that the dead can do any damage. Damage is done so preponderantly by the living that this latter conception will not tolerate a rival conception easily." Almost all his supernaturals are "dependent", functioning only through magic formulas. His almost "religious", respectful attitude to these supernaturals in his formulas proves on the other hand the only relative value of such labels as "magic".

When we now turn to medicine proper in Dobu, not much is left after a general survey in Dobuan life. As disease is the principal magical weapon, as everybody fights against everybody with magic and knows disease incantations, as necessarily the sorcerer is also the healer in Dobu, there is no special medicine man and no special medical department.[40] Disease (and "medicine") are everywhere. Death from old age or accident is not accepted as such by the Dobuans. All illness, disease and death are attributed to jealousy and provoke recrimination. We have already described the usual magical production of disease by spells introducing animal spirits into the foe's body in connection with the tree taboos. Excepted from that rule are only minor troubles like ulcers and the diseases introduced by the white man (measles, tuberculosis, influenza, dysentery) for which no incantations exist. While the sorcerer always proceeds by uttering his spell over some personal leavings of the victim, the Dobuan witch may also act by spirit abstraction. There is no tender feeling for the deformed and incurable in Dobu. He is "bad". His magic was weak. His ghost will not even be admitted in Bwebweso. The only professional in Dobuan medicine is the diviner who acts by water gazing or crystal gazing (after preliminary inquiry). He detects the witch or sorcerer and the economic background of the conflict paying strict regard to native justice. He is rather a justice of the peace than a medical man. The healing procedure is quite simple. Each taboo has its lola (exorcizing spell). The publicly exposed and publicly appeased witch or sorcerer breathes in a vessel of water and the patient is bathed with it. If he dies nevertheless, not the detected, but another, still undetected sorcerer is held responsible. Since all disease spells are believed to lead inevitably to death, the curative exor-

40 The strange multiplicity of "specialists" in Eddystone Island, described by Rivers in *M. M. R.*, p. 43 ff., may perhaps have similar bases.

cisms are automatically credited with more power than they deserve. In rare cases where a crystal instead of an animal spirit is believed to be projected, it is removed by suction.

The unity of Dobuan culture cannot be denied, sinister as it may seem to us.[41] Supernatural beliefs enforcing lawful behavior towards neighbors are nothing unusual in Oceania.[42] But nowhere else than in Dobu do they seem to have attained such forms which almost defeat the purpose. Nowhere is every evil attributed with such consequence to human agency, nowhere else does there result a similar spirit of jealousy and thievery, of witch obsession (even in daytime the Dobuan does not dare to wander alone) and aggressiveness. Neighbor cultures (in the geographical and cultural sense) showing relatively small formal differences like Basima (patrilocal residence of the family) or Trobriand (rank system and chiefs, patrilocal residence) exhale quite a different spirit. Dobuan medicine owes its special features to its perfect integration with the pattern. In Dobu there is only and one cause of disease, witchcraft or sorcery. There is no possible intervention of supernaturals, independent from human agency, imposing a more impersonal sanction, acting mostly by soul abstraction, no influence of ghosts, no taboo infraction as elsewhere in Melanesia.[43] Diagnostic knows neither dreams nor trance nor the sacrifice to the ancestor.[44] Treatment in Dobu is deprived of drugs as almost everywhere in Melanesia,[45] but on the other hand it is also deprived of the characteristic Melanesian mixture of spells and massage.[46] Nor are there bone setters, etc.; it is strictly reduced to the exorcising spell. Dobuan "medicine" needs no

41 We have to be cautious with such appreciations given from outside. It seems worth while to remember here Seligman's commentary to another Melanesian culture: "Indeed, as far as I have been able to ascertain, the Papuasian of this district regards the existence of sorcery not as has been alleged as a particularly terrifying and horrible, but as a necessary and inevitable condition of existence in the world as he knows it. So that the Roro speaking tribes look on sorcery in the abstract with no more horror and fear than Europeans in their prime regard old age and death" (*l.c.*, p. 279). Even Fortune remarks once: "Dobuans prefer to be infernally nasty or else not nasty at all." On the other hand, we have even omitted a good many Dobuan horrors. Even a study of their only esthetic product, their beautiful songs, treating mostly of "love", mourning and sea-accidents leaves one deeply depressed.

42 Fortune, R. F., Manus Religion, 1935; Firth, R., pp. 340–362; Malinowski, 1922, p. 75

43 Codrington, *l.c.*, p. 208; Rivers, *M. M. R.*, p. 15 (Banks Isl., Gazelle Peninsula), p. 37 (Eddystone Isl.); Fortune, *l.c.*, p. 7, 28 (Admiralty Isl.); Seligman, *l.c.*, p. 183 (Koita).

44 Codrington, *l.c.*, p. 208, 209; Rivers, *M. M. R.*, p. 31; *Report Cambridge Exp.* (1908), V, 362; II, 266.

45 Codrington, *l.c.*, p. 199.

46 Rivers, *M. M. R.*, p. 100; Wedgwood, C., 1934/35, p. 280; Hocart, *l.c.*, p. 232.

special practitioners; it is generalized, and its outstanding feature is that disease-making counts more than disease-healing.

THONGAS[46a]

The Thongas are a Bantu speaking tribe, living around Lourenço Marques and numbering about 750,000 souls. They are divided into six dialect groups; each group is composed of 3 to 7 clans of several thousand members. The most solemn oath of the Thonga is that which is taken with earth. The same word "tiko" means soil and clan. The monkeys are considered degenerate human beings who lost the habit of working and of tilling fields, and thus fell into their present miserable condition. That is a typical peasant view. Although they lack the plough, manure and irrigation, Thongas have a rather manifold agriculture of different cereals. The country is rich in wild fruit trees. From cereals and fruits they make beer. They have also some cattle, goats, pigs, and fowl. They do a little fishing. Hunting of big game (lion, elephant, crocodile, hippopotamus) is in the hands of specialists. But in spite of these various resources there is always the danger of famine in case of drought. Women besides taking care of almost the whole agriculture are potters; men make the famous baskets, build the houses, supervise the cattle. The Thongas know iron. They know how to work and how to enjoy life. There is a real culinary art among them. Storytelling and singing is greatly cultivated. Musical instruments are highly developed. A good poet is able to make a living as a wandering minstrel. Although there is warfare, there is no genuine interest in war. Not heroic deeds give a social standing, but the number of wives! This is because more wives mean more tilled soil, more cooked food and more children to propitiate the ancestor later. Love is of little importance in Thonga life. Marriage is first and foremost an economic transaction between two families. The family of the bridegroom has to pay the "lobola" (a number of hoes) for the bride. With that lobola, the brother of the bride will buy his wife. Lobola debts are guaranteed by the whole village. Lobola debts are a permanent problem with the Thongas and poison the relations of the in-laws and the whole social life. Women have no property and form, after the death of the husband, the main bulk of an inheritance. They are distributed among his brothers and his sister's sons. Very old people are neglected.

46a Except when other references are given, the facts of this chapter are taken out of
    H. A. Junod: *The Life of a South African Tribe*, 2 vols., London, 1913.

The elementary unit of Thonga society is the village, inhabited by the headman, his wives, his younger brothers, his sons and their wives. When the headman dies, the village dies. His brother-successor builds a new one with the same population. In the village food-communism reigns, but the ancestor gods can only be approached by the headman. The villages depend on the king. The king lives materially almost at the same level as his subjects but he is a magical being, the incarnation of the country. His ancestors are the gods of the country. The soil is the king's property, justice is distributed by him. He is guided by his counsellors. He receives taxes and other services. The long custom of organized jurisdiction gives to the people a strong sense of justice and makes them rather peaceful and law abiding.

The religious world of the Thonga is based on the same principle of familial hierarchy; as gods of the individual serve the ancestors not only of the paternal but also of the maternal line. The ancestors of the king are the gods of the whole tribe. The notion of another supernatural force, the heaven, exists only in a most rudimentary form.

Thonga religion is a strong religion without idols, temples, professional priests, special days of worship, based exclusively on prayers and sacrifices. Except in case of rain making, the sacrifice consists of fowl, goat or ram and not of men. It is somewhat surprising and perhaps shocking to some whites that the Thonga uses with his relative-gods also a more terrestrial "family" language which sometimes is more frank than respectful. Human life is for the Thonga a sequence of stages like the agricultural year. Every change seems surrounded by supernatural dangers. Thus numerous taboos have to be kept, especially in the period of these changes; numerous rites and ceremonies connected with prayer and sacrifices have to neutralize the dangers. The week after birth is full of taboo for child and mother. The baby is regarded in a supernaturally dangerous state up to its weaning. Not less than four ceremonies are performed with him and it continually receives magic medicine. Puberty brings circumcision and a hard initiation school for boys and minor rites for girls. Menstruation is always highly dangerous. Marriage ceremonials and taboos are well elaborated. Adultery is taboo and will result in protracted labor of the guilty wife and other diseases. Before the first fruits and mealies are eaten, the chiefs have to perform the luma rites, thus doing justice to the gods and guarding the hierarchic priority in consumption. Exceptional events like war, hunt, return from the Johannesburg mines, convalescence from disease, are similarily connected with taboos and ceremonials. Before marriage boys and girls enjoy sexual freedom. After marriage sexuality becomes a somewhat official affair. There is almost no event which is not connected with a sexual taboo (hunting, fishing, war, village building, mourning, menstruation, child growth, disease of a village inhabitant, etc.), almost no purification rite without a special kind of ritual sex-intercourse. The most terrific defilement is death, the most elaborate ceremonial, mourning, ends after a year with the destroying of the hut of the deceased and the distribution of the heritage. The sons of the sister play a special rôle in the mourning ceremonial. The sadness and restrictions of the mourning period are in a strange way combined with drinking and feasting and the ritual use of an otherwise impossible obscene language.[47] This custom seems a psychological safety valve like under other circumstances the continuous praise of the wisdom of the little ones and the triumph of the weak in the stories of the rather highly hierarchized Thonga society. The taboos are not man made like Melanesian taboos; they are god made and are connected with prayer and sacrifice. On the other hand they have gained a kind of independence, attracting the whole fear complex, rather missing in Thonga religion proper. All Thonga life is suspended in a big net of taboos. These taboos avenge themselves almost automatically and without intervention of the gods, mostly through disease and death. The most terrible reaction against a taboo transgression is drought in the case of miscarriage and improper burying of a young child which requires a complicated purifying ceremonial again connected with obscenity. Rain and lightning are the only supernaturally important celestial events. Dreams are of little importance.

The will of the gods is revealed to the diviners through the throwing of bones, a kind of dice. The diviners have a set consisting of dozens of bones of beasts. This set is a real "microcosm". Every bone represents an element in Thonga life. Innumerable combinations of positions are possible. The Thongas are very proficient in the art of bone throwing and greatly revere these bones.

While divining, as other magic elements, is strongly integrated in Thonga religion, magic acquires a certain independence (although even witches are controlled by the ancestor-gods) in the terrible witchcraft beliefs which the Thongas share with most other African tribes.[48]

47 Evans-Pritchard, E.D., 1929, 311 ff.; Herskovits, M.J., 1938, vol. I, p. 387.
48 With the disintegration of native culture witchcraft beliefs seem rather to increase

Thongas differentiate strongly between the black magician (sorcerer) and the white magician (witch-doctor). They also make some distinction between the hereditary witch (hereditary in the case of evil eye in the maternal line!) acting at night unconsciously,[49] and the sorcerer, acting consciously by black art, motivated by envy, jealousy and greed. Sorcerers form societies. The admission fee often consists of the sacrifice of his own child. (It is not clear if these facts are actual as for instance with the Manos,[50] or mere delusions as probably with the Gas.[51]) Witches kill by eating the spiritual part of the bewitched (a kind of "vada"), they enslave the killed,[52] they produce accidents especially with wild animals, they send disease producing foreign bodies or animals into the body of the bewitched, they make him go to Johannesburg and die there, and they steal the crops. Amulets, magical fences, etc. are used to protect against witchcraft. The main fighter against witchcraft is the witch doctor, who thus gains great importance in upholding the social order.[53] His methods for smelling out the sorcerers are: questioning, trance and ordeal. As in many other parts of Africa the ordeal in Thonga is a poison-ordeal, the drinking of the mondjo. The mondjo is a plant of the Solanacea family with intoxicating properties. At the same time the witch doctor hypnotizes his victims. Astonishing confessions are obtained,[54] which emphasizes the general belief in witchcraft.

Disease is either itself one of the mysteriously dangerous situations in Thonga life or it is the outcome of such a taboo-situation. Thongas

than to decrease (see Junod II, 488; Field, M. J., 1937, p. 135; Evans-Pritchard, E. E., 1937, p. 446). "The secularization of modern life has proceeded at the expense of religion and its gods rather than at the expense of magic" (R. Benedict, *Encycl. Soc. Sc.*, vol. X, p. 41). This phenomenon perhaps gives the answer to the famous question of "degeneration of religion into magic". – Generally in the course of this article we were unfortunately obliged to treat primitive societies as static. We tried first to describe the place of the institution in a given society. We had to disregard the shifting of interest from one institution to another in one society, described for instance by R. K. Merton, *Osiris* IV, 1938, 360–632, for the 17th century in England, which of course exists also in primitive society!

49 See also Field, *l. c.*, p. 135. But Thongas have not the elaborate anatomical ideas in hereditary witchcraft which are reported from the Azande (Evans-Pritchard, *l. c.*, 387–391), the Liberian Manos (Harley, G. W., 1941, p. 23, 185) and the whole "likundu" district (Baumann, H., 1928).

50 Harley, *l. c.*, p. 23.
51 Field, *l. c.*, p. 139.
52 This old African idea is still flourishing even among the Haitians (Herskovits, *l. c.*, II, p. 244).

53 See below, p. 131.
54 Junod II, p. 486; see also Field, *l. c.*, p. 129; Harley, *l. c.*, p. 27; Lowie, *l. c.*, p. 37.

are ridiculed for having only a few disease names and calling the rest of the diseases after the diseased organ. But could not that custom be the consequence of a taboo against disease names such as exists elsewhere in Africa?[55] Anyway, they know syphilis, gonorrhoea, consumption, "fever", smallpox, scarlet fever, leprosy, rheumatism, tonsilitis, hematuria, dysentery, colic, headache, hydrocele, bilharzia, lumbago, scabies, cough worms, and most feared of all, mental diseases and epilepsy. Except for the few cases caused by witchcraft or the "heaven", diseases are sent by the ancestor gods; they are a consequence of taboo transgression (for instance consumption for not respecting mourning ritual; insanity for not purifying after hunt, hydrocele when men enter Kafir peafields) or the taboo situation (defilement of death, birth, etc.). Leprosy and consumption are regarded as magically contagious to the relatives. Death in old age is regarded as natural. Children are not allowed to mock cripples.

Diagnosis of course is obtained from the bones, which also prescribe prayers and sacrifices. There are no incantations. The central element of Thonga therapy is the medicine, a mixture of drugs and other magical substances. The medicine is given by the gods but its acting element seems a special mystical, purifying force circumscribed by such general notions as "moya" (signifying also wind, breath, spirit of alcoholic beverages) or "muri" (meaning tree, plant, herb, but also any means of producing any effect of any influence). This dynamic conception suggests somewhat the Liberian "nye"[56] or even the Melanesian "mana". Junod counted 40–50 drugs and 20 prescriptions. None seems to have the immediately convincing actual value of other African drugs and poisons with which undoubtedly the drug and not suggestion work. Anyway there is no differentiation between actual and only magically efficient drugs. Thonga inoculate against snake-bite by rubbing snake ashes into the incisions.[57] They also inoculate against smallpox.[58] Together with medicine the Thonga also use cupping, cauterizing and the sweat bath. A most ingenious procedure is the bringing up of premature children in warm pots. Surgery does not exist.

55 Harley, *l.c.*, p. 39; Field, *l.c.*, p. 120, etc.

56 Harley, *l.c.*, p. 13.

57 This apparently successful and rather astonishing procedure is described also by Harley for the Manos (*l.c.*, p. 213) who quotes there 6 other African testimonials for the same custom. See also Lebzelter, V, 1928, p. 305; Hewat, M.L., 1906, p. 94.

58 For Manos and literature on other tribes, Harley, *l.c.*, p. 217.

Every grave disease is "closed" by the hondlola rite. The hondlola rite (a rite of purification, performed also after weaning, for unsuccessful girls, in mourning, after the diviners initiation) seems to show that for the Thonga a serious illness constitutes a marginal period after which the patient must be aggregated afresh to society.

The profession of the medicine man is hereditary, descending from the father or the maternal uncle. Sometimes the heritage of knowledge is small but a good medicine man tries to combine the activities not only of the diviner and therapist, but also of the witch doctor, the rain and the war-magician-priest, and thus gains a high social standing. There are no pure herb doctors and no woman in the profession. There is no ecstatic behavior or special dress. The forked pole in the village of the medicine man is a kind of altar where he prays to the ancestors and suspends the medicines, the knowledge of which he inherited from them. Once a year in a special feast the medicines are renewed and a kind of luma of the medicines is celebrated. The medicine man charges a considerable fee.

Witchcraft, which acts by soul abstraction as well as by spirit intrusion, is of course treated differently. The witch has to recall his spells. Quite a special chapter in Thonga medicine is possession. A foreign spirit (generally of a dead Zulu) takes possession of the patient and produces a nervous crisis which has some resemblance to hysteria, but also to schizophrenia and to amuck. An exorcism ceremony – there are different "schools" of men and women specialists in exorcising – with a lot of drumming, singing, medicine, blood drinking and vomiting expells the spirit. But the patient has to celebrate protective rites which represent a worship of the spirit, during his whole future life. He enters a society of exorcised and becomes himself an exorciser. Practically he still seems ill, but is converted to a kind of new "religion". It is quite typical that possession, like witchcraft, increased enormously in Thonga during the last 80 years. Conversion to Christianity heals in Thonga but that seems rather the consequence of conversion as such than of the special creed thus acquired; in Ga a similar accident with people already converted to Christianity is healed by their becoming a professional medium, mouth-piece of the heathen gods.[59]

In Africa similar cultures are covering large sections and sharp cultural limits are less developed than among Oceanic islands.[60] Nevertheless, seen against the background even of African cultures with

59 Field, l.c., p. 101.   60 Ankermann, B., 1905.

similar tendencies, Thonga society has quite a silhouette of its own. There is neither the economic richness and differentiation in trade and crafts, the accumulation of property for heritage, the conspicuous consumption in sacrifices, the esoteric knowledge of an enormous "Olympus" by a priestly class, nor the harsh but perfect political organization of absolutism as in Dahomey. There are no Zande classes, no Ga towns, no Zulu warrior kings, no Liberian secret societies. Dreams are of small importance, witchcraft never becomes a universal factor. There is neither the pananimism of the Manos nor the complete absence of spiritualism of the Kpelle. There is a society of families of peasants, governed by their dead elders and one outstanding family, with a celestial world as simple and undifferentiated as their own family, with a wealth of terrestrial and supernatural rule, a certain amount of anxiety as in all men, but a well developed ability to enjoy a hard and simple life.

Thonga medicine is consistent with this picture. The family organizes the daily life, the ancestors rule that life; they give taboos and they give disease. The fundamental attitudes of the Thonga: his relation to the ancestors, to legal order in the natural and supernatural world, his behavior to woman, pervade also medicine. In its grouping around the taboo idea,[61] Thonga medicine lacks some traits typical of other African cultures. There is no differentiation into natural and supernatural diseases,[62] not the wealth of surprisingly efficient poisons and drugs (antispasmodics, diuretics, abortives), specifics against venereal diseases, malaria, anthrax, and perhaps even leprosy.[63] There are no bonesetters, no sick-huts. On the other hand no fetishes, no spells, no drug revealing dreams and ecstasies exist. Spirit-intrusion acts only in the relatively rare possession. Thonga medicine guards the simple and law-abiding character of its society.

*

We hope that our material brings out with sufficient clarity the following three points:

There is primarily not one "primitive medicine", but there are numerous different primitive medicines. Although the choice of our tribes was purely incidental, dictated only by the availability of good material,

---

61 Observed in a less central position naturally also in other African tribes. See Harley, *l.c.*, p. 39; Field, *l.c.*, p. 7; Herskovits, *l.c.*, I, p. 397; Westermann, D., 1912, p. XXIII.
62 Harley, *l.c.*, p. 197.
63 See Harley, Lebzelter, and Delobsom, D., 1934.

both general and medical from one author – a thing unfortunately much rarer than is generally supposed – no one of our tribes seems to correspond to the time-honored scheme of "primitive medicine". Although incidentally all three tribes emphasize the spiritual rather than the technical element (we would appreciate very much if in discussions on primitive medicine the misleading term "rational" could be replaced by the more exact term "technical"), they are still different enough the one from the other.

The differences between primitive medicines are much less differences in "elements" (they have a lot of common elements), *than differences in the medical "pattern"* which they build up and *which is conditioned fundamentally by their cultural pattern.* There is no inevitable position which illness and the healing art must take in society. Disease may be regarded in its narrowest physiological limits and even below them or may become a symbol for dangers menacing society through nature or through its own members. It may seem a mere incident or reach the rank of a goddess. Society unconsciously gives these different places to disease in the course of history.

This fact may also throw some light on the question why the rhythm and the lines of development in medicine were and are so different, uneven and unequal. Were medicine but a quasi-biological reaction of society towards the general fact of disease without interference of general cultural trends, the striking neglect of the obvious, the painful and costly adherence to the inefficacious or obnoxious in certain societies, the miraculous insights and progress in others would be hardly understandable. It is not the special amount of intelligence or stupidity in a given culture to which we can attribute the responsibility for these facts, but the existence of fortunate or unfortunate cultural attitudes, often in no way connected with healing, which give us the correct explanation.

The degree of integration of the different elements of medicine into a whole and of the whole medicine into the cultural pattern varies considerably. There is no doubt, for instance, that the integration is more complete in Dobu than in Thonga and in Thonga than in Cheyenne.[63a] In

63a Incidentally the three cultures described all reach in the field of their medicines a certain degree of integration, so that one can speak of a "typical" disease cause (e.g. Cheyenne: spirits; Dobu: sorcery; Thonga: taboo-transgression), of a "typical" way of diagnostics or therapeutics, etc. But that is by no means necessary or general. There are numerous tribes (e.g. Dahomey-personal communication of Prof. Herskovits) where different ideas concerning the cause of disease, the ways of

the present state of our knowledge the reason seems historical. Rivers [64] explained this fact by the tendency of borrowing culture elements and the blending of cultures. [65] Even when we suppose an isolated development in the tribe, the fact that different sections of tribal life do not advance at the same rate may at least partly explain our phenomenon. Medicine in primitive society is incidentally part of the spiritual section which often seems more conservative than the purely technical.

We abstained consciously from general deliberations like evaluation of the worth of primitive medicine or of the deeper meaning of magico-religious practices. We have dealt elsewhere with these questions. [66] We consciously abstained from creating definite "types" of primitive medicine or from accepting one of the existing classifications, not because we deny the possibility or necessity of such a classification, but because answering that question can never be the object of an article and seems to be premature before a thorough-going reexamination of the material, including a study of medical *objects* and of *time relations* in primitive culture. We are rather sceptical concerning the possibility of evolutionary schemes, but we think that already a large comparative study of primitive medicine would be a great value for medical history and medicine as a whole. We even sincerely believe that general anthropology would profit from such studies. As the study of the handwriting of a person, an isolated and rather insignificant trait, can throw a new light on the knowledge of the whole personality, so sometimes the study of an art, law, language, object, family-system, religious belief throws light on a whole culture. And why not medicine? General historians at least begin to accept this argument for historical research. We tried to be extremely careful concerning the *causal* implications of the whole pattern as well as of the medical practices. It is sometimes a great temptation to explain the causal necessity of things in terms of psycho-biology, [67] environment or material culture instead of simply

healing etc. are coexistent without one of them being considerably more important than the others.

64 Rivers, *M. M. R.*, p. 98 ff.

65 Concerning the "incessant tendency of borrowing" see also Lowie, R., 1929, p. 435.

66 See below, p. 128,, 132.

67 In an extremely interesting article "The probable origin of man's belief in sympathetic magic and taboo" (1931), Dr. E.J. Kempf describes in terms of nervous physiology (conditioned reflexes, etc.) how magic works, thus greatly enlarging our understanding of the process. But the fact that magic acts in this way is no explanation why humanity chooses first the way of magical thinking instead of another way physiologically not less "natural".

stating the connection of the facts. Such an explanation may even be possible for simpler traits.[68] In a complex phenomenon like medicine, not to speak of a culture pattern, one realizes soon enough that one took for a real cause what was a mere occasion which permitted the observed development. The unconscious subjective factor of choice and decision, which characterizes all human activity and the real tendency of which so far we do not know, generally spoils such plain causal considerations. We think that in spite of these our subjective and objective limitations the simple study of the *various possibilities and connections in culture and medicine* exemplified here by the Cheyennes, Dobuans and Thongas already has its value.

68 Hobhouse, L. T., Wheeler, J. C., Ginsberg, M., 1930.

THE SHAMAN AND PRIMITIVE
PSYCHOPATHOLOGY IN GENERAL*

ON PSYCHOPATHOLOGICAL LABELS

One of the characteristic mental traits of our culture is the labeling of phenomena with psychiatric diagnoses. This trait has become so very common that we are hardly any more aware of it. Persons and crowds, historic personalities and periods, cultures and societies, magic procedures and religions are "neurotic", "sadistic", "schizophrenic", etc., or in the plain and less dignified vocabulary of the common man "mad", "lunatic" and "crazy". Even the child in the cradle has not been spared and is supposed by some to undergo a "normal neurosis".

This trait is not so very new. Vesalius was called Vesanus. Goethe complained about its occurrence in literary criticism. As a more general phenomenon it may be traced back at least to the beginning of the last century, to the reactionary French historians, to Chateaubriand and his generation, and later on to Taine and his school.[1] Full of the strongest moral indignation against the revolution of 1789, but lacking already at that time a common moral basis, as e.g. religion, from which to appeal to the public, they arrived, probably rather unconsciously, at the ingenious solution of condemning the revolution as a case of mental illness. In a culture oriented towards and penetrated by an almost religious respect for science, deeply impressed by great medical progress, the procedure proved to be efficient and has thus survived in full vigor. Their adversaries did not remain inactive and devoted much time to a pious analysis of the more or less authentic mental defects of dead monarchs. Both parties immediately mobilized against the other the meanwhile rather outmoded but once so handy psychological and anatomical concept of the "degenerated".[2]

This quality of a hidden moral judgment may still be easily detected in a number of contemporary, apparently objective and scientific psychopathological labels.[3] The deep resentment against our own culture

---

* This article was published first under the title "Psychopathology, Primitive Medicine and Primitive Culture" in the *Bull. Hist. Med. 14*, 30–67 (1943).

1 Cabanès, A., Paris, 1920, p. 13, 230.

2 See for this side of psychopathological labeling the masterly study of O. Bumke, 1922; Walton, G.L., 1904.

3 A very meritorious contemporary sociologist still thinks that "the normal is but a variant of the concept of the good and the proper". Young, Kimball, 1940, p. 736.

is very often manifested in this way. To avoid misunderstandings: we are not opposed to moral judgements at all. On the contrary, we cannot resign to this modern "Ersatz" for moral norms and judgments. We think that the custom of covering moral judgments with a pseudoscientific psychopathological nomenclature is no advance at all and is equally bad for both of them: morals and science. But quite apart from the scientific "value" of this labeling, by the development of our attitude towards the mentally ill the once powerful weapon has paradoxically become very often a weapon against the one who uses it. It makes him now powerless instead of more efficient. Transferring a famous dictator, for instance, out of the political into the psychopathological sphere means to transfer him out of the field of normal political action. We pity the ill, and to fight and to hate one who is insane has become utterly unfair and senseless in our society. Thus from being an instrument of intolerance, psychopathological labeling has sometimes become an expression of tolerance or even over-tolerance. It may, on the other hand, serve just the opposite purpose and soothe moral scruples for ruthlessness following the old French dictum: Si on veut tuer son chien, on dit qu'il a la rage.

Psychopathological labeling is in part simply an expression of the very old penetration of our entire speech and thought by medical, physiological and anatomical terms and metaphors. Today it is to a large extent an involuntary tribute to the great achievements of psychiatrists in the field of general psychology during the last decades.[4] We cannot blame psychiatrists like Freud or Kretschmer[5] that they made their great discoveries with ill people. But we suffer from the fact that this procedure has formed the terminology. "Paranoids", "schizoids", "sado-masochistic characters" to us are unfortunately much less primary normal forms than people suffering from an extremely mild degree of mental disease. Looking at a character and classifying him as "paranoid", "schizoid", etc., we usually see in him at least the potential paranoiac, schizophrenic, etc., while the actual probability that he ever

But William James already has shown that the mere fact even of a true psychopathological origin decides nothing concerning the value of a phenomenon ("The Varieties of Religious Experience", Lecture I: Religion and Neurology).

4 Zilboorg (1939) seems to look mainly in this direction for the reasons of psychopathological labeling and calls it "an expression of the fundamental narcism of man who naively overestimates the arms he himself has invented".

5 It is interesting to notice that Kretschmer created the unequivocal normal notion of the "schizothym", but the pathological "schizoid" became the usual term.

will develop a psychosis is infinitesimal.[6] Of course, there are authors who, speaking e.g. of paranoid or megalomanic traits[7] in cultures or individuals, are fully aware of the fact that they deal with normal and not pathological phenomena; but in this awareness unfortunately they seem to represent rather the exception than the rule. Attempts by modern psychologists to change the terminology are therefore far from being vain stylistic exercises and deserve the fullest approval and encouragement.[8] This part of the history of psychopathological labels is almost tragicomic. The pathologists, embittered by the pertinacious lack of anatomical findings in certain mental and other diseases, had stigmatized them as "functional", had deprived them (and the unfortunate sufferers from them) of the legitimate title of honest diseases and driven them out of the realm of the scientifically abnormal; but the functional diseases have returned by the backdoor and have not only reconquered their deserved places, but also inundate the normal world with their terminology.

In psychopathological labeling there is also much lingering of older psychiatric thought. Older psychiatry was based on a concept of "normal" mentality which became not less efficient by the fact that it was never clearly formulated. From the counterparts of the pathological symptoms, from the ideals of past philosophers there was constructed an ideal "mentally normal" man who, very much like certain "ideal" anatomical pictures, has never existed and compared to whom not only every one of us but also – as the study of numerous "historical" psychiatric or psychological articles shows – every outstanding personality of the past is hopelessly "psychotic" or "neurotic". It is still not yet realized how extremely difficult it was to gain a realistic concept of the normal in a field as inaccessible to morphological, physical, chemical, even statistical methods, and what enormous an advance in our understanding of the mentally normal and abnormal has been reached by the functional method, the introduction of the notion of "integration", "adjustment", etc.

Nevertheless, all these explanations, true as they are, do not touch the fundamentals of our phenomenon. *Psychopathological labeling seems to be foremost an expression for helplessness, a specific attitude of*

6 This procedure has of course served the understanding of the insane, being regarded so far as something absolutely unhuman. But it has had ugly consequences for the normal, after all the majority.

7 E.g. Benedict, Ruth, 1934, pp. 151, 190, 216, 222.

8 Fromm, E., 1941, p. 164.

our culture towards the unknown. While the savage regards the incomprehensible as supernatural, the "civilized" Western man regards it as psychopathological. This reaction of our culture seems to occur in whatever field it may be. Whether Moreau de Tours declares "le génie n'est qu'une névrose" or one of our most intelligent and influential businessmen can see in the economic crisis of 1929 but "crowd madness",[9] in both cases the psychopathological "diagnosis" gives, perhaps, emotional relief, but not a scientific solution of the incomprehensible.

Our culture is unique in its consequent outlawing of the irrational, the emotional, the ecstatic. These phenomena have thus become most uncomprehensible and unknown to our society.[10] The bedroom, the liquor store and the office of the psychiatrist are their last sanctuaries, but only the last of these three places is not tabooed for public expression. Thus it is no wonder that an almost unlimited number of phenomena has acquired a psychopathological label.[11] Without hesitation the irrational is now very often called simply psychopathological and sometimes actually made psychopathological by this procedure. The same banishment of the irrational into the barren fields of psychopathology explains also the unmeasured and otherwise almost incomprehensible interest of the large public in psychopathology as the only means of satisfying an innate metaphysical need.[12]

We cannot agree with those who see in psychopathological labeling but a mere variant of the "psychological manoeuvres" of "bourgeois ideologists" to hide fundamental economic facts. Social psychology in itself did by no means ignore those facts and was on the contrary born out of the impotence of exclusive biological or economical materialism to explain fully the social process in past and present. As long as it does not fall into the monopolistic attitude of its forerunners, it is a sound reaction.

9 Bernard Baruch, 1932, p. XIV.
10 And this in spite of the most extensive and intensive study of these phenomena and in spite of the official, scientific recognition, nay, overemphasizing of the rôle of the emotional in our psychic economy!
11 "Many psychiatrists, including psychoanalysts, have painted the picture of a "normal" personality which is never too sad, too angry or too excited. They use words like 'infantile' or 'neurotic' to demonstrate traits or types of personalities that do not conform with the conventional pattern of a 'normal' individual. This kind of influence is in a way more dangerous than the older and franker forms of name-calling. Then the individual knew at least that there was some person or some doctrine which criticized him and he could fight back. But who can fight back at 'science'?" Fromm, *l.c.*, p. 246.
12 Concerning the problem of the metaphysical need see Ackerknecht, E.H., 1942, p. 516–518.

The mechanism of psychopathological labeling in itself is obvious and the paralogism very easy to detect. The concept of the *different* is simply identified with the concept of the pathological although the latter should be limited to the socially incompatible. But we are very far from underestimating the attractiveness of this trend, from despising its followers. Its emotional roots are too deep, the step from analyzing analogies between psychopathological thought and other forms of behavior to identifying those phenomena is too short and easy, that it should not be a very great temptation to make it. But, as we have already seen, it is very bad for the labeled, for the labeler and – what we are most concerned about here – for science. Once we stop at a typical statement of the "psychopathological school" as the following: *"Primitive religion and in general 'quaint' primitive areas are organized schizophrenia"*,[13] and think it over, it is not very difficult to realize the full consequences[14] of this tendency for science. When (primitive) religion is but "organized schizophrenia", then there is left no room or necessity for history, anthropology, sociology, etc. God's earth was, and is, but a gigantic state hospital and pathography becomes the unique and universal science. Absolute subjectivism has thus conquered science again. It needs the gigantic helplessness and vanity, the terrible "uniqueness" of our culture to come to such statements.

One of the main contributions of anthropology was to throw new light on the concept of the abnormal[15] and to invalidate older misconceptions of an universal type of "abnormality". The tendency of psychopathological labeling in our culture and science is thus a chal-

---

13 Devereux, G., 1939, p. 338. It is sad to see – but one reason more to take up the problem – that this statement – apparently an "improvement" of the older slogan that religion is a neurosis – comes from an author who, on the other hand, has done so much to elucidate problems of primitive psychopathology (e.g. 1939–40, 1940; 1942).

14 An analysis of the degree of reality in such a statement is not the object of these short introductory notes, but of the whole article.

15 See Sapir, E., 1932, p. 325; Hallowell, A.I., 1934, pp. 1–9; *Am. J. of Psychiatry*, 1936, pp. 1291–1330; Kroeber, A.L., New York, 1934; but especially Benedict, Ruth, 1934, pp. 59–82, and her *"Patterns of Culture"*, pp. 258–288. In 1930 in his "Psychopathologie und Kulturwissenschaft", H. E. Sigerist already warned against the projection of present psychopathological notions into history very much on the line of argumentation which was developed here by anthropologists. The above mentioned article of Zilboorg and remarks of Fromm, *l.c.*, p. 140, Kardiner, A., 1939, pp. 84, 418, seem to show that at least some more "enlightened" psychoanalysts become aware of the danger.

16 Concerning the problem of the sincerity of the medicine man see Ackerknecht, *l.c.*, p. 510.

lenge to medical anthropologists to begin charity at home and to reexamine their material to find out the actual rôle psychopathology plays in primitive medicine and primitive cultures.

THE MEDICINE MAN AND PSYCHOPATHOLOGY

When the medicine man first became known to Europeans, he generally was regarded as a humbug. With an increasing knowledge and understanding of primitive cultures this opinion has since been abandoned.[16] But it is still quite usual to see the medicine man characterized as a kind of madman. The diagnosis varies from epilepsy[17] to hysteria,[18] from fear neurosis[19] to "veritable idiocy".[20] As a matter of fact he is one of the preferred targets of psychopathological labeling in anthropology. We observe in his case again the passing from moral judgment to clinical diagnosis already described above.

Before analyzing how far the mentality of the medicine men may be regarded as abnormal or psychopathological, it may be useful to define how in our sense this diagnosis can only be applied in a legitimate sense. From the medical point of view mental diseases have the great disadvantage that the overwhelming majority of them cannot be defined in terms of anatomy or biochemistry. A cancer or a diabetes is everywhere the same, not only in its disabling consequences, but also in its objective symptoms and bodily changes.[21] A neurosis or a psychosis

17 McKenzie, D., 1927, p. 8; Gillin, J., 1939, p. 682; Bartels, M., 1893, p. 79. The epilepsy diagnosis implies besides the appreciation of the medicine man as mentally ill, which we are discussing, a special psychiatric error. Closer examination of these cases hardly ever reveals true epilepsy, but symptoms which would be classified in our society either among schizophrenic or hysteric syndromes. We will discuss this problem all the less as the identical error of historians is dealt with in great detail in O. Temkin's "Falling Sickness" (1945). We want to express to Dr. Temkin here our gratitude and indebtedness for many stimulating discussions on our problems. We also are very grateful to Dr. H. A. Loewald for his inspiring criticism of the psychiatric implications of this article, for which, of course, the author is only responsible.

18 Jennes, D., 1938, p. 52; Maddox, J., 1923, p. 40.

19 Hambly, W. D., 1926.   20 Wissler, C., 1922, p. 204.

21 Of course so many social and cultural factors enter directly and by psychological ways even the genesis and effects of these diseases that the above statement is only valid in the limited context of the artificial confrontation of mental and bodily disease! *Primarily every disease is a social phenomenon and is defined socially.* Then only the incapacitated or maladjusted are analyzed in terms of anatomy or biochemistry. Thus the paradox occurs that an anatomically slight deformation is "disease", while a much graver one like the deformed feet of Chinese women never is regarded as such, because it is never socially singled out to be submitted to pathologico-anatomical analysis.

most probably has also an organic basis or components,[22] but those are not known to us and we can diagnose mental disease exclusively by observation of changes in behavior and mental content, incompatible with successful social activity; such changes are not biological but socio-cultural phenomena. Our psychiatrists have empirically classified as special diseases and belonging to the realm of abnormality and psychopathology a number of such changes and attitudes which (and because they) are incompatible with normal functioning in our society. The anthropological study of other cultures has now produced the great surprise that these notions of abnormality judged from the only possible criterion, social integration, deserve by no means the absolute value we imputed to them. A man, e.g., with paranoid behavior and ideas, unlike a man suffering from tuberculosis, may in another cultural set-up where almost everybody shares his attitude, be by no means socially disabled, but a normal and even ideal participant of his society.[23] Ruth Benedict has analyzed in her "Anthropology and the Abnormal" and "Patterns of Culture" trances in the Shasta, Zulus and Siberians, homosexuality in the berdache-customs, paranoiac behavior in Dobu and "megalomania" among the Kwakiutl, and shown that the normals of those cultures look like abnormals in our culture while the abnormals in Dobu, among the Crow and Zuñi could be perfectly normal with us.[24] *"Normality within a very wide range is culturally defined."* [25] That means that we cannot any longer regard as abnormal a

22 Those mental diseases where organic changes are well known like general paralysis, alcoholic psychoses, have played the trick on us of appearing only in our civilization, thus stressing the importance of the cultural component even in those mental diseases where the organic basis is obvious, but depriving us again of possibilities of comparative study of mental diseases on a given organic basis.

23 "It is clear that culture may value and make socially available even highly unstable human types. If it chooses to treat their peculiarities as the most valued variants of human behavior, the individuals in question will rise to the occasion and perform their social rôles without reference to our usual ideas of the types who can make social adjustments and those who cannot. Those who function inadequately in any society are not those with certain fixed abnormal traits, but may be well those whose responses have received no support in the institutions of their cultures. The weakness of these aberrants is in great measure illusory. It springs not from the fact that they are lacking in necessary vigor but that they are individuals whose native responses are not reaffirmed by society. They are as Sapir phrases it 'alienated from an impossible world'." Benedict, 1934, p. 270.

24 Benedict, 1934, pp. 258–260. See also Mead, M., 1935, Ch.: The Deviant, pp. 290 ff.

25 Benedict, *J. of Gen. Psych. I,* 73 (1934); "Psychiatric diagnosis cannot be made without regard to cultural environment", Kroeber, A. L., 1934, p. 347; "Psychosis can only be stated in relation to culture pattern", Hallowell, 1934, p. 3.

person only on the basis of certain fixed symptoms, disregarding the historical and cultural place of this person, but that we can only regard as abnormal a person whose character reactions hinder social integration in a given period and society.

As anthropologists we deal with societies, cultures separated in space. But the same is true for separation in time, for different periods of the "same" culture. A normal of the Middle Ages would easily be an abnormal today.[26] This statement even holds good for the different horizontal culture areas[27] or subcultures,[28] in stratified (non-primitive) societies, in which for normality only "social personalities of the same level"[29] or "status"[30] should be compared.[31] We call in the following *"autonormal"* and *"autopathological" those who are defined in their normality and abnormality by their own society, the only true definition of normality we recognize.*

We call *"heteronormal"* or *"heteropathological" those who are regarded as normal or pathological according to the scale of our society,* a scale which is inadequate as long as we lack truly general notions of human psychopathology. We would like to warn from the very beginning that of course even the "autopathological" in a non-literate society is never to his brethren "mentally ill" in our sense, as most of these societies lack the conception of special mental or bodily diseases. He is simply "ill" and his illness is explained by the general disease concept, in the respective society. But for our purpose here it is essential that he is regarded as pathological and it would be an unnecessary burden for our present study, to analyse in every case the exact meaning of his disease in his society.

We are fully aware of the intricacies of the problem. We know that our solution is a provisory one and an expression of our limited knowledge. Our knowledge allows us to see that those members of primitive societies who behave like our psychopaths may be perfectly normal. But there may be a fundamental state of mental disease, common to all those who are mentally ill, as after all we are all men.[32] But we ignore it.

---

26 See Sigerist, *l.c.*, p. 145. Only such an approach elucidates the paradox why the majority of us, although apparently descendents of (pseudo) "neurotics" and "psychotics" are nevertheless rather normal persons.

27 Benedict, 1934, p. 230.   28 Sapir, E., *l.c.*, p. 36 ff.   29 Warner, L., 1939, p. 280.

30 Linton, R., Introduction of Kardiner, p. xiv.

31 See also Scheunert, G., 1930; Davis, K., 1938.

32 "The problem of understanding abnormal human behavior in any absolute sense independent of cultural factors is still far in the future... When data are available

There may be a morbid type condemned to become mentally ill in every society and changing only the forms of his disintegration in different cultures. But we are unable to diagnose this type, as we do not even know truly and to a necessary extent the normal of our own society. We are only able to state integration and non-integration every time they occur. It is almost certain that among the members, e.g., of a culture with paranoid or schizoid orientation there are those who are simply following the pattern [33] and there are those who are following it by "vocation", by inner structure, by a kind of organic necessity, and that both types, though normal, are different. But we have no instruments to differentiate them in quantity and quality.[34] We know that while between the former type and our paranoiac and schizophrenic there exists *but an analogy*,[35] because their "delusions" grow from different sources, *the one being formed by society, the other having grown against society*,[36] there may be more intimate relations between the latter and our psychopath. But without new criteria we can but produce more or less meaningless speculations on the problems. We are fortunate enough to have learned at least that the member of a primitive society, although he behaves exactly like the psychopath of our own society, may be perfectly normal (auto-normal) because functioning well in his society, while the abnormal, the nonintegrated, of this society may be normal (heteronormal) in the eyes of another society. The insight in the incompleteness of our equipment must not stop our endeavor, but encourage us to clear and prepare the field for new advances by using

in psychiatry, this minimum definition of abnormal human tendencies will be probably quite unlike our culturally conditioned, highly elaborated psychoses such as those that are described, for instance, under the terms of schizophrenia and manic-depressive." Benedict, *J. genet. Psychol. 1*, 79 (1934).

33 "The small proportion of the number of the deviants in any culture is not a function of the sure instinct with which society has built itself upon the fundamental sanities, but of the universal fact, that, happily the majority of mankind quite readily take any shape that is presented to them." Benedict, *l.c.*, p. 75.

34 This field of research has so far not yet been explored. It is not surprising that a single attempt on a dogmatic basis (W. Sachs, 1937, The psychoanalysis of a South African Medicine Man) has not yielded many results.

35 Hallowell, 1936, p. 1294; Wegrocki, H.J., 1939, pp. 169/170.

36 Gallinek, A., (1942, p. 54) in spite of using the heteropathological terminology, observes this fact very clearly on a historical level: "This hysteria was productive and of cultural significance in contrast to modern hysteria. It was different and it affected other personalities, personalities, who nowadays hardly would have a tendency toward hysteria and psychogenic disturbances. It affected those persons who needed a stimulus and a tool in order to embody and express completely the essence of their era."

the valuable although limited criteria we already have for analyzing concrete material.

*

For some decades now it has become customary to apply to medicine men all over the world the Siberian term "shaman". This use of terminology – or more exactly, misuse, as a rapid examination of the peculiarities of the shaman will show immediately – has undoubtedly to a very large extent contributed towards creating the psychopathological reputation of the medicine man. It seems too late to attempt or to obtain a change of this terminology; but an exposition of the facts may perhaps help to reduce the faulty conclusions springing from an uncritical use of the term shaman.

The Siberian shaman, as a matter of fact, is by no means the model of a medicine man, but a very special type of medicine man. Loeb[37] asked in 1929 that a differentiation at least be made between "shaman" and "seer". He wanted to retain the term "shaman" for the inspirational type of medicine man; the (voluntarily) possessed, *through* whom the spirit speaks; the man, who exercises and prophesies; as he occurs in Siberia, Asia, Africa, among the Dravidian tribes of India, the Veddhas, in Melanesia, Fiji and Polynesia. He created the term "seer" for those "non-inspirational" non-possessed medicine men, *with* whom the guardian spirit speaks and who do not exorcise or prophesy: the medicine men of North and South America, Australia, New Guinea, and of the Negritoes. He observed personally both types in Indonesia.[38] The proposition of Loeb becomes particularly important when his opinion can be confirmed that the seer is an earlier type and the shaman a later product of development.[39]

But not only in this sense is the Siberian shaman different from a great number of other medicine men. Not only is his possession of such a peculiar type (ventriloquism) that Oesterreich in his fundamental book – it is true on the basis of very incomplete material – even denies to him the character of possession.[40] Not only does the Siberian sha-

37 Loeb, E., 1929, p. 61/62.
38 It seems not to be place here to discuss in detail Loeb's classification. It is obvious that of course Africa and Asia are full of non-inspirational medicine men and that in North and South America, in New Guinea and among the Negritoes exist some rather rare occurrences of inspirational medicine men.
39 The study of disease concept distribution by Clements (1932, p. 223) leads to similar results.
40 Oesterreich, T.K., 1930, p. 305.

man belong to that restricted group of medicine men where previous illness in general is a condition of his vocation [41] where the vocation has an absolutely compulsory and obsessional character,[42] but he is the *outstanding representative of that small group of medicine men where the medicine man passes indeed through a stage of grave mental illness* before becoming a shaman. This fact has undoubtedly given more than anything else the special psychopathological tint to the term "shaman".

Of course mental illness is not the only way to become a shaman. Young orphans may voluntarily become shamans.[43] A special adventure accompanied by great danger may lead to shamanism.[44] Shamanism, e.g., among the Buriats may be simply hereditary and transmitted by instruction.[45] Or the "inspiration" may even be sold (Ostjak).[46] But as far as we are able to judge from the scanty documents mostly collected in a period of decay of shamanism,[47] a kind of mental disease seems to be most common during the preparatory period of the shaman. The first signs may appear in childhood. The outbreak occurs generally in the late puberty. "The preparatory period is compared by the Chukchee to a long severe illness and the acquirement of inspiration to a recovery."[48] "He who is to become a shaman begins to rage like a raving madman. He suddenly utters incoherent words, falls unconscious, runs through the forests, lives on the bark of trees, throws himself into fire and water, lays hold on weapons and wounds himself, in such wise that his family is obliged to keep watch on him. By these signs it is recognized that he will become a shaman."[49] Bogoras knew a woman shaman who had been violently mad for 3 years and whose hands were mutilated[50] as a consequence of these paroxysms. He reports of this tendency towards isolation, the changing periods of excitement and calm. One man slept during two months.[51] Sternberg reports a Giljak who was "unconscious" during two months.[52] Sieroszewski

41 As e.g. among the Zuñi: Benedict, *Patterns*, p. 72; Kwakiutl: Benedict, *l.c.*, p. 211; Pawnee: Linton, *Field Mus. Leafl.* VIII: 5; Africans: Harley, G., *Native African Medicine*, Cambridge, Mass., 1941, p. 199.

42 Sternberg, L., Divine Election in Primitive Religion, 1924; Yakuts: Sieroszewski, W., 1902; Abyssinians: Leiris, M., Paris, 1934; Yavapeis: Aitken, B., 1930; Maida: Corlett, W.Th., 1935, p. 92; Mentawei: Loeb, E., *l.c.*, p. 62.

43 Bogoras, W., 1904–1909, p. 424.

44 *Id.*, p. 421.

45 Klementz, D., p. 15.

46 Czaplicka, M.A., 1914, p. 178.

47 Bogoras, *l.c.*, p. 444.

48 *Id.*, p. 421.

49 Mikhailowsky, V.M., 1895, p. 85.

50 Bogoras, *l.c.*, p. 43.

51 Czaplicka, *l.c.*, p. 181.

52 *Id.*, p. 420; see also Jochelson, W.I., 1907, p. 47.

tells the story of Tiuspiut who had auditory and visual hallucinations during 9 years before recovering by becoming a shaman.[53] "If the man designed to become a shaman (by the spirits of dead shamans) opposes the will of the predecessors and refuses to shamanize, he exposes himself to terrible afflictions, which either end in the victim's losing all his mental powers and becoming imbecile and dull or else going raving mad and generally after a short time doing himself an injury or dying in a fit."[54] It is clear why a person should try to avoid the terrible shamanistic call and in spite of Radloff's general statement a few succeed in recovering without becoming shamans.[55]

It is not quite clear which one among the numerous Siberian psychoses the pre-shamanic psychosis is, nor can it be classified exactly as one of our mental diseases; it is not the convulsionary disease called epilepsia by Sieroszewski and Bogoras, and leading more or less rapidly to death.[56] It is certainly not amürakh, the "arctic hysteria" (see following chapter). On the contrary an amürakh cannot become a shaman and a shaman who gets amürakh has to give up his profession.[57] It seems to come closest to what Sieroszewski calls the "crying disease"[58] He saw these lunatics guarded in cages because they sometimes kill, and it sometimes seems necessary to kill them.[59] Although the preparatory madness of the Siberian shaman is generally regarded as hysteria, these descriptions would rather fit into our picture of schizophrenia insofar as they fit into one of our pictures at all.

Similar phenomena may occasionally be observed with Eskimo medicine men,[60] or in Indonesia.[61] They seem to have been rather common in the life history of medieval saints.[62] But *with a like clearness we have found the preshamanistic psychosis only among South African Bantu tribes.* We have the old but very graphic description of Rev. C. H. Calloway in his "Religious System of the Amazulu".[63] A man falls ill, does not eat, becomes "a house of dreams", weeps, has convulsions. He is treated for years, all his wealth is eaten up by the practitioners. He is but skin and bones. His death is daily expected. But then he

53 *L.c.*, p. 310.
54 Radloff, W., 1884, 2: 16.
55 Czaplicka, *l.c.*, p. 173.
56 Sieroszewski, *l.c.*, p. 218; Bogoras, *l.c.*, p. 42; see concerning a similar disease in Fiji, Spencer, D. M., 1941, pp. 29/30.
57 Czaplicka, *l.c.*, pp. 320, 325.
58 Sieroszewski, *l.c.*, p. 229.

59 Bogoras, *l.c.*, p. 43.
60 Kind of Amok of the future Anjagok. Ch. F. Hall, 1864, 2: 251; Weyer, E. M., 1932, p. 431.
61 Loeb, *l.c.*, p. 67.
62 Oesterreich, *l.c.*, p. 85; Gallinek, *l.c.*
63 1870, pp. 259–267.

becomes able to detect hidden (or stolen) things and after a purification ceremony he is a medicine man (inyanga) and well again. "If the relatives of the man who has been made ill by the Itongo do not wish him to become a diviner, they call a great doctor to treat him, to lay the spirit that he may not divine. But although the man no longer divines, he is not well; he continues to be always out of health."

Laubscher's [64] very recent studies among the Tembu and Fingu tribes present a rather similar picture. Numerous people fall in a state called "ukutwasa" [65] where they undergo a call from the mythical "River People" to become a "Doctor". They have visions, run wild, some commit suicide in this state. If one is refrained during ukutwasa from becoming a "Doctor", or if he is not properly treated by native methods he becomes mad. It is not quite clear if ukutwasa is already definitely regarded by the Tembu as mental illness or more as a mental state comparative to those of our examination candidates; but anyway the consequences of an ukutwasa not ending in doctoring activity are clearly hetero- and autopathological.

Mention should here also be made of the Wyo, male and female mediums among the Ga people of the Gold Coast. [66] Although not medicine men themselves, they are important assistants of both, medicine men and priests. They also pass through a preparatory state of mental disturbance (in this case closer to our "hysteria") and if their call is not followed they become plain mad (the Ga themselves differentiate between plain undirected madness and spirit possession). Following their call they undergo a long training period by a medicine man ("treatment"?) and function then as full-fledged mediums, being able to undergo voluntary possession, and being otherwise perfectly normal! [67]

Among the South African Thonga the ordinary medicine man is highly "non-inspirational". His office is purely hereditary. But those

---

64 Laubscher, B.J., 1937.

65 See also Hoernle, W., 1937, p. 231.

66 Field, M., 1937, p. 100–109.

67 Anyone who gets to know Wyo in their everyday lives cannot but be struck with the *lack* of any imbalance or hysteria in their everyday behavior. They are often serene and good tempered and not selfish or in the least 'difficult'. Seeing them again when excited by the spirit one cannot doubt that they are working off volumes of 'steam' which others must dispose of quietly and perhaps less thoroughly: The Wyo system is probably satisfactory from the Western medical point of view, as well as having the social satisfactoriness of providing a dignified niche for the type of person who in Europe would be the unfit and plague of society." Field, *l.c.*, p. 109.

who have suffered from possession by a spirit ("bubayiby psikwembu" = "the madness of gods") enter after the exorcism a special group of practitioners, who now themselves treat possession. [68] The possessing spirit has been won as a friend and protector.

This recovery by becoming a shaman is certainly a very strange fact. While it is easy enough to understand in simple hysteria-like states of possession where conversion to a creed and becoming an exorciser is well known to heal (Thonga, Ga),[69] it is rather difficult to do so in the above described Siberian, Tembu and Zulu cases. But even Laubscher, who generally is rather inclined to diagnose full blown schizophrenia everywhere, states: "The 'witch doctors' conform broadly to the class of abnormal characters known in our culture as psychopaths. They display in conduct all shades of deviation from the average person and it is not unlikely that many of them are psychotic persons in remissive phases or *improved or relieved without insight*."[70] He even recognizes that a whole category of them (the isanuse – they all have gone through ukutwasa!) is *not psychotic or psychopathic at all*.[71] We cannot adopt Nietzsche's principal refusal to recognize religious healing as real healing, which is based on the very personal philosophy of a minister's son, but he incidentally has pointed to an important, special trait of these healings: they rather stupefy than eradicate the evil.[72] In our cases too it is symbolical that the disease spirits are not "expulsed" but only pacified and even worshipped.[73] This seems to explain in a certain way why during old age some shamans seem to have a relapse,[74] while others

68 Junod, H. A., 1913, 2: p. 439.
69 Oesterreich, *l.c.*, pp. 272, 219 ff.; Ackerknecht, E. H., this volume, p. 52.
70 Laubscher, *l.c.*, p. 227.
71 *Id.*, p. 32. Similar preshamanistic pathological stages exist among tribes of Southern California (Kroeber, A. L., 1939/40, p. 205). *Id.*, 1925, p. 425). Devereux (1942, p. 82) seems to allude to these tribes in the following rather sensational statement: "Many native tribes believe that a seizure of insanity precedes the acquisition of shamanistic powers, and that a person receiving these powers, but unwilling to practice will become psychotic. One cannot but wonder how many Indian psychotics have turned into shamans while hospitalized in an institution, and been retained there, although they are ready to return to their tribes and to function as useful members thereof."
72 Nietzsche, F., p. 160.
73 Junod, *l.c.*, 2: 454.
74 "Dès que l'âge affaiblit les sorciers, les esprits se vengent de l'abaissement dans lequel ils les ont tenus. Ils les tourmentent, les agacent, les empêchent de dormir, volent incessamment autour d'eux en criant, en les raillant, en les mordant, en les piquant. Personne ne les entend, à l'exception du chamane qui souffre en silence, en général délaissé lâchement de tous." Sieroszewski, *l.c.*, p. 324.

retire, completely calmed.[75] On the other hand we cannot disregard the fact that the shaman is functioning socially while those who do not become shamans stay unadapted. We have to remember what a tremendous psycho-therapeutic power magic has not only for those for whom it is performed, but above all for the performer himself.[76] It is a kind of psychological safety valve where too strong psychic pressure can be released. We thus have to recognize that in primitive societies there perhaps exist outlets for mental conditions with which we are not able to deal. It seems as if we will have to accept the fact that *shamanism is not disease but being healed from disease.*

In stating that the shaman after having passed through an auto-pathological stage is autonormal,[77] we could stop our argument. But in order to convince sceptics we would like to discuss some points which show how little the shaman fits even in our scheme of a psychopathological (disintegrated) personality, as soon as we study not only some traits analogous to those of our psychopaths but his whole (integrated) personality. Although the preshamanistic mental crisis during puberty is unparalleled elsewhere in its deepness, we would become perhaps somewhat more comprehensive towards it, if we would remember that even in our society we accord to youngsters of that age an amount of mental unbalance, which is by no means physiologically justified but culturally conditioned.[78] The prophetic crisis is regarded as non-pathological, is highly respected and looked for; it is *voluntarily* induced, prepared and always kept in certain limits. Some minutes afterwards the shaman is perfectly calm, without signs of exhaustion. "Although hysteria lies at the bottom of the shaman's vocation, yet at the same time the shaman differs from an ordinary patient suffering from this illness in possessing an extremely great power of mastering himself in the periods between the actual fits which occur during the ceremonies."[79]

The professional shaman besides is not such an exceptional being in his culture, he is only a variety of the family-shaman. Where family-shamanism still exists, to a certain extent everybody

75 Bogoras, *l.c.*, p. 419. Bogoras regards this as complete "recovery from nervous conditions".

76 Kempf, E.J., 1931, p. 25.

77 "But neither to the institution of voluntary death nor to the hysterical fits of the shamans are we justified in applying the name of disease since these are not so considered by the natives themselves." Czaplicka, *l.c.*, p. 319.

78 See Mead, M., 1928.   79 Czaplicka, *l.c.*, p. 169.

shamanizes. Noise is as comforting to the Siberian in case of illness, as calm is to us.[80] Bogoras, who always insists on the nervosity of the shaman, reports himself a very rare act of self-control in Chukchee land: the refusal of alcohol perpetrated by a shaman (Scratching Woman). The existence of *self-control* is also evident in the rules for a model shaman: "Un véritable chamane doit posséder les vertus qui forment le trésor du cœur humain; il doit être sérieux, avoir du tact, savoir convaincre son entourage; surtout il ne doit pas se montrer présomptueux, fier, emporté!"[81] "In answer to persons seeking advice Chukchee shamans often display much wisdom and circumspection."[82] In refusing to treat tuberculosis, dysentery, scarlet fever, measles, syphilis and other diseases inaccessible to their therapeutical means they certainly display a good deal of *judgment*.[83] Perhaps they would be better understood if one would realize that they are not only priests and healers but also great dramatic artists.[84] This trait has impressed observers from the very beginning (v. Wrangel 1839, Castren 1853). One of the preferred arguments for the psychopathology of the shaman is his bad economic status. One forgets too easily that this poverty is imposed on the shaman by society. The mentally similar Eskimo angagok and Bantu isanuses by no means suffer from this evil for the simple reason that they are not instructed like the Siberian shaman to go first to the poor and not even to ask much from the rich![85] The adoption of woman's clothes by the shaman, another "psychopathological" trait, appears after closer examination in the overwhelming majority of cases socially conditioned and not temperamentally. Very few of these transvestites are true homosexuals and marry another man.[86] And besides even homosexuals are rather biological variants and by no means psychopaths by nature, but only become psychopathic through their outlawed position in our society.[87] Just the two latter points remind us to what an extent the shaman is formed by society, how impossible it is to identify his socially created mentality with that of our psychopath which has grown asocial. It is typical that he cannot work in a trance without an "ocitkolin", a person who gives him answers and applause during the séance.[89] As elsewhere he probably could not give up his

80 Bogoras, *l.c.*, p. 463.
81 Sieroszewski, *l.c.*, p. 318.
82 Bogoras, *l.c.*, p. 429.
83 Sieroszewski, *l.c.*, p. 323.
84 *Id.*, p. 325. We accord even to our own artists a certain amount of ecstatic behavior as normal.
85 Klementz, *l.c.*, p. 16.
86 Bogoras, *l.c.*, p. 450.
87 Benedict, 1934, p. 262 ff.
89 Bogoras, *l.c.*, p. 434.

wretched profession even if he wanted to do so.[90] "The magician is a being determined by society and pushed by it to fulfil its rôle." [91]

Certainly the shaman is very sensitive, nervous, has a special look, etc. He may be called supernormal, an "abnormal of fulfillment" as Benedict terms it,[92] but he cannot be regarded as subnormal, abnormal in the psychopathological sense. He is not an outcast, but privileged by the gods. He is normal in the sense of being well adapted to his society. He is "autonormal", and even those who would like to have him heteropathological, cannot deny that he is far from presenting the disintegrated personality which our psychopaths present.

*

Already the rest of the inspirational medicine men, although they undergo ritual possession, offer much less difficulty to our psychological understanding than the real "shaman" type. Possession may be a mental disease among primitives, truly autopathological and most often compared to our hysteria (see following chapter). But the *ritual possession* of the medicine man is *autonormal*. Melanesians clearly differentiate it from the possession-disease (and other pathological conditions: fever-delirium, etc.).[93] As already described, it is voluntarily induced by drumming, singing, dancing, gazing, etc., and rather well controlled. It may even be of actual value "setting free the healing instinct".[94] It seems to be a state of *autohypnosis* and even quite far from hysteria (not to speak of epilepsy).[95] Hysteria or other psychoneuroses may be entirely absent in the tribe where ritual possession is practiced.[96] On the other hand death from exhaustion and over-exertion of the devoted medicine man has been described, a trait rather inconsistent with our conception of hysteria.[97] While the possessed medicine man by his technique comes thus rather close to our spiritual mediums, he does not participate in their psychopathology. This is not

90 Sumner-Keller, 1927, 2:1368, 4:747.
91 Hubert-Mauss, 1907; Benedict, *Journ. Gen. Psych.*, 1934, p. 76.
92 The Giljak quite naively symbolize this in according him four souls instead of one (Czaplicka, *l.c.*, p. 272), the Samoyeds in singling him out for a life after death (*id.*, p. 163).
93 Codrington, R.H. 1891, p. 218; Müller-Wismar, W., 1917, vol. 1, p.378.
94 Saintyves, P., *Les origines de la médecine*, Paris, 1920, p. 83.
95 Intoxication, probably the active factor in epilepsy, is by no means the only agent able to mobilize the *latent tendency towards convulsion*, present in every brain. Bumke, *l.c.*, p. 29.
96 Seligman, C.G. and B., 1911, p. 135.
97 Field, *l.c.*, p. 105; Oesterreich, *l.c.*, p. 272.

so very surprising if we remember that the psychopathology of our mediums is due – as the psychology, e.g., of our homosexuals, mulattoes, hunchbacks and not so long ago onanists – much more to their ambiguous position in society than to their organic structure. *Where possession does not occur as an illness but as a requisite of the "medical" profession, it neither needs an ill person to become possessed nor does it make one mentally ill.* The missionary Warneck in his "Die Religion der Batak", Göttingen, 1909, p. 8, on the basis of long personal experience makes the following clear statement: "This state *in a person otherwise completely sane* has nothing to do with epilepsy or other nervous affections, for those who suffer from mental troubles are well known and clearly distinguished from the shamans; no one of the diseases of the mind, found among the Bataks, presents the same symptoms."

Mariner [98] says in his classic "Account of the Natives of the Tonga Islands", concerning the "inspirational" medicine men: "If there was any difference between them and the rest of the natives, it was that they were rather more given to reflection and somewhat more taciturn and probably greater observers of what was going forward." The Seligmans found no special nervous irritability either among the Vedda medicine men or their pupils. [99] These artificially possessed men are of course venerated. The confusion between them and the spontaneously possessed (mentally ill) seems to be the main source for the myth of "veneration of the insane and his sayings" by the primitives.

*

With the "non-inspirational" medicine man (the non-possessed: Loeb's "seer") the elements which may suggest psychopathological conditions fade out still more. Their visions and trances lack almost all objective "symptoms" like fits and seizures. They are easier to understand as the effects of an early implanted conception of a world where the natural and supernatural are not firmly separated, as dramatized day-dreams than as "auditory and visual hallucinations" in otherwise normal persons. A real analysis of our normal individuals would perhaps reveal even there a surprising number of such tendencies, hidden only by the structure of our culture pattern. Besides, the ways of producing these experiences are very often frankly artificial, from fasting to alcohol and other drugs, and show them as momentary consequences of intoxication in normal people. Or we deal with simple

98 London, 1817, vol. II, p. 146.   99 Seligman, *l.c.*, p. 129.

dreams which are not different from ours, but are only differently interpreted. The strange standardization, the stereotype of these subjective experiences betrays also their social origins. The elements of tradition, social heredity, and learning – objectively decisive in the making of every medicine man – also become officially more prevalent and visible. In the procedure of these medicine men the accent is more on the objective and fixed parts of their rite: spells, drugs, fetish objects than on their inspiration, their state of mind.

Of course the activity even of the most "non-inspirational" medicine man still involves magico-religious acts which appear strange enough to us. Fundamentally, the medicine man as the outstanding representative of primitive mentality can only be understood by those who have grasped the essentials of this mentality. But as long as one does not make the rather radical step of regarding the belief in magic qua such as pathological, these magic acts do not justify heteropathological evaluation.

The strongholds of the "non-inspirational" medicine man are, as mentioned above, America and Australia. Already Bourke stated, that "our native tribes do not believe that the mildly insane are gifted with medical or spiritual power".[100] Autopathological and even heteropathological behavior is not very likely when a majority performs the acts in question and as a matter of fact is absent in all those Indian cultures where leechdom is not hierarchized, where almost everybody in reaching adulthood has a vision governing his future behavior, and where the vision of the "medicine man", who stays a rather common man, differs only slightly from the other visions.[101]

But more psychopathological traits are not observable when the medicine man becomes the leader, as, e.g., among the Cherokees.[102] Among Olbrechts' numerous and detailed character studies of Cherokee medicine men there is not a single psychopath.[103] The fact that only such individuals are accepted as pupils who seem apt to live up to the high moral standards of the profession,[104] that, e.g., the quarrelsome and the lazy are excluded in advance[105] is of course a very efficient preventive measure in this direction. A. J. Hallowell states expressly of Salteaux conjurers: "My impressions of Salteaux conjurers were quite

100 Bourke, J. G., 1892, p. 460.
101 E.g. Cheyenne: Ackerknecht, this volume, p. 39; Chiricahua Apache: Opler, M. E., 1941, p. 200.
102 Olbrechts, F., and Mooney, J., 1932, p. 83.
103 L.c., p. 109 ff.
104 L.c., p. 95.
105 L.c., p. 99.

the reverse (of Bogoras' impressions concerning Chukchee shamans). Nothing seems to distinguish them, as a group, from other Indians in respect to psychological type or psychic peculiarities of major significance."[106]

Even in Mohave culture, where dream experience is so dominant that it is actually confused with ordinary life experience,[107] where the medicine man seems to occupy a peculiar position, going into a special heaven[108] and provoking his own murder,[109] Devereux comes to the following result: "Under ordinary circumstances Mohave shamans seem as extroverted as any run-of-the-mill Mohave... The average Mohave shaman is neither obviously neurotic nor obviously maladjusted."[110]

Concerning Australian medicine men B. Spencer and I. G. Gillen in their classical book on the native tribes of Central Australia state that "the medicine men are characteristically the reverse of nervous and excitable in temperament".[111] Recent studies among the Murngins by so sophisticated an observer as W. L. Warner bring out the same results. The white magician among the Murngins has such supernatural qualities as seeing the spirits of the killer near the dead man; he prophesies, sucks out disease objects, etc. Nevertheless: "The individuality of the white magician is not different from that of the ordinary man. The only noticeable tendency in all the observed healers was their joviality and pleasantness in their ordinary social relations. There were no indications of the psychopathic personality, for psychologically and physically they were a very normal group." [112]

And even the black magician who daydreams the most awful magic murders, "is individually not different from the ordinary men in the community. He participates in the culture and in the daily round of affairs exactly like other men".[113] Of one of these men (Laindjura) Warner states expressly: "There was nothing sinister, peculiar or psychopathic about him; he was perfectly normal in his behavior." [114]

When the call for the medical profession is absolutely hereditary, when the (magic but mostly objectively efficient) drug is more important than the medicine man, as among the Manos of Liberia, where

106 1942, p. 13.
107 Kroeber, 1925, p. 754.
108 Bourke, l.c., p. 470.
109 Devereux, G., 1942, p. 529.
110 Id., 1939/40, p. 107.
111 1899, p. 278.

112 Warner, W. L., 1937, p. 210.
113 Id., p. 197.
114 Id., p. 198. Even G. Roheim, the well known psychoanalyst-anthropologist, states the normalcy of Australian medicine men (1939, p. 381).

advanced techniques and elementary ignorance (no method of lighting a fire) are strangely mixed,his behavior may take the following forms: "In treating disease... there is no special dress, no fuss, no shouting, singing or chanting. There is even a bedside manner, dignified, confident..."[115]

The mentality of medicine men all over the world, conditioned by their respective culture patterns, can hardly be caught by one general label, and least of all by the term "shaman" (the healed madman, as we have seen) or other psychopathological labels like epilepsy, hysteria, etc. (Nor can the different mentalities be arranged in an evolutionary scheme.) It is more or less in the nature of things that the medicine men are autonormal. Closer analysis shows the psychological soundness of such an approach, in revealing a surprising amount even of heteronormalcy, where superficial and premature labeling had seen but psychopathology.

PRIMITIVE CULTURE AND PSYCHOPATHOLOGY

The medicine man owed his psychopathological label mostly to the fact that he was the best known representative of primitive mentality. When this mentality became better known as a whole, the same "logic" which had made him a madman characterized also primitive mentality, especially the belief in magic, and primitive cultures as psychopathological.[116]

Of course primitive mentality looks at first glance strange enough to those who are brought up only with the (incomplete) knowledge of the "white, adult and civilized" man. There is no limit between the natural and the supernatural. The natural is supernatural and the supernatural is quite natural.[117] Perception may not be different,[118] but values are

115 Harley, *l.c.*, p. 39.
116 See e.g. an outstanding psychiatrist as A. Hesnard, 1924. But even A.L. Kroeber occasionally speaks of "magic as the pathology of culture" and of "the abnormal primitive cultures, which are perhaps not less numerous than the normal ones" (in Bentley, *l.c.*, p. 350). Roger Money Kyrle (1939, p. 71) states bluntly: "The savage is indeed an obsessional neurotic", with the benediction of the *Psychoanalytic Quarterly* indeed (11: 563, 1942).
117 Garrison, F.H., 1929, p. 20; see also the whole work of Lucien Lévy-Bruhl.
118 But even in the field of perception differences often enough develop e.g. "To the Tanala ghosts are thoroughly individualized and entirely real. Every native will report seeing ghosts and talking with them. It is very often difficult for the people to distinguish between dream states and waking states. Hearing ghosts talk to one is so common an experience that natives often will not pay attention to you if you call them only once. If you call twice, they will know it is a man and pay attention,

just the reverse of those of our culture.[119] "What high cultures stigmatize as purely personal, non-real and non-social, abnormal and pathological, lower cultures treat as objective, socially useful, and conducive to special ability."[120] The ideas concerning "causality" which are generated by this approach are of course as different from ours as possible.

But being different is not yet being psychopathological. To regard primitive culture and the primitive qua such as "neurotic" because of certain analogies is as intelligent as to regard childhood as a kind of neurosis.

As long as there are no more objective criteria for mental health in cultures as in individuals our main criterion has to be the criterion of *function.*[121] Now, primitive cultures, in spite of numerous supernaturally conditioned regulations which seem to "work against the practical wisdom of conservation",[122] have well sustained the ordeal of existence. Cultures, where the fear complex and the corresponding "regulations" are much more overt than in our own, like Navaho, Apache, Eskimo society[123] have even proved to be extremely vigorous. *A culture cannot be called pathological except under one condition: when the culture is driven to self-destruction by its own mental structure or by changes in its mental structure.*[124] Such cases and "diseases" exist, as we will see, but they are very rare – their diagnosis is mostly possible only post mortem – and have nothing to do with the superficial and fashionable talk of "neurotic cultures".[125]

since ghosts call only once." Linton in Kardiner, 1939, p. 269. See also for the Mohave, Kroeber, 1925, p. 754, etc.

119 Kroeber, 1939/40, p. 209. See also Warner, *l.c.,* p. 24: "I had not been able to obtain this information (the ideas on natural conception) earlier because the ordinary savage is far more interested in the child's spiritual conception... He would far rather talk about ritual and myth than about ordinary human affairs."

120 Kroeber, 1939/40, p. 205.

121 See Fromm, *l.c.,* p. 140.

122 Weyer, *l.c.,* p. 455; such regulations are besides by no means lacking in our "rational" society.

123 Leighton, A. and D., 1941, p. 517; Opler, M. E., 1936, p. 1374; Weyer, *l.c.,* p. 238.

124 In culture there is so far only the possibility of differentiating between these two tendencies: life or death, but no objective criterion for judgments of neuroticism as those proposed by Devereux (if energy expenditure is "most fruitful" or less or "permits an optimum survival in proportion to the energy expended" or less than an optimum, etc.).

125 Kardiner has rightly opposed to this conception the genetic criterion. "The elaboration of these basic frustrations in neurosis and in a cultural trait are very different. In neurosis the representations of frustrated needs usually indicate coexisting inhibitions; in cultural constellations they depend on actual or institutional barriers." *L.c.,* p. 418.

The faulty conclusions spring from the supposition that a society is only able to function normally insofar as it is rational. History proves that this "criterion of rationality" is but a delusion. As Kroeber has pointed out again and again, in this belief our difference from the primitive consists not so much in the complete absence of magico-irrational attitudes in our own culture, than in our bias of not seeing in our own culture, what we so easily discover and condemn in others.[126] Only a society which is based entirely on rationality according to plan would be entitled to apply the criterion of rationality in stigmatizing others as abnormals. Whether such a society will ever exist is unknown. But one has only to look at the history of the two great revolutions started under the banner of rationality, the French and the Russian, both of which proved to be such a deadly surprise in the most literal sense of the word to their initiators, to know that it certainly has not yet arrived.

The problem of psychopathology in primitive culture cannot be solved by cheap generalizations and paralogisms. It has to be approached by an examination of the existing material, scanty and highly contradictory as it unfortunately still is. While the psychopathological labels have suggested nothing but madmen among our august ancestors and their primitive cousins, the first exact researches have put quite another problem: *does mental illness exist to any considerable extent among primitives?*

A fact which badly hampers every study in this field, is that most cultures that we regard as still primitive have already entered the stage of *acculturation* when they become observable. It is now well known, for individual as well as mass psychoses, from ethnographical studies as well as from "transition periods" of our own history or between our different subcultures, that man in such situations – "marginal man" in the terminology of R. Park[127] – is particularly liable to fall a victim of disease in general and especially of mental disease.[128] As soon as it is

126 Kroeber in Bentley, *l.c.*, p. 346. *Id.*, 1939/40, *l.c.*, p. 205.
127 Park, R.E., 1928, p. 881; Stonequist, E.V., 1937.
128 See Bumke, *l.c.*, p. 87; Hallowell, 1934, p. 6; Lamson, 1935; Mead, M., 1932; Revesz, B., 1907, and Baumann, E.D., 1934, p. 57, concerning Japan. It is noteworthy that magic in such situations not only generally becomes relatively stronger in relation to religion as has been pointed out, e.g., by R. Benedict (*Encyl. Soc. Sc.*, vol. X, p. 41) or M. Field ("If centralised, disciplined faith is weaker, vagrant credulity is stronger", *l.c.*, p. 133), but undergoes a definite change, gaining all the characteristics, which differentiate so strongly, e.g., medieval from primitive magic. (For an excellent description of this process see Redfield, R., 1942.) It would per-

thus possible to prove that a primitive culture is definitely in an acculturation situation, a large occurrence of mental disease in such a culture loses every relevance to the problem of frequency of mental disease in actual primitive societies.

The mere existence of mental disease in primitive societies is, of course, established beyond doubt.[129] For those who have realized the impact of social factors on the genesis of mental disease, this fact is not surprising or mysterious. One would be a belated victim of the belief in the "good savage" to think that primitive society does not also contain sufficient psychic tensions to produce mental disease.[130] Hallowell has well pointed to the ambivalent character of primitive society in this behalf: "It is quite possible that the decline of supernaturalism in Western society has forever undermined the status of a generic culture pattern which, in a multitude of forms, has been an effective, although to us naive authority, previously available to the individual as a means of resolving various forms of psychic stresses. *At the same time, certainly, one must not forget the potent rôle that supernaturalism has played in causing psychic stresses.*"[131]

While there is no doubt concerning the existence of mental disease in primitive society, its frequency, especially in *its Western forms, has become extremely questionable.* Seligman's statement[132] that among Papua-Melanesians, schizophrenia is absent, neuroses are rare, and only occasional manic conditions are observable, has raised great interest. But there are and have been already rather numerous similar statements concerning the scarcity of mental disease among primitives.[133] On the other hand primitive tribes are sometimes reported as

haps be useful to differentiate this kind of magic as "*secondary magic*" from primitive magic, as generalizations on magic often suffer from a confusion of the two types.

129 For collection of data see Bartels, M., 1893; Westermarck, E., II: p. 269, 1906–10; Brinton, Crawley, A.E., *JAI* 24: 223; especially Koty, J., 1934; see also Winston, E., 1934 (the second part of W's article which tries to solve the problem on the basis of five (5) cases is valueless).

130 Such a naive assumption has existed at least concerning suicide, making part of the degeneration "myth". G. Zilborg (1936, p. 1347) has demolished the equation suicide – mental disease – civilization. The equation seems by now as wrong in its second as in its first part and the existence of mental disease is no more an exclusive feature of our society than is suicide.

131 *L.c.*, p. 1308.

132 1926, p. 196.

133 E.g. Plehn, F., 1898, p. 271; Krause, F., 1911, p. 338; Faris, E., 1937, p. 286 (concerns the Forest Bantus); Donnison, C.P., 1937; Dhunjibhoy, J., 1930, p. 254.

presenting a particular high incidence of mental disease.[134] Hirsch quotes both kinds of sources.[135] All these statements are too vague to enable us to reach any definite conclusions. Fortunately we dispose at least of one document based on the records and observations of 80 years in the District of Astrachan which gives some more articulate *local* conclusions (Skliar, N., and Starikowa, K., Zur vergleichenden Psychiatrie, *Arch. Psychiat. Nervenkr. 88,* 554–585, 1929). Skliar and Starikowa compare the psychopathology of seven nations among which two: the Kalmucks (100,000) and the Kirghizes (300,000) were at least primitive for a long time. Their research brings out the following results:

1. The incidence of mental disease was extremely low, almost non-existing among these tribes (Kalmucks 1850; 0.01 per cent; Kirghiz admission rate 1890: 0.4 : 100,000

2. Contact with civilization, established around 1850, means steady increase of disease rates (Kalmucks 1898: 0.07 per cent; Kirghiz admission rate 1927 from 0.9 to 3.0 : 100,000). The farther a Kalmuck division is from civilized areas, the less the disease rate. The disease rate in both tribes is still far below that of the surrounding civilized people (Kalmuck 2-14 : 100,000; Tartars 30-60, Armenians 90, Jews 50, Russians and Persians100:100, The influence of civilization is independent of alcohol and syphilis. In both tribes syphilis is endemic but both lack general paresis. The Kalmucks were always alcoholics, the (Islamic) Kirghizes still do not drink alcohol.

3. Dementia praecox is still rare (Kalmucks 2.6 per cent of all mental diseases; Kirghizes 1.9 per cent compared to 6.4 per cent among the Russians and 20 per cent among Armenians). There is no hysteria and no general paralysis.

4. While these tendencies are common to both tribes there are considerable differences in frequency and male-female ratio. While among the Kalmucks there are twice as many insane women as men, the Kirghizes have the usual higher male ratio (8 times more diseased Kirghiz men than women). Between 1890 and 1902 there were from 5 to 30 times more admissions among the Kalmucks than the Kirghizes, in 1925 to 1927, from 3 to 10 times more.

134 E.g. Devereux, G., 1939, p. 316 (Indoch. Moi); Klementz (Siberia); Cooper, M., 1934, p. 14.
135 1886, vol. III, p. 361.

These conclusions emphasize the scarcity of mental disease in certain primitive tribes and the differences in this belief among primitives themselves. They confirm the statements of Revesz, Seligman, Gordon, Lopez, Dhunijibhoy, Overbeck-Wright, Faris, Cooper [136] about the absence of schizophrenia among primitives and relative prevalence of manic-depressive conditions, if there is any psychopathology at all.[137] Devereux has built on these facts a rather speculative "Sociological Theory of Schizophrenia", which comes close to Donnison's thought of the diseasing effect of isolation in civilization [138] and to the older sociological ideas on psychopathology expressed by the late Charles Blondel.[139]

These reports on the scarcity of mental disease in *certain* primitive societies may partly be due to the fact that for social or biological reasons some cultures actually enjoy a greater *mental health* (with some it seems to be just the opposite). In others it may be due to a more effective psychotherapy [140] (the wealth of psychotherapeutical methods in primitive medicine, although such methods are of course also efficient in "pure" bodily disease, nevertheless suggests a certain amount of mental disease). But those reports may also sometimes be the result of misunderstandings. In a culture where there are a number of "native" forms of mental disease and a lack of its western forms, two observers may come to opposite results, the one including, the other

136 Revesz, Dhunijibhoy, Seligman, *l.c.*; Overbeck-Wright, A.W., London, 1921, p. 3; Gordon at Donnison, *l.c.*, p. 33/34; Lopez, C., 1932, p. 706; Faris, 1942, p. 5.

137 It is easy to rule out the opposite thesis of L. Stern (1913) as it is definitely based on irrelevant acculturation material like Kraepelin's Java observations, etc. More difficult is the case of Laubscher who after very extensive studies among the Tembu has concluded to an enormous incidence of schizophrenia among the Tembu and the black race in general (the latter statement is certainly wrong, see Lewis, J.H., 1942, p. 260). One could easily oppose to Laubscher that his Tembus are acculturated. But to me the error seems still deeper and Laubscher's whole study the result of a gigantic misunderstanding produced by his bias towards an exclusive "heredity" theory of schizophrenia. To him ukutwasa (see p. 69), a very frequent phenomenon, is equal to mental disease and particularly to schizophrenia. Thus he obtains his result. But it is very doubtful whether in most cases ukutwasa is a disease at all. It is even very doubtful if his "schizophrenics", who are, e.g., "rarely ever readmitted to the hospital" and *obey* generally tribal interdiction of suicide, are schizophrenics at all! Laubscher basing his whole thesis on the frequency of ukutwasa in the family of his "schizophrenics" has even omitted the most elementary controls on the frequency of ukutwasa in the family of normals which probably would have ruined his whole theory from the very beginning.

138 *L.c.*, p. 134; on the problems of isolation see also Fromm, *l.c.*

139 Blondel, Ch., 1913.

140 In this connection see also O. Klineberg on Buddhism and schizophrenia (1940, p. 510).

excluding the former cases. The main source of misunderstanding is probably the fact that *the primitive not only in his medical concepts*[141] *does not separate diseases of the body and the mind, but also does not produce such separate units.* His "body" ailments may very often hide very strong "mental" elements[142], which may have escaped some observers.

That such "native" mental diseases, as alluded to above, exist, mental diseases which do not fit into our classification, seems by now fairly certain. The best known is the almost proverbial *amok* or amuck of men, first described among Malays, but meanwhile observed in other different parts of the world: among Fuegians, who ask to be bound before the onset of the attack,[143] among Melanesians, where the maniacs seem to be less murderous and consequently are not killed,[144] among Siberians,[145] among Kalmucks and Kirghizes,[146] in India.[147] The very fact that amok has been so differently classified, is to a certain extent in favor of its being a special disease.[148] Another Malay diesease mostly mentioned together with amok is *lattah*, which also was first studied in Indonesia and later detected in Siberia and among Eskimos as so called "arctic hysteria".[149] A similar disease was also found in the Philippines.[150] Lattah is mostly a disease of women and characterized by echolalia and echopraxia. To call it hysteria, as Kraepelin did, is insofar not very enlightening as our hysteria just lacks these two main traits of lattah. It has more than only a local connection with amok insofar as an attack of lattah may end with amok-like paroxysms, e.g., in its Ainu form Imu.[151] Winiarz and Wielawski identify not only Imu with lattah, but also the Meriachenie of the Siberian Russians, the Ra-

141 Ackerknecht, 1942, p. 514.
142 Laubscher, *l.c.*, p. 28.
143 Coriat, F.H., 1915, p. 201.
144 Seligmann, *l.c.*, p. 198; Fortune, R., 1932, p. 55.
145 Czaplicka, *l.c.*, p. 310.
146 Skliar and Starikowa, *l.c.*, p. 573.
147 Overbeck-Wright, *l.c.*, p. 46.
148 Gimlette (1901) considers it a form of somnabulism. Kraepelin thought it to be epilepsy. F.H.G. Van Loon (1926/27) calls it "an agony of fear on the basis of fever". Cooper (*l.c.*, p. 13) doubts whether it is a disease at all or simply a custom, which seems unlikely.
149 Not all cases of "arctic hysteria" in the literature are "lattah". Czaplicka warns rightly (*l.c.*, p. 320): "It would seem that the name 'arctic hysteria' has been given by travellers partly to religio-magical phenomena and partly to the nervous ailments which are considered by the natives to be disease."
150 Deniker, 1926.
151 Winiarz, W., and Wielawski, J., 1936. Imu, sometimes very frequent (12 cases in a village of 1000 inhabitants) is regarded as possession by a serpent spirit *and as healing another morbid state.*

maneniana of Madagascar, the Yuan of Burma and the Bah-tchi of Siam. Revesz mentions also the Mali-mali of the Tagals. Lattah is a rather serious condition insofar as it may lead to considerable damage of the victim itself or that done by the victim to others. The *Piblokto* of Eskimo men and women [152] comes closer to our own hysteria and seems on the other hand related to the Saki-si-djoendai of Sumatra.[153]

While we probably are not entitled to classify the "madness of starvation and cannibalism" [154] among the hungry Eskimos as a special *cannibalistic psychosis*, such psychoses seem to exist elsewhere among primitives where the food supply is satisfactory [155] and to a larger extent than among us. The relatively best known is the *windigo psychosis* of the Cree and Ojibwa Indians.[156]

Devereux has recently described the "Hiwa-Itck" of deserted older Mohave men [157] and Linton, the tromba, a dancing mania among the Tanala of Madagascar.[158] There are special psychoses on the basis of exotic narcotics like the Indian hemp, etc. If the problem would be followed up by field workers, probably many more such diseases would be discovered and thus the basis created for a more satisfactory discussion of the problem.

While we much more often regard as heteropathological what is autonormal, the case also occurs that the primitive sees disease where we see only character difficulties. A. I. Hallowell has described a very interesting case of this sort in his "Shabwan, a Dissocial Indian Girl" (*Amer. J. Orthopsychiat. 8*, 329, 1938), and M. J. Field gives very plastic descriptions of the treatment of such cases among the Ga people (*l.c.*, p. 94-96). In general this field of the autopathological and heteronormal states is still less studied than the "native" diseases which are auto- and heteropathological.

To us perhaps the most interesting native "mental disease" is what the late W. E. Roth called "*thanatomania*",[159] the death from magic, the

152 Brill, A., 1913; Czaplicka, *l.c.*, p. 314.
153 Bartels, *l.c.*, p. 215.
154 Weyer, *l.c.*, p. 118.
155 Marquesas; Linton in Kardiner, p. 142; Kwakiutl; cannibalistic possession during initiation, Kardiner, *l.c.*, p. 118.
156 Hallowell, J., 1934; *id.*, 1936; Cooper, J. M., 1934; *id.*, 1933. The renaissance has known mental epidemics with similar contents: the Vaudoisie of 1436, etc. See Cesbron, H., 1909, pp. 134 ff.
157 1940, p. 1198.
158 Linton in Kardiner, *l.c.*, p. 270.
159 W. B. Cannon has collected in a recent article "Voodo death" (1942) the material of Soares de Souza and Varnhagen for South America; Mirolla and Leonard for Africa; Brown for New Zealand; Lambert, Cleland, W. E. Roth, Basedow, Warner (interesting for a social theory of thanatomania, *l.c.*, p. 242), Porteus for Australia,

death from autosuggestion without other visible pathological reason. The importance of autosuggestion for health and disease of primitives has always been emphasized,[160] striking examples have been quoted.[161] But in thanatomania undoubtedly the phenomenon reaches a magnificence which can only be compared with the voluntary sterility of Polynesian women[162] probably based on the stopping of ovulation.[163] *Thanatomania seems to illustrate best what we meant when we spoke of the impossibility of separating mental and body diseases in primitive man* (a separation which, of course, even with us is only gradually less artificial). Thanatomania makes Bilby[163] say concerning the medicine man: "A propos of the extraordinary command the conjurors universally exercise over the people and of the paramount psychic influence they establish in the community, it is not too much to say that they hold every man's life in their hands." Suicide may also sometimes be effectuated by the mechanism of thanatomania.[165] But otherwise we are not entitled to list *suicide* – unknown to some primitives[166] – under mental disease except in the rare cases when it is attributed by the primitives themselves to insanity.[167] We have already quoted Czaplicka's judgment: "But neither to the institution of voluntary death nor to the hysterical fits of the shamans are we justified in applying the name of disease since these are not so considered by the natives themselves."

The "hysterical fits" of the shamans of which Czaplicka is speaking, are the cases of artificial, ritual "possession" already discussed in the previous chapter and which we think to be autonormal as well as heteronormal. But there is another form of *possession*, involuntary,

and tried to give a physiological explanation of the phenomenon. Besides the material collected by Cannon and another collection in Sumner-Keller, pp. 1326 ff., or Webster, H., 1942, pp. 24 ff., further cases may be found, e.g., in Brough-Smyth (*l.c.*, II: 468), Codrington (206), Czaplicka (260), Field (118), Fortune (284), Howitt (*JAI* 16: 42), Laubscher (105), Linton-Kardiner (187), Mariner, Seligman (192), Weyer (237, 460). Benedict's cases of shamans dying of shame (1934, 210, 214) probably also belong here.

160 E.g. Malinowski, B., 1922, p. 465. See the survey by Otto Stoll, 1904.
161 E.g., suggested dumbness in taboo transgressors, Harley, *l.c.*, p. 127; rashes in food-taboo transgression, Herskovits, M.J., 1938, vol. 1, p. 161; an incurable "trembling sickness" as consequence of taboo transgression among the Batamba (Uganda), M.A. Condon, 1911, p. 377, etc.
162 Pitt-Rivers, 1927, p. 147.
163 Personal communication Dr. J. Gillman, Johannesburg.
164 Weyer, *l.c.*, p. 459.
165 Zilboorg, *l.c.*, p. 1353. For the strange suicides by conscious taboo violation which then kills by autosuggestion, see Handy, E.S.C., *Berenice P. Bishop Mus. Bull. 9*, 279; Ivens, W.G., 1927, p. 121.
166 Kardiner, *l.c.*, p. 113.
167 Linton-Kardiner, *l.c.*, p. 275 (Tanala of Madagascar).

spontaneous, distinguished from the former even by the natives, which we think is clearly heteropathological as well as autopathological and which is generally regarded as a form of hysteria. The "asocial" tendencies of the individual becoming too strong, they get split off and speak with another voice out of the mouth of the innocent "patient". It is thus no wonder that *periods of situations of heightened social tension like acculturation make for a tremendous increase in possession.*[168] But possession, although very widespread among primitives, does not belong to the discussed "native" mental diseases, as it also pervades all civilizations through antiquity up to the middle of the last century.

Possession epidemics are only one subspecies of other "pathological" mass movements, *"psychic epidemics"*, as our forefathers used to call them. They certainly are not specific for primitive society as the history of civilizations in transition periods abundantly proves. It is even highly *doubtful* if they exist in *primitive* societies properly speaking although they too have had their transition periods; in any case we lack pertinent material. The twenty messianic movements occurring among American Indians prior to 1890 and listed by Barber,[169] the Melanesian "mass neuroses" mentioned by Seligman,[170] the Madagascan dancing mania of 1863[171] are all *typical acculturation phenomena* and another attempt of the natives besides rebellion and depopulation to deal with the new situation. It is highly doubtful if they deserve the title of *"neuroses"*. When they are autopathological the case is, of course, clear. But most of them are autonormal. Concerning the psychopathological character of historical as well as exotic "psychic epidemics", even conservative authors such as Friedman, Hirsch, Irland or Oesterreich[172] have been extremely sceptical. Lowie, treating two of the outstanding ones: the Ghost Dance and the Peyot cult purely as religious phenomena, seems to have hit the right point.[173] Much more for the understanding of *most of them is gained if we regard them as attempts of a disturbed culture to produce a new equilibrium by producing a new religion.*[174] Nothing in their forms is found which could not be found in

---

168 Oesterreich, *l.c.*, pp. 137, 139.
  Historically speaking *epidemics* of possession are limited to a period between the 13th and the 18th century!
169 Barber, B., 1941, p. 663; see also: Mooney, J., 1893; Parker, A. C., 1913; Phister, 1891; Ray, V. F., 1936; Spier, L., 1935.

170 Chinnery, E. W. P., and Haddon, A. C., 1917, p. 446; Williams, F. W., 1923.
171 Hirsch, *l.c.*, 3: 367.
172 Friedmann, M., 1901, p. 20; Hirsch, *l.c.*, p. 363; Ireland, W. W., 1906/07; Oesterreich, *l.c.*, p. 190.
173 Lowie, R. H., 1936, pp. 88 ff.
174 Chapple, E. D., and Coon, C. S., 1942, p. 411.

the rite of other religions: dances, trances, etc.[175] The fact, so often quoted against them, that they are caused by suggestion, they partake with numerous other normal beliefs and ideologies, even scientific ones. (The pathological character of some *sects* is not based on these elements, but on their living outside of society.) The clearly self destructive messianic movements, which could be regarded at least as heteropathological, are extremely rare.[176] And even those like the mass suicide of Caribbean Indians[177] bear sometimes rather the mark of a rational decision than of neurosis.

In speaking of *sorcery* too many are somewhat hypnotized by the great witch-smelling wave in our Renaissance or in some African cultures, probably both acculturational.[178] And they forget too easily that the belief in magic and sorcery and its execution are common to the majority of mankind and thus already most unlikely to be psychopathological.[179]

The fear complex, expressed in some cultures by the sorcery belief (by no means in all)[180] is after all rather well founded and its expression a matter of convention. While for some renaissance witches the psychopathological assumption can at least be based on reports of hysteric stigmata, we know already of the perfect mental health of numerous primitive black magicians.[181] Others should rather be regarded in the same way as primitives do for them; as criminals, choosing the best known native way of crime. And the criminal is until further notice not yet identical with the psychopath, sometimes rather an alternative. On the other hand, the black magician, far from being antisocial, may just

---

175 Concerning dance see, e.g., Herskovits, *l.c.*, 1:133; dance is by now even regarded as a very valuable psychotherapeutic element of group treatment (Marsh, L. C., 1935).
176 Only one of the five cults reported by Chinnery and Haddon (*l.c.*, p. 458) is self destructive; then of course the two famous African catastrophies of Usambar (Meinhof, C., 1926, p. 6) and of Mulakaza (Schapera, J., 1937, p. 253; Brownlee, Ch., 1898). In the former case the seed was stopped in the latter all cattle slain, in both famine followed.
177 Zilboorg, *l.c.*, p. 1352.
178 For self destructive witch hunt in Africa see Sumner-Keller, p. 1321; Talbot, P. A., 1926, 2: 219.
179 For Laubscher, of course, "Witchcraft and mental disorder are practically synonymous" (p. 29) and "a study of the histories of a few witches bore ample evidence that they were suffering from schizophrenia" (*l.c.*, p. 17).
180 "When a man suffers from misfortune due to witchcraft his emotional reactions generally range from annoyance to anger rather than from fear to terror." Evans-Pritchard, E. D., 1937, p. 84. See also Seligman, C. G., 1910, p. 279.
181 Warner, *l.c.*, pp. 197/98; Fortune, *l.c.*, p. 163.

enforce the tribal law by his threats and maintain the public order without coercion.[182] Even the enormous acculturation increase of sorcery[183] would perhaps sometimes be better understood when regarded as a kind of *"negative" new religion*, as Michelet did, than as "neurosis". A heteropathological element may indeed pervade the strange, *spontaneous self-accusations* of witches and sorcerers, which must have clearly self-destructive consequences[184] and form one of the most disturbing psychological problems of all time. But Lowie has given a rational explanation even to them, which may fit some cases, others not.[185] Here in the sorcery question as everywhere in anthropology, things are complex and not very accessible to generalizations and it is always wiser to look first for a normal explanation instead of choosing the way of least resistance in ceding too quickly to fashion and adopting a probably erroneous psychopathological one.

We do not know enough of the so-called "disease worship" to decide whether it belongs at least heteropathologically to native mental diseases. Caution seems necessary since we have lately learned that there is no disease worship at all in some of these cases. "Small pox as such is not worshipped. It is the earth gods who are worshipped. Small pox is merely their most severe penalty for wrong doing."[186]

We have thus come to the end of our short survey of psychopathology in primitive society.[187] We have tried to correct some current preju-

---

182 E.g., Fortune, *l.c.*, p. 175; Loeb, *l.c.*, p. 83; Linton-Kardiner, *l.c.*, p. 139; Pitt-Rivers, *l.c.*, p. 201; Rivers, W.H.R., 1926, p. 87; Spencer, D.M., *l.c.*, p. 76; Whiting, J.W.M., 1941, p. 219.

183 Friedman, *l.c.*, p. 247; Junod, *l.c.*, 2: 488; Evans-Pritchard, *l.c.*, p. 446; Field, *l.c.*, p. 135; Redfield, *l.c.*, p. xx. This kind of sorcery is the cornerstone of "secondary magic" (see above).

184 For those confessions see for Africa, Harley, *l.c.*, p. 27; Field, *l.c.*, p. 128; 139; Lowie, *l.c.*, p. 37; Talbot, D.A., 1915, p. 50; Meek, C.K., 1936, p. 84; for America: Sumner, Coll. Essays I, ch. IV; Karsten, R., 1926, p. 492. Here belong also the self-provoked murder of the Mohave sorcerer (Devereux, 1942, 529) and the self-execution of the New Caledonian sorcerer (Turner, G., 1889).

185 Lowie, *l.c.*, p. 39.

186 Herkovits, *l.c.*, 2: 136, for a similar statement concerning the Shilluk, where a god and illness bear the same name, because the god gives it, see Westermann, D., 1912, XL. See, e.g., also for leprosy in Bali, which is called the "holy disease" while being the most terrible punishment of the gods: Weck, W., 1937, p. 159.

187 The fact that "race" was not mentioned at all in this article is by no means caused by forgetfulness or because we deny in advance the possibility of racial factors in mental disease. It is exclusively conditioned by our inability to find during our research a single reliable fact which actually demonstrates the influence of race on mental disease.

dices by confronting them with facts. We are very well aware of the shortcomings of our essay, conditioned to a certain extent by the scarcity of good material. Psychiatry and anthropology have many common problems and are even genetically closely connected. Suffice it to recall the names of Benjamin Rush and J. C. Prichard. The collaboration of psychiatry and anthropology has yielded rich results, but it also threatens now to produce, from a scientific point of view, rather unwelcome consequences. This is a problem coming up everywhere where sciences try to collaborate. It would perhaps be useful to remember what Kroeber once wrote (in another context, concerning the scientific and historic approach in anthropology): "But precisely if they are to cooperate, it seems that they should recognize and tolerate each other's individuality. It is hard to see good coming out of a mixture of approaches, whose aims are different."[188] Just because we believe in the necessity of cooperation between the two sciences we have tried to eliminate some misconceptions, and we sincerely hope to have thus furnished a modest contribution to a future fertile collaboration of psychiatry and anthropology.

APPENDIX

Since publication of this article I have collected dozens of references, confirming my statements. While in general I have simply added such references to the bibliography, I would like to call particular attention to the work of Jenness on the Carrier Indians (1933 and particularly 1943). Jenness describes here the preshamanistic psychosis (which happens to be of the windigo type!) with a clarity and richness of detail not found elsewhere. Shirokogoroff (1935) has not only collected numerous details on Siberian shamans, analogous to those quoted above, but regards the shaman as normal. To the same conclusion came Stoll (1904) and Zucker (1934), the latter offering a most original psychobiological analysis of the shamanistic trance.

The description of amok, lattah, and koro by van Wulffen (1936) is superior to those quoted in the text. The observation that amok stopped in Java after Japanese occupation (personal communication of Dr. R. v. Koenigswald) deserves notice.

As far as my remarks on population decline in the South Seas on the basis of psychogenic stopping of ovulation are concerned, I would like to make two additional remarks. That psychogenic stop of ovulation does exist in man seems to have been established meanwhile (Whitacre & Barrere, 1944). On the other hand, the greater part of population decline in the South Seas seems to be explainable by far more prosaic factors like the spread of venereal disease (Powdermaker, 1931, Roberts, 1922).

188 1935, p. 547.

AUTOPSIES AND ANATOMICAL KNOWLEDGE*

It is a well known fact that the anatomico-physiological knowledge of primitives is extremely scanty. As a matter of fact it is much more scanty than their knowledge in other technical or "scientific" branches.[1] They may recognize and name an organ, but most of the time neither an inkling of its real function nor of its regular occurrence and position enter their mind. Suffice it here to remind our reader of two significant observations: many primitives are even unaware of the causal relations between sexual act and pregnancy[2] and of the specific function of the sexual organs, even when castrating animals at the same time for taming and fettering. Primitives place the vital principle ("soul", "intelligence", etc.) in such different and altogether rather irrelevant places as the stomach,[3] the kidney fat,[4] the larynx,[5] the pelvis,[6] or even the great toe.[7] Even when more correctly the head is chosen as seat of the "soul", it is generally done for quite "unrealistic", "unscientific", mystical reasons.[8]

We derive our anatomical knowledge from dissections. Primitives generally are very much afraid of dissections[9] and do not dissect. They abstain from dissections for the same mystical reasons (fear of having to live mutilated in the world of the dead, fear of becoming ritually unclean, etc.) which hinder them also from developing any considerable active surgery in spite of great manual skill[10]. Thus without a detailed

---

* This article was published originally as "Primitive Autopsies and the History of Anatomy" in the *Bull. Hist. Med. 13*, 334–339 (1943).
1 Browne, C. A., 1935.
2 This fact and the strange anatomical representations of primitives were much emphasized by the late B. Malinowski concerning the Trobriands, e.g. in Malinowski, 1927. For an analysis of the conception problem see Ashley-Montagu, M. F., 1938. See also Nieuwenhuis, A. W., 1928, pp. 289 ff., for a good survey of this problem among Australians, Malays, etc., and interesting observations concerning the absence of anatomical knowledge among the Dajaks of Middle Borneo. For misinterpretation of the rôle of the uterus and other anatomical errors among the Thongas see Junod, H. A., 1913, vol. II, p. 332.
3 Trobriands and Dobuans, see Fortune, R., 1932, p. 148.
4 Brough-Smyth, R., 1878, vol. II, p. 289.
5 Ellis, A. B., 1894, p. 126.
6 Herskovits, M. J., 1938, vol. II, p. 237.
7 Sumner, W. G., and Keller, A. G., 1927, vol. 2, p. 817.
8 Ackerknecht, E. H., *Ciba Symposia*, 1947, p. 1654.
9 Junod, *l. c.*, II, p. 332.
10 Junod, *l.c.*, II, p. 418; Harley, G. W., 1941, p. 74; Johnston, James, New York, 1893, p. 335; Lévy-Bruhl, L., 1927, p. 400. In primitive societies the same reasons also make of body mutilations a terrible punishment for criminals and a humiliating form of vengeance on the enemy.

analysis the conclusion would seem rather obvious and well founded that their lack of anatomical knowledge is simply a consequence of the absence of dissections.

The argument that hunting and its variation, cannibalism, could replace dissection for gaining anatomical knowledge is convincingly dismissed by Olbrechts who gives in addition a very vivid picture of the anatomical ignorance of the Cherokee medicine men (who, at the same time, have such a rich knowledge of drugs). "The hunter who cuts up the game in the forest to bring home the better morsels is not engrossed in anatomical speculation and his wife who disembowels the rabbit or the groundhog is too anxious to have the meat barbecuing before the fire to be able to afford the time for scientific observations."[11] Similarly human or animal dissection for such entirely different purposes as sacrifice or divining are not prone to further anatomical studies, and as a matter of fact have not done so in the overwhelming majority of cases.

Relevant for our problem and worthwhile to be analyzed are the very rare cases where primitives really dissect for medical purposes: to find out the seat of disease. We were only able to collect three such cases in the whole literature.[12]

One of the earliest reports of primitive autopsies is found in G. Turner's classic on *Samoa*:[13]

If the person had died of a complaint which carried off some other members of the family they would probably open the body to "search for the disease". Any inflamed substance they happened to find they took away and burned, thinking that this would prevent any other members of the family being affected with the same disease.

Forty years later Margaret Mead observed the very same custom[14] as well as the much more widespread cutting out of the fetus from the corpse of a pregnant woman,[15] both customs being apparently unchanged.[16]

11 Olbrechts, F. H., and Mooney, J., 1932, p. 90.
12 There may be some more such cases as the remarks of Marrett (London, 1920, p. 210) and Malinowski (1927, p. 20) suggest, but altogether they cannot be very numerous. Dissections, identical in all their implications with those described below are also mentioned for the Mapuches in E. A. R. Smith, 1855.
13 Turner, G., 1884, p. 145. See also Ella, S., 1892, p. 639.
14 Mead, M., 1924, p. 134.
15 Mead, *l.c.*, p. 133, p. 156. The sense of the operation is a mystical one – avoiding of bad actions of the fetus' ghost. Junod describes the same custom for the Thongas (*l.c.*, II, p. 332) and is startled by their simultaneous ignorance of anatomy. Concerning the distribution and the later rationalizations of postmortal sectio Caesarea see MacKenzie, D., 1927, p. 333, and Ploss-Bartels, 1895, vol. II, p. 291.

In a very different natural and cultural setting, among the Chuk-chees of *North-Eastern Siberia*, it is part of the mourning ceremonial to rip the body of the deceased and to see from the state of the organs whether he has died from sorcery or the attack of bad spirits *(kelets)*. These *kelets* seem to be especially fond of attacking the liver.[17] Similar customs are reported from the neighboring Koryaks.[18]

Undoubtedly the most extensive area of primitive autopsies is found in *Western Equatorial Africa*. Following Hermann Baumann, who has given a rather complete survey of the custom among 42 tribes in the *Zeitschrift für Ethnologie*, Berlin, 1929, pp. 73-85, we would like to call this area the *"Likundu"* area. Likundu is a widespread Lingala word which is used for the magic force which is sought for in these autopsies.[19] The area covers, roughly speaking, the region from Cameroon in the north to the lower Congo in the south, and goes as far east as the Bahr el Ghazal.[20] Autopsies are performed on persons who are suspected either to have been sorcerers themselves or to have been killed by sorcery. It is thought that both facts would become visible by alterations in the organs, changed organs representing either the magic force of the born sorcerer or the destruction caused by his magic in the victim. They look for hyperemia or anemia of the organs, tumors, stones, especially of the gall bladder, ulcers, quality of the gall, enlarged spleens, stomachs, etc. Perfectly normal organs as the uterus and ovar-ies may be regarded as pathological "witch-tumors".[21] The technical procedure generally consists of a longitudinal incision in the middle of the chest and abdomen. The "pathological" parts are cut out, buried

16 It is of great general importance that these customs seemed *unchanged;* no change, neither of the form nor of the content of the ceremony, had occurred. Dr. Mead was kind enough to confirm this statement for me. This is rather surprising when we realize what transformations and influences Samoa has undergone during these 40 years in general culture as well as in the medical field (see e.g. Keesing, F.M., 1934, pp. 375 ff.). Dr. Mead in a personal communication makes the following pertinent remarks on Samoan medicine: "In spite of the attitude towards the super-natural in Samoa, the Samoans were exceedingly unreceptive to any form of Euro-pean rational medicine... It had not occurred to me before but I am inclined to think that perhaps mildly rational medicine may be more resistive than definitely supernatural. People who are accustomed to shop around among religious practi-tioners often add the doctor without resistance."

17 Bogaras, W., 1904–1909, pp. 258, 527.
    Iden-Zeller, O., 1911, p. 855.
18 Jochelson, W., 1907, p. 130.
19 See also Evans-Pritchard, E. E., 1937, Chapter II, "Witchcraft substance is revealed by autopsy."

20 The remarks of Harley (*l.c.*, p. 23) concerning the Manos of Liberia suggest still other African centers of the custom outside this area.
21 Yaunde; see Nekes, 1913, pp. 134–143.

apart or destroyed, or used as medicine in the form of powders.

When we now compare these three sets of autopsies, the magical background seems fairly common to all of them. In spite of a quasi rational opening and examining of the body the goal of the examination is quite different from our search of diseased organs. One should suppose that these autopsies performed through centuries have nevertheless had some positive consequences on the anatomical or pathological knowledge of these tribes. But there is the interesting fact that *not only nowhere is such better knowledge reported, but there is, in some cases, positive evidence of an extremely bad anatomical knowledge among these dissectors.* We have already mentioned the appreciation of uterus and ovaries as "pathological" growths with the Yaunde. There is a report of Pechuel-Lösche [22] concerning the dissecting Bawili of Loango who describe "a bundle of threads near the vertebral column of sorcerers". When these threads are pulled, the corpse moves the ears or twinkles! There is the evaluation of the normal appendix equally as a pathological growth, particularly to sorcerers,[23] among the Azande. These dissectors are a nice example of what Jonathan Wright called "the blindness to nature in the interest of art, of the ideal, of religion exhibited in primitive civilization".[24] It becomes evident that the mere technique means nothing for scientific progress as long as it is not pervaded by the scientific spirit. With this spirit the opening of bodies is an inexhaustible source of anatomical knowledge. Without it, in the atmosphere of magic, it is a gesture of no importance for knowledge because the essential element for the formation of scientific knowledge is missing. *Only in the context of a culture pattern oriented towards a kind of "science" do dissections furnish anatomical knowledge.*[24a] Then even hunting or sacrificing may provide such knowledge. In other, for instance magically orientated, culture patterns dissections may have any other meaning but the increase of anatomical knowledge. Our observations are an impirical corroboration of the ideas of Daniel Essertier, who opposed to the Frazerian speculations of gradual growth from magic to science the idea that magic even in its most progressed stages can never engender but pseudo-sciences and that a revolutionary transformation of the spiritual approach is necessary to bridge the cleft between magic and science.[25]

22 Pechuel-Lösche, 1907, p. 337.
23 Gayer-Anderson, 1911, p. 253.
24 *Med. Life*, 1925, p. 183.

24a For the general theoretical implications of this statement see Ruth Benedict, 1934, pp. 46, 244.

But in this little essay we are more concerned with the bearing of our examples on medical history than with its anthropological connections. The fundamental importance of the renaissance of anatomy in the 16th century for the great adventure of modern medicine-which is still going on, has rightly been stressed [26] and can hardly be overestimated. The simultaneity of the renaissance of anatomy and a freer and larger use of human dissection has not been overlooked; rather has this more technical point been taken by us children of a technical age and under the influence of certain general theories to be the essential cause.[27] In the light of our study of primitive autopsies this seems to be rather an error. Without falling in premature generalizations concerning the role of the technical element in all places and all times, it may at least be safely stated that its role in the history of anatomy is quite secondary. To understand fully the development of modern anatomy our interest should be concentrated rather on the fundamental cultural and spiritual implications and orientations than on secondary technical problems.

APPENDIX

The article describes three centers of primitive autopsies. In a footnote a fourth (Araucanos of Chili) is added (see also Aichel, 1913, p. 183, Métraux, 1942). It is worthwhile to be mentioned that Araucano shamans perform in the same time the old trick of "opening the body" during the curative rite.

A fifth center of primitive autopsies seems to have existed in Madagascar (Dubois, *Anthropos 21*, 118; Grandidier, *L'Anthropologie 23*, 320, 325). Such magic autopsies were performed in Western society up to 1632 and 1817 (Stoll 1904, 463).

W. Schilde has added to Baumann's report on Likundu much new material (ZE 1938).

25 *Les formes inférieures de l'explication*, Paris, 1927.
26 Sigerist, H. E., 1932, p. 8. Idem, 1924, pp. 194–200. Sigerist states here concerning Babylonian "anatomy": "A people that was able to represent the finest movements of the animal, that was accustomed to observe the smallest variations of the animal liver, would also have been able to unveil the secrets of the organism to a certain degree – *if it had felt the urge to do so*. Religious restraints would have been overcome if the anatomical urge had been present. Vesalius took bones from the gallows."
27 Fortunately I do not need to discuss here the motes in my brothers' eyes, having produced once myself a little beam; 1932, p. 155.

SURGERY AND ITS PARADOXES*

Speaking of "primitive surgery" is one of those arbitrary procedures which are to a certain extent unavoidable if we try to analyze primitive phenomena for a better understanding of our own cultural processes, and which are justifiable as long as we remain aware of their arbitrary character. Not before the second half of the Middle Ages were surgery and its practitioners regarded as different from or inferior to other methods or practitioners of the healing art. Then for 700 years they remained separated from the body of medicine. In modern society "surgery" has again become part of medicine – but as one of its "specialties". This again is without precedent. Though we find "specialists" also in primitive and archaic medicine (Egyptian, Peruvian, etc.), specialization there has other reasons and proceeds along dividing lines different from those observed in modern scientific medicine.[1] Surgery is, therefore, not a special field defined by the primitives themselves. We simply deal in the following with such procedures as would be mainly in the domain of the surgeon in our society. Practically, it means that we deal primarily with therapeutic measures which are of a definite technological interest.

WOUND TREATMENT

There is no tribe on record which does not in some way or other treat wounds. It would lead us too far to go into details here of the hundreds of different treatments recorded, the principles of which are very similar. Herbs or roots, often with astringent or disinfectant qualities, are applied to the wound in form of powders, infusions, or poultices. In rare cases animal substances, like powdered insects or cow dung, are used. Heat is rather widely employed to speed the healing process.[2] Wound treatment by primitives is in general regarded as "good".

"In the treatment of wounds the Cherokee doctors exhibit a considerable degree of

* This article was published first under the title "Primitive Surgery" in the *American Anthropologist 49*, 25–45 (1947). Parts of this article were given as a paper at a Viking Dinner Conference on March 22, 1946. I wrote this article while working in the Institute of Human Morphology (Department of Anthropology, American Museum of Natural History, New York), a project financed by a grant from the Viking Fund. I am glad to express on this occasion my appreciation to the Fund and to its Director of Research, Dr. Paul Fejos.

1 Rosen, 1944, p. 5 ff.; Ackerknecht, 1945, p. 37; Ackerknecht, 1946, p. 479 ff.
2 Martius, 1844, p. 182; Harley, 1941, pp. 220, 222; Warner, p. 221.

skill, but as far as any internal ailment is concerned the average farmer's wife is worth all the doctors in the whole tribe."[3]

Similar appreciative judgments can be easily collected from Oceania,[4] South America,[5] or Africa.[6] They are, of course, mainly based on the prompt healing of wounds, which can be explained equally well through the constitution of the patients or the absence of the highly "cultivated" germs of our cities and hospitals. To evaluate wound treatment in primitive society in such a general way is all the more difficult when we see in our own medicine rather different treatments applied with about similar results. Reports of deaths occurring during initiation rites in Melanesia and Africa[7] from infected scarification wounds should not be omitted from a general picture.

It is easier to appreciate certain isolated technical procedures in the course of wound treatment. For instance, the suturing of wounds (with sinews among North American Indians like the Carrier, Mescalero, Dakota, Winnebago;[8] with thorns among the Masai and Akamba,[9] and with the heads of termites among the Somali and Brazilian Indians)[10] is a very respectable accomplishment. Wound drainage too is reported from North American Indians.[11]

The stopping of hemorrhage is a difficult problem for primitives. That they do not know the ligature[12] is not surprising, as it appeared in our own culture only with Celsus (1st century A. D.) and was rediscovered by Ambroise Paré (1510–1590). Primitives do use, more or less successfully, such diverse materials as powdered gum, charcoal, ashes, eagles' down, and bandages of bark or coconut fibre. Tourniquets are known in Africa, North America, and Oceania.[13] One of the best styptic methods is cauterization, practised in Africa, America,[14] and Oceania.[15] The only tribe known to suture *vessels* (with tendons) is the Masai.[16] We will encounter the Masai again and again as the primitive master surgeons. They are atypical, as their surgery is incomparably

3 Mooney, 1891, p. 323.
4 Landtman, 1927, p. 227.
5 Koch-Grünberg, 1923, III, p. 274.
6 Driberg, 1923, p. 55.
7 Linton, 1945, p. 301; Harley, 1941, p. 131.

8 Morice, 1900/01, p. 22; Stone, 1932, p. 76.
9 Lindblom, 1920, p. 312; Merker, 1910, p. 181.
10 Pardal, 1937, pp. 50, 161; Monfreid in Stephen-Chauvet, 1936, p. 76.
11 Stone, 1932, p. 76.

12 The ligature of an artery with copper wire among the Ba-Yaka mentioned by Tardy and Joyce, 1906, p. 50, and ligature of North Carolina Indians are likely to be borrowed from the whites.
13 Malcolm, 1934, p. 200.
14 Bartels, 1893, pp. 282, 287.

15 Hagen, 1899, p. 285.
16 Merker, 1919, p. 181.

superior not only to that of all other primitive tribes reported, but also to the surgery of most civilized peoples up to the Renaissance. That even this highly developed surgery is not free from magic becomes obvious from such examples as the Masai, putting a dead fly into the wound and binding one testicle around the left anterior leg of their cattle after castration so that the wound might close more quickly. [16a]

Occasionally, deep-seated arrows seem to be extracted skillfully and successfully.[17] In a limited area in East Africa, natives are *even able to suture intestines* opened by arrows or spears.[18] Intestinal wounds may heal sometimes,[19] but treatment in general seems inept.[20] Incarcerated hernias die. Umbilical hernias are, in many places, regarded as a sign of beauty. In North America hernias are occasionally bandaged.[21] The Déné bring a prolapsed uterus back into its original position and bandage it.[22]

The oldest document in the German language, the so-called "Merseburger Zaubersprüche", is wound incantations. Homer's "Odyssey" (XIX, 457) mentions an incantation against bleeding. It is, therefore, not surprising that, in addition to dressing, wounds are treated with magic songs among, e.g., the Apache,[23] Havasupai,[24] or Creek.[25] The Creek submit the wounded to the same kind of isolation as women after childbirth.[26] The wounded among the Banyankole can be nursed only by women without sexual relations.[27] The latex used in the treatment of wounds among the Mania plays a magic role.[28] The Maori exorcised arrowheads which they could not touch.[29] Heat used in the treatment of wounds, be it in the form of the "moxa" or not, has often a symbolical meaning and makes the disease spirit fly away.[30]

FRACTURES AND DISLOCATIONS

To base judgments concerning the quality of primitive surgery on mere excavation material has become impossible since Adolph Schultz has

16a *Id.*, p. 159.

17 E.g., Chartier in Stephen-Chauvet, 1936, p. 76; Routledge in Harley, 1941, p. 221; Grinnell, II, p. 147.

18 Merker, 1910, p. 181; Monfreid and Maurice in Stephen-Chauvet, 1936, 76–80; Roscoe and Talbot in Harley, 1941, p. 222.

19 Bartels, 1893, p. 284.

20 Webb, 1933/34, p. 95; Catlin, 1876, I, p. 39.

21 Morice, 1900/01, p. 23; Opler, 1941, p. 217; Malcolm, 1934, p. 200.

22 Morice, 1900/01, p. 24.

23 Opler, 1941, p. 349.

24 Spier, 1928, p. 284.

25 Swanton, 1928, p. 617.

26 Swanton, 1928, p. 625.

27 Roscoe, 1923, p. 161.

28 Vergiat, 1937, p. 171.

29 Parham, 1943, VI.

30 Morice, 1900/01, p. 20; Sieroshewski, 1901, p. 105.

shown that well-healed fractures are numerous among wild gibbons and other primates which are not likely to enjoy treatment by professional bonesetters.[31]

As in the case of wounds, numerous reports emphasize again the good treatment of fractures, e.g., among the Creek, Winnebago,[32] the Barundi,[33] Bavenda,[34] Duke of York Islanders,[35] and Maori.[36] From these, and from the following tribes, the use of splints is reported: Chippewa,[37] Nez-Percé,[38] Hottentot,[38a] Tahitians,[39] Eskimo.[40] Original casts, made from leather, chicle, or clay, are used by the Shoshone,[41] the Lango,[42] the Jîvaro,[43] and South Australian tribes.[44] That splints do not prevent bad healing was already emphasized by Martius.[45] Morice[46] sees the reason for such failures in the absence of proper setting of the fragments. As experience in Nias shows, even relocation does not always seem to prevent bad results.[47] The Cherokee[48] and the Dakota[49] are credited with poor fracture treatment, without further comment. When on the other hand fracture treatment is associated with systematic traction (Liberian Manos[50]) or absolute immobilization, the limb being fixed to the floor with pegs (Akamba[51]), it is most likely to be successful. The absence of splints in fracture treatment is by no means rare. The Polynesian Tubnai[52] give only medicine and recommend immobility. The Murngin use only poultices and heat.[53] The Tanala apply heavy bandages, but no splints.[54] Dislocations are reduced, e.g., in North America,[55] Oceania,[56] and Africa.[57] There is much less enthusiasm among observers about the treatment of dislocations than about fracture and wound treatment.

31 Schultz, 1939, pp. 571 ff.; *id.*, 1944, p. 115 ff. Dr. Schultz' publications have very important implications on the problems of primitive pathology in general and natural selection, with which I have been unable to deal in this context. They should be perused by all interested in these problems.

32 Bartels, 1893, p. 290.
33 Meyer, 1916, p. 142.
34 Stayt, 1931, p. 273.
35 Brown, 1910, p. 185.
36 Parham, 1943, p. VI.
37 Densmore, 1928, p. 334.
38 Spinden, 1908, p. 257.
38a Schapera, 1930, p. 408.
39 Ellis, 1853, III, p. 42.
40 Weyer, 1932, p. 329.
41 Stone, 1932, p. 82.
42 Driberg, 1923, p. 56.
43 Stirling, 1938, p. 120.
44 Bartels, 1893, p. 290.

45 Martius, 1844, p. 182.
46 Morice, 1900/01, p. 22.
47 Kleiweg, 1913, p. 133.
48 Olbrechts, 1932, p. 71.
49 Bartels, 1893, p. 290.
50 Harley, 1941, p. 95.
51 Lindblom, 1920, p. 311.
52 Aitken, 1930, p. 89.
53 Warner, 1937, p. 221.
54 Linton, 1933, p. 225.
55 Morice, 1900/01, p. 22.
56 Ellis, 1853, p. 42; Aitken, 1930, p. 89.
57 Schapera, 1930, p. 408.

Fracture treatment of primitives seems to be more active than ours. Massaging seems to start relatively early.[58] As the use of massage is by no means restricted to surgical cases among primitives and is not a surgical procedure, properly speaking, we prefer not to deal with this subject in detail in this connection. Massage as a therapeutic procedure seems to be almost universal.[59] This is not surprising in view of the fact that it can be easily derived from the behavior of sick animals (scratching, rubbing) and presupposes no technological accomplishments whatsoever.

Fracture treatment like any other primitive treatment is, even if objectively effective, pervaded with magic elements. The plants used so frequently as internal medicaments or poultices have implications of magic power.[60] Gio bonesetters use much mimic magic in setting bones.[61] The success of an otherwise "rational" fracture treatment depends entirely on the fate of a chicken whose bones are broken and treated like those of the patient.[62] A blacksmith tong is employed magically for reducing a dislocated mandible.[63] The bonesetters among the Azande use splints, massage, and "mystic" ointments.[64] Magic fracture treatment is reported from the Ubena[65] and the Tanala.[66] At Nias, fractures and dislocations are preferably reduced by those born with their feet forward,[67] among the Zuñi by those struck by lightning.[67a] The Tarahumare apply peyote and bind the heads of lizards around the fracture.[68] The Havasupai use splints – and songs.[69]

BLOOD-LETTING

Though not used primarily in surgical diseases, bleeding is a surgica procedure itself. Bleeding again is an almost universal trait in primitive medicine. As we automatically identify bleeding with venesection, which is actually not too frequent among primitives, we tend to have a somewhat exalted idea of the technical excellence of primitive bleeding. The confusion between venesection (phlebotomy) and blood-letting makes a propper evaluation of source material difficult. If a source says that a tribe does not practise phlebotomy, does that mean

58 E.g., Harley, 1941, p. 95.
59 See Sumner-Keller, 1927, II, pp. 1401 ff.; IV, pp. 799 ff.
60 Vergiat, 1937, p. 166.
61 Harley, 1941, p. 17.
62 Id., p. 95.
63 Id., p. 118.
64 Evans-Pritchard, 1937, p. 498.
65 Culwick, 1935, p. 397.
66 Linton, 1933, p. 225.
67 Kleiweg, 1913, pp. 132, 203.
67a Spier, 1928, p. 285.
68 Hrdlicka, 1908, p. 250.
69 Spier, 1928, p. 284.

that there is no bleeding at all? If a source speaks of "blood-letting" in general, we do not know which technique is really used.

Actually, there exist four bleeding techniques in primitive cultures: scarification, cupping, venesection, and leeching. Scarification is undoubtedly the technique most widely used. In some regions scarification is used so freely that everybody is covered with scars resulting from the treatment.[70] A great variety of instruments is employed.[70a] Scarification is reported particularly from Oceania (e.g., Samoa, d'Entrecasteaux Islands, Nias, Australia, New Guinea) and America (e.g., the Tlingit, Ten'a, Chippewa, Omaha, Cherokee; Central America and Brazil).[70b] Cupping with a horn over incisions is so generally applied in Africa[71] that it has almost completely replaced scarification for bleeding, and sucking for the production of local hyperemia. Outside Africa cupping is found but rarely, e.g., in British Columbia and Nias.[72] Venesection is not very frequent and is mostly found in America (Alaska, California, Honduras, Peru; the Déné, Chippewa, Carajá);[73] though in some places the technique may be adopted from the whites, at least for Peru it is certain that the custom was pre-Columbian.[74] Venesection is found occasionally in Africa[75] and Oceania.[76] Leeching is extremely rare.[77] A queer variation of bleeding techniques is the shooting of little arrows into the skin, reported from New Guinea,[78] Africa,[78a] Central and South America,[79] and Greece(!);[79a] it is probably magical in origin.[80] The magico-religious background of bleeding in primitive culture has so often been commented upon that it seems unnecessary to deal with this question here in detail.[81]

INCISION

Not so widespread as the above-mentioned practices, but still fairly

70 Ehrenreich, 1891, II, p. 33; Haddon, p. 113.
70a Lillico, 1940, p. 135.
70b Sumner-Keller, 1927, II, p. 1401; IV, pp. 801 ff.; Haddon, 1901, p. 113; Hagen, 1899, p. 257; Martius, 1844, p. 182; Fletcher-La Flesche, 1911, p. 582; Kleiweg, 1913, p. 133; Lillico, 1940, pp. 135 ff.
71 Harley, 1941, p. 217.
72 Sumner-Keller, 1927, IV, p. 799; Kleiweg, 1913, p. 133.
73 Bartels, 1893, p. 209; Morice, 1900/01, p. 18; Martius, 1844, p. 182.

74 Pardal, 1937, p. 49/50.
75 E.g., Smith and Dale, 1920, p. 231.
76 E.g., Ray, 1917, p. 273; Haddon, 1901, p. 223; Lillico, 1940, pp. 137 ff.
77 Lillico, 1940, p. 135.
78 Haddon, 1901, p. 223.
78a Merker, 1910, p. 182; Driberg, 1930.
79 Karsten, 1926, p. 159; Wafer (1699), 1934, p. 18.
79a Heger, 1928, p. 275.
80 Karsten, 1926, p. 160.
81 Id., pp. 155 ff.; Lillico, p. 133; Sumner-Keller, 1927, II, p. 1403.

frequent, are operations by incision. Technically akin to scarification and venesection, such operations are still conservative and not concerned with anatomical change, but they come much closer to "active" surgery. The most frequent one is, of course, the opening of boils and abscesses with a great variety of instruments. Boils are lanced, e.g., among the Eskimo,[82] the Thompson Indians,[83] and Zuñi,[84] among the Barundi, Akamba and Dama,[85] in the Shan states,[86] in New Guinea, Samoa, Tahiti, and Vaitupu.[87] The Masai operate even on abscesses of the liver and spleen.[88] In the same direction lies the lancing of a hydrocele in Vaitupu[89] or of an inflamed testis in Uvea. Fatal outcome of the incision of a hernia is reported by the same author.[90] Rare operations along similar lines are the opening of an empyema (Great Lakes);[91] pneumothorax by cautery in pleurisy and pneumonia in Uganda;[92] scarification of inflamed tonsils by the Masai;[93] multiple piercing of goiters,[94] and tenotomy.[95]

MEDICAL AMPUTATION AND EXCISION

With these operations we enter the field of the very rare. Observers of even the more surgery-minded tribes in America,[96] as well as in Africa[97] and Oceania,[98] emphasize the absence of amputation. Amputation seems most likely where nature, by freezing limbs, has already prepared the procedure. Thus we hear of the (very crude) amputation of frozen fingers among the Eskimo and Chippewa.[99] The Dama represent an isolated case of amputating crippled fingers and toes.[100] Whether the penis amputation photographed by Neuhauss[101] is of a medical nature is doubtful. The Masai enucleate eyes and, for instance, amputate limbs with hopelessly complicated fractures with great skill.[102] They have

82 Weyer, 1932, p. 328.
83 Teit, 1900, p. 370.
84 Freeman, 1924, p. 32; a masterly description of the opening of an abscess in Stevenson, 1904, p. 386.
85 Meyer, 1932, p. 142; Lindblom, 1920, p. 314; Vedder, 1923, II, p. 90.
86 Milne, 1924, p. 251.
87 Whiting, 1941, p. 52; Turner, 1884, p. 141; Ellis, 1853, p. 44; Kennedy, 1931, p. 241.
88 Merker, 1910, p. 183.
89 Kennedy, 1931, p. 241.
90 Ella, 1874, p. 50.
91 Stone, 1932, p. 84.
92 Harley, 1941, p. 222.
93 Merker, 1910, p. 190.
94 Milne, 1924, p. 251.
95 Kaysser in Neuhauss, 1911, III, p. 77.
96 Morice, 1900/01, p. 22; Grinnell, 1923, II, p. 147; Swanton, 1928, p. 625.
97 Meyer, 1932, p. 142; Van der Burgt, 1903, p. 363.
98 Ella, 1874, p. 50.
99 Weyer, 1932, p. 328; Densmore, 1928, p. 333.
100 Vedder, 1923, II, p. 90.
101 Neuhauss, 1911, I, p. 436.
102 Johnston, 1902, II, p. 829; Merker, 1910, p. 193.

protheses.[103] They are thus apparently the only primitives to equal in this field the accomplishments of the ancient Peruvians[104] who, according to Roy Moodie, were far better surgeons than "any other primitive or ancient race of people."[105] We are not dealing further with the surgery of the ancient Peruvians because neither can they be regarded as "primitives", nor is it clear whether the numerous mutilations of nose, lips, and extremities seen on Peruvian pottery are spontaneous (a consequence of lepra, syphilis, or, most likely, leishmaniasis), or, if artificial, whether they are of a medical, religious or juridical nature.[106]

A remarkable local surgical accomplishment, reported by six different authors, is the excision of neck glands by native African doctors in the case of sleeping disease (trypanosomiasis).[107] Neck tumors are cauterized in Rhodesia.[108] The Galla and the Akamba remove the uvula.[109] The Tembu and Fingu operate vaginal polyps.[110]

I have been able to find only one place outside Africa where surgery reaches similar levels, Vaitupu (Ellice Islands) in Polynesia. There subcutaneous lipomata, the elephantoid scrotum, tubercular glands in the neck, old leprotic or yaw ulcers are removed successfully.[111] While the Africans at least have iron knives at their disposal, these Polynesians operate exclusively with shark teeth.

I would regard with the greatest distrust the marvelous stories of the abdominal surgery of the Araucanians, based on old sources.[112] We know now that the shamanism of the Araucanians shows the closest resemblances to Siberian shamanism. The Araucanians practise the rare postmortem opening of the body, typical of Siberia,[113] as well as the old shamanistic trick of opening the body and cleaning the intestines.[114] It is most likely that early observers have mistaken both customs for operations.

Equally spurious are reports on primitive "cataract operations".[115] The only clear-cut case in the literature is no less clearly of Arabic provenience.[116] If a case is described in sufficient detail, as by Morice,[117]

103 Merker, 1910, p. 196.
104 Pardal, 1937, p. 160.
105 Moodie, 1927, p. 278.
106 Pardal, 1937, Chapter VII, pp. 217, 234.
107 Bartels, 1893, p. 300; Harley, 1941, pp. 45, 219.
108 Harley, 1941, p. 222.
109 Paulitschke, 1896, I, p. 184; Lindblom, 1920, p. 312.
110 Laubscher, 1937, p. 11.
111 Kennedy, 1931, pp. 241 ff.
112 E.g., Corlett, 1935, p. 242.
113 Ackerknecht, 1943, p. 336.
114 Czaplicka, 1914, p. 233.
115 E.g., Teit, 1900, p. 370.
116 Harley, 1941, p. 38.
117 Morice, 1900/01, p. 27.

it becomes obvious that we are not dealing with the operation of a cataract but of a pterygium! Actually, I do not think that the one report on ovariotomy in Australia [117a] justifies counting this operation among the accomplishments of primitive surgery.

CAESAREAN SECTION

The Caesarean section is technically even more difficult than the operations mentioned above. It may be very old, but the earliest authentic reports of it stem from the 16th century, and only during the last sixty years has it become a routine procedure. One is thus inclined to dismiss reports of primitive Caesareans as mere fable or misunderstanding. Neither self-inflicted rippings of the belly by desperate mothers, as have occurred even in our time,[118] nor the widely practised cutting out of the fetus when the mother has died can qualify as "surgery". The latter measure was prescribed by law in Rome as early as 715 B.C., and seems to be rather common in parts of Africa [119] and Oceania.[120] This performance, based mostly on magic representations, leads by no means automatically to the true Caesarean section. We might even disregard van der Burgt's repeated statements that the Kurundi do practise Caesarean section,[121] and dismiss primitive Caesarean section with a shrug of our shoulders if there did not exist a well-dated, most detailed, and most positive description of a Ceasarean section coming from an observer whose reliability has, to our knowledge, never been challenged. The skill with which the operator acted leaves no doubt that he did not improvise, but followed a well-established procedure.

The observer was Robert Felkin and he saw the operation performed upon a 20-year old woman in Kahura in Uganda in 1879.[122] Banana wine served as an anesthetic and disinfectant. Hemorrhage was checked with a red-hot iron. The incision was made in the midline, between symphysis and umbilicus, and closed with iron nails. Temperature never rose above 101° F in the postoperative stage, and the wound was closed on the eleventh day.

Unfortunately, I feel unable to explain why in 1879 there existed in Kahura in Uganda a black surgeon performing the Caesarean section

117a Miklucho-Maclay, 1882, p. 26.
118 Young, 1944, pp. 12 ff.
119 Balima Unjoro (Emin Bey, 1879, p. 393); Barundi (Meyer, 1916, p. 442); Kisiba (Rehse, 1910, p. 117); Thonga (Junod, 1927, II, p. 332).

120 Mead, 1924, pp. 133, 156; Mackenzie, 1927, p. 333; Ploss-Bartels, 1899, II, p. 310.
121 Van der Burgt, 1903, p. 363.
122 Felkin, 1884, p. 928 ff.

safely and, in some respects, better than many of his contemporary white colleagues. It is suggested that, as we have already seen, East Africa shows generally a better surgery than any other region inhabited by primitives; that the widespread embryotomy[123] seems particularly frequent in East Africa;[124] but all this, of course, does not constitute a real answer to our question.

TREPANATION

The common surgical procedures described in the 1st to 4th sections, and even the rare ones noted in the 5th and 6th, create a picture of primitive surgery which would be fairly consistent if we did not encounter among primitives, and not rarely but fairly frequently, an operation which up to the second half of the 19th century was regarded by modern surgeons as extremely dangerous and difficult: trephining of the skull. It is, of course, neither possible to survey here the extensive literature on primitive and prehistoric trephining, nor is it necessary for our purpose. We need not deal with technical details, and we can almost entirely omit European prehistoric trephining as not belonging properly to our subject. (In another context this material is of the highest importance as it is the sole existing tangible evidence of prehistoric medicine.) Peruvian trephining I have included to a limited extent. I do not think that Inca medicine can be called "primitive",[125] but trephining in the Andean region preceded Inca civilization[126] and survived it into the 20th century.[127]

The practice of trephining has been directly observed among the following tribes and nations: in the Balkans, in Daghestan,[128] and among the Berber; in Abyssinia,[129] Uganda,[130] and Nigeria.[131] It seems to be particularly frequent in Oceania (New Caledonia,[132] New Zealand,[133] New Guinea,[134] Uvea and the Loyalty Islands,[135] the Gazelle

123 Ploss-Bartels, 1895, p. 306; Parham, 1943, p. VI.
124 Ploss-Bartels, 1895, p. 307; Roscoe, 1911, p. 54; id. 1924, p. 121.
125 See my article on the medical practices of the South American Indian in the Handbook of the South American Indian, Smithsonian Institution, vol. V, p. 621–643, Washington (1949).
126 Means, 1931, p. 446. My colleague, Junius Bird, was kind enough to inform me that the trephined skulls found at Paracas most likely come from the beginnings of the Christian era.
127 Bandelier, 1904, p. 442.
128 Guiard, 1930.
129 Wölfel, 1925, p. 1.
130 Roscoe, 1921, p. 147; id., 1923, p. 161.
131 Driberg, 1929, p. 63.
132 Guiard, 1930.
133 Wölfel, 1925, p. 14.
134 Hagen, 1899, p. 257.
135 Ella, 1874, p. 51; Ray, 1917, p. 273.

Peninsula and New Ireland,[136] New Britain,[137] the Solomons,[138] and Tahiti.[139] The center of trephining in the Americas was undoubtedly the Peruvian highlands. But isolated evidences of trephining have been found all over North, Central and South America, from British Columbia down to Chile.[140] In the latter respect the situation is similar to the one encountered in European neolithic trephining: besides numerous finds in France, we encounter isolated ones from Russia to Spain, from Sweden to North Africa. Although success in this complicated operation is explainable where it is a routine procedure, genesis and success of such isolated operations are hard to unterstand.

Prehistoric trephining was interpreted by Broca and many subsequent authors as largely magical (to liberate the disease spirit). Wölfel, on the other hand, regards trephining as a purely surgical measure in the case of skull fracture, caused mainly by two weapons – the slingshot and the club. The little we know of actual motivations of primitive trephining, however, does not allow a clear-cut decision.

In New Britain the operation obviously is used in the case of combat fractures of the skull – and yet it is also a means to obtain longevity.[141] In New Ireland, trepanation is applied in the case of skull fractures, as well as against "headaches" and "epilepsy" (both magically explained), and in children as a prophylactic against ill health in general.[142] In the Gazelle Peninsula the indication is surgical, but success depends entirely on magic remedies.[143] In Tahiti the indication seems purely surgical; in Uvea, purely magico-medical ("headache"). Almost all men are trephined there. The Uveans also trephine the tibia and ulna in cases of rheumatism.[144] In most Peruvian trephinings, the slingshot, club, or accident seems to have been the causative agent. Yet the form of some trephinings suggests "medical" indication, a fact which is admitted even by Wölfel.[145] Sometimes tumors or gummata seem to have been the reason for the operation.[146] It is remarkable that even such an apparently rational procedure as the Peruvian one was so carefully hidden by the natives for almost four hundred years that no chronicler or traveler recorded it before Bandelier (1904).

136 Parkinson, 1907, p. 108; Crump, 1901, p. 167.

137 Crump, 1901, p. 167.

138 Wölfel, 1925, p. 10.

139 Ellis, 1853, p. 43.

140 Leechman, 1944; Shapiro, 1927; Wölfel, 1925, p. 19 ff.

141 Crump, 1901, p. 168.

142 Parkinson, 1907, p. 133; Crump, 1901, p. 168.

143 Parkinson, 1907, p. 110.

144 Ella, 1874, p. 51.

145 Tello, 1913, p. 81; McCurdy, 1923, p. 251; Wölfel, 1925, p. 32.

146 Freeman, 1924, p. 24; Wölfel, 1925, p. 14; Tello, 1913, p. 79.

It has been shown repeatedly that diverse pathological conditions may produce lesions very similar to trephining.[147] That the bulk of our archaeological material consists nonetheless of true trephinings is suggested by the numerous unhealed trepanations which can be easily identified, and by the ethnographic record.

For Oceania, survival has been estimated by observers as high as 50,[148] or even 80 or 90 per cent.[149] For Peru, McGee concludes from his series of skulls a survival rate of 50 per cent, which is equal to European results in the second half of the 19th century.[150] The results of Tello and McCurdy are even more favorable.[151]

RITUAL AND JUDICIARY MUTILATIONS

With trephining we have reached the limits of surgery proper in primitive societies, but by no means the limits of activities which, objectively, are on the same level with amputations and incisions. On the contrary, in numerous places we see the same primitives who only rarely use a knife in the case of disease or traumatism fall into a veritable frenzy of cutting and chopping off when ritual or judiciary motives are involved.[152] Of this enormous field of ritual and judiciary mutilation I can here, of course, give only a very sketchy survey which, however, I hope will help us to a better understanding of primitive surgery.

I need scarcely mention such minor interventions as dental mutilations, ritual cicatrization, or head deformation. Amputation of the fingers for ritual reasons is well known to us from South and North American Indians.[153] The custom seems even more widespread in Africa and Oceania. In an excellent survey, Lagercrantz mentions no less than fourteen tribes in black Africa practising ritual finger mutilation.[154] Söderström gives almost the same number for Oceania.[155] Next to the fingers, the genitalia seem to offer a convenient target for religious zeal. No less than fourteen methods of operating upon the male genitalia are known.[156] There is no need to give details on circumcision

147 Alajouanine and Thure, 1945, pp. 71 ff.
148 Ella, 1874, p. 51.
149 Crump, 1901, p. 168.
150 Shapiro, 1927, p. 266.
151 Tello, 1913, p. 83; McCurdy, p. 259.
152 In this respect trephining fits much better into the ritual than into the medical field, and this is one of the reasons why I would feel hesitant to discard Broca's old hypothesis as eagerly as Wölfel did.
153 Dembo-Imbelloni, 1938, p. 203; Morice, 1900/01, p. 23; Grinnell, 1923, II, p. 196; Karsten, 1926, p. 186; Preuss, 1890.
154 Lagercrantz, 1935, pp. 129 ff.
155 Söderström, 1938, pp. 24 ff.
156 Malcolm, 1934, p. 200.

and its variations.[157] Subincision, the opening of the male urethra, is, curiously enough, eminently unsuccessful when practised for purely medical reasons.[158] Its medical character in Fiji and Tonga is, to say the least, somewhat confused. Its magic character in Australia is clear. So far the most satisfactory explanation for its true nature has been brought forth by Dr. Ashley Montagu.[159] A surgically most remarkable genital mutilation, monorchy, the removal of one testicle, has been reported from the Hottentot, the Dama, from Abyssinia, the Loyalty Islands, the Carolines, Tonga, etc.[160] The female genitalia are submitted to clitoridectomy, infibulation, etc.[161]

For punishment, the fingers again become convenient objects[162] if the whole hand is not sacrificed.[163] The Seneca Indians performed a very neat amputation of half the foot upon their captives.[164] Offenders may be deprived of their tongues,[165] or of their genitalia in case of adultery.[166] Compared to the rare incisions and even rarer amputations, ritual and judiciary mutilations are of an almost universal character in primitive societies.

THE SURGICAL PERSONNEL

Unfortunately most observers have failed to inform us about the not unimportant item of who actually performs the operations described.

Only among the Masai[167] do we hear of a definite class of surgeons (treating humans and animals alike). In West Africa surgery is not in the hands of the witch doctors, but of the herbalists (mostly female), who operate with the mysterious assistance of a white fowl.[168] One of the religious societies of the Kiowa, the Buffalo Doctors, specialized in the treatment of wounds.[169] The Omaha Buffalo Society concentrated upon the magic treatment of accidents.[170]

It seems less surgery which is set apart as a specialty than bonesetting. We hear of Zuñi bonesetters (mostly people struck by light-

157 Hastings Encyclopedia of Religion and Ethics, III, p. 659 ff.
158 Steinen, 1886, p. 129; Harley, 1941, p. 59.
159 Montagu, 1937, pp. 193 ff.
160 Lagercrantz, 1938, pp. 199 ff.
161 Hastings Encyclopedia of Religion and Ethics, III, p. 659 ff.
162 Eleven African tribes mentioned by Lagercrantz, 1935, pp. 129 ff.; for Oceania see Söderström, 1938.
163 Uganda (Roscoe, 1921, p. 278); Bahr-el-Ghazal (Anderson, 1911).
164 Packard, 1901, p. 29.
165 Malcolm, 1934, p. 200.
166 Hrdlicka, 1908, p. 251; Lagercrantz, 1935, p. 132.
167 Merker, 1910, p. 181.
168 Kingsley, 1899, p. 157.
169 Marriott, 1945, p. V.
170 Fletcher-La Flesche, 1911, pp. 487 ff.

ning);[171] of a clan of bonesetters among the Azande, using splints, massage, and mystic ointments;[172] of efficient, though much magic-using bonesetters among the Gio and Manos;[173] of bonesetters in Melanesia,[174] and at Ontong Java.[175]

Most frequently surgery seems to be done by the otherwise supernaturalistic medicine man. It is the "wizard" who trephines in New Britain,[176] as well as in Bolivia.[177] The famous abscess-opening among the Zuñi is done by the "theurgist".[178] One of the first things a Creek medicine man learns is how to treat gun-shot wounds with "songs" and medicines.[179] Paviotso shamans cure wounds and injuries as well as illness.[180] Jíbaro medicine men set bones.[180a] In Kenya, surgery and bonesetting are in the hands of the medicine man,[181] and in Uganda the medicine man first chops the limbs off as an executioner, to treat the wounds later as a surgeon.[182]

It would lead too far to go here into the characteristics of medical specialization among primitives in general, which differs considerably from medical specialization in our society. As far as the separation between medicine and surgery is concerned, it seems not to have advanced very far, if we are to judge from our scanty material. Our picture of the primitive surgeon as being probably more realistic and socially inferior is strongly influenced by the later medieval and early modern situation in our own society. Such an expectation does not seem to be confirmed by the data available.[183]

DISCUSSION AND CONCLUSIONS

Primitive surgery has never reached the level of, for example, Alexandrian surgery as it is reflected in Celsus (1st century A.D.). Celsus speaks of the excision of tumors, of operation for aneurism, hernia, and stone, of plastic surgery, of the amputation of the larger limbs and the resection of bones (the jaw included). The typical "surgery" of a Guarani tribe consists of cutting the umbilical cord, perforating the earlobe and the lower lip, and of opening abscesses.[184] Tribes with a

171 Spier, 1928, p. 285.
172 Evans-Pritchard, 1937, p. 498.
173 Harley, 1941, pp. 17, 93.
174 Codrington, 1891, p. 199.
175 Hogbin, 1930/31, p. 165.
176 Crump, 1901, p. 167.
177 Bandelier, 1904, pp. 442 ff.
178 Stevenson, 1904, p. 386.
179 Swanton, 1928, pp. 617 ff.
180 Park, 1938, p. 59.
180a Stirling, 1938, p. 120.
181 Barton, 1923, p. 74.
182 Roscoe, 1911, p. 278.
183 See Rosen, 1944, pp. 5 ff.; Acker-knecht, 1946, pp. 479 ff.
184 F. Müller, 1928, p. 502.

very developed medicine, like the Liberian Manos, "are extremely conservative when it comes to surgery".[185] Their surgery is limited to
bonesetting, blood-letting by small shallow incisions, circumcision and
scarification of tribal marks.[186] There is no surgery in the Bhar-el-
Ghazal;[187] neither surgery nor autopsies in Madagascar.[188] "Surgical
cases are treated in the worst possible way, any intervention with a
knife being looked on as absurd if not culpable... Medical cases are
generally treated more rationally than surgical cases."[189] There is no
substantial difference between such isolated judgments of observers
and the results of our foregoing survey. *Primitive surgery is indeed poor
in scope and quality.* Only in the more southern parts of East Africa and
in certain Polynesian localities do we encounter a relatively well-devel-
oped surgery. The East African focus of good surgery is not limited to
the Masai. Among their neighbors we have found such outstanding
accomplishments as Caesarean section, intestinal suture, trepanation,
excision of glands, etc. It is to be hoped that regional specialists will be
able to throw more light on the reasons why we find these two local
centers of a more highly developed surgery.

Logically there exist four possibilities why primitive surgery has not
advanced further: that there was no need of surgery; that primitives
lack technical skill; that they lack certain elements of knowledge; that
other elements of their socio-mental make-up have been unfavorable to
the development of surgery among them. All these possibilities undoubtedly play a certain rôle, but their relative importance is by no
means the same. It is a fact that one of the main objects of our surgical
endeavors, cancer, is rare among primitives, whether for racial reasons,
or simply because most of them never reach the cancer age. On the
other hand, the ills from which the savages are not exempt are sufficiently
numerous to have furnished enough incentive for a more developed
surgery.

Surgery undoubtedly presupposes a considerable manual skill. But
many primitives show such skill and yet, like the Eskimos, are very
poor surgeons.

The great progress in modern surgery was made possible by an
enormous increase in our knowledge concerning anatomy, anesthesia
and asepsis. *The anatomical knowledge of most primitives is notoriously*

185 Harley, 1941, p. 74.
186 *Id.*, p. 40.
187 Anderson, 1911, p. 264.

188 Grandidier, 1908, IV, p. 428.
189 Junod, 1927, II, pp. 458/459.

bad.[190] Yet explaining the lack of surgery by the lack of anatomy is only reformulating the problem in other terms. The lack of anatomy is undoubtedly due to certain objective limitations. Anatomical knowledge becomes valuable only when organized. The possibilities of organizing knowledge depend largely on the structure of society in general. Not accidentally have ideas concerning the social body so often colored anatomical ideas, and vice versa. And many primitive societies are rather amorphous. But this is only part of the truth. The knowledge of people is not only a question of what they are able to learn, but also one of what they want to learn – a question of interests and values. In this respect a comparison between the anatomical knowledge of primitives who make autopsies and those who do not has been very revealing to me. Surprisingly enough, both categories are equally ignorant of anatomy,[191] because even the dissectors are so strongly under the influence of supernaturalistic ideas that they overlook the anatomically obvious.[192] Anatomical ignorance of primitives seems mainly due to their supernaturalistic orientation. We must not forget that our own way of looking at the human body and bodily functions is rather unique compared to the attitude not only of primitives but also of most ancient civilizations.

The absence of anesthesia and asepsis in the modern sense is perhaps less important in the lag of primitive surgery than it appears at first sight. In spite of the lack of anesthesia and a very rudimentary asepsis, the Masai have developed a quite creditable surgery. Many primitives have a considerable number of general and local anesthetics at their disposal.[193] All observers agree upon the relative ease with which primitives overcome wound infection.[194] It is immaterial here whether this increased resistance is primarily constitutional or, as I am inclined to think, primarily due to the fact that no hospitals are at the

---

190 E.g., Dené (Morice, 1900/01, p. 21); Omaha (Fletcher-La Flesche, 1911, p. 107); Chorti (Wisdom, 1940, p. 307); Brazilian Indians (Martius, 1844, p. 128); Pangwe (Tessmann, 1913, II, p. 128); Thonga (Junod, 1927, II, p. 332); Ba-Ila (Smith and Dale, 1920, I, p. 224); Kiwai Papuans (Laudtman, 1927, p. 281); Sinaugolo (Seligman, 1902, p. 301).

191 See above, p. 90.

192 Mere dissection did not improve medieval anatomy either. More than 200 years of dissecting before Vesalius under scholastic auspices did not reveal the obvious errors of Galenic anatomy till the Renaissance shattered the authoritarian principle in science and replaced it by observation.

193 Ellis, 1945. See also Stevenson, 1904, p. 386; Bandelier, 1909, p. 445; Freeman, 1924, p. 32; Harley, 1941, p. 70; Felkin, 1884, p. 928; Angus, 1897/98, p. 324.

194 Malcolm, 1934, p. 201; Bartels, 1893, p. 307.

disposal of primitives for the cultivation of particularly virulent strains of strepto- and staphylococci. The fact remains that primitives do, as far as wound infection is concerned, labor under less odds than did modern surgery in its beginning, and this might explain their comparatively excellent results in complicated operations like trephining whenever they did attempt them.

It seems, therefore, that the most satisfactory explanation for the particular character of primitive surgery lies in the direction of the limiting influence which supernaturalistic ideas among primitives exert upon the development of the operator's art. It seems the only way to explain the "mystery" of primitive surgery,[195] that is, the occurrence of major operations such as trephining and of wholesale ritual and judicial mutilation among people who otherwise possess but the rudiments of surgery.

We have mentioned already the presence of magico-religious elements in surgical practice in their proper place. We hope that it has become obvious that primitive surgery is, as little as primitive midwifery, the purely empirical half of primitive medicine, and different in principle from a much more supernaturalistic internal medicine (as to a certain extent it is in Egyptian medicine). "Superstition affected more or less all surgical operations."[196] Yet this *active* rôle of the magicoreligious in primitive surgery is only a part, and perhaps the smaller one, of the influence of magico-religious representations on primitive surgery in general.

The *negative* influence of supernaturalistic ideas on surgery is very clear in all those cases where bodily mutilation in general is dreaded because of its detrimental influence in the future life of the ghost. "A Central African will not consent to an operation (not even tooth extraction), as it conflicts with the anticipation of his dismembered spirit.[197] For the same reason, the Tanala have no fear of death, but are very much afraid of mutilation.[198] To the Arab and Shawia, death is preferable to the loss of a limb.[199] It is obvious that amputation or other major surgery can hardly develop or be "diffused" under such circumstances. It is also clear that punishment by bodily mutilation in such tribes is damaging far beyond the physical disability it leaves. And it is understandable that in regions where mutilation is a customary form of

195 Bartels, 1893, p. 281.
196 Morice, 1900/01, p. 22.
197 Johnston, J., 1893, p. 335.
198 Linton, 1933, p. 314.
199 Hilton-Simpson, 1913, p. 717.

punishment, people will dislike to undergo operations which externally would identify them with criminals.[200] Such attitudes of fear are not restricted to primitive societies. The Chinese, for instance, dislike for magic reasons the spilling of blood to such an extent that they did not adopt blood-letting or a quite excellent surgery from the Hindus, though they did learn a great many other medical practices from them.[201]

Yet, as we have seen, this fear of mutilation is not general. In numerous tribes ritual mutilation is widely practised, and yet these tribes generally fail to develop medical amputation or other major surgery.[202] The same holds good for most of those who practise trephining. It is most likely that ritual mutilation is so far removed in their thoughts from practical considerations, their general orientation and their thinking about the human body, and the most appropriate ways of treatment so different from ours, that it just never occurs to them that this mutilating technique might be useful or even life-saving when applied to infected complicated fractures, focuses of septicemia, tumors, etc.[203] The medical use of trephining or Caesarean section seems to be arrived at not as a result of a general approach, but on magic or empiric grounds in such an isolated way that it cannot influence the general status of surgery. The fact that relatively high technical accomplishments remain isolated without influencing the general level or orientation is rather frequent in primitive societies and by no means restricted to surgery. It is mysterious only as long as we suppose such technical accomplishments to be the result of more or less scientific thought or research as they would be in our society. In the case of the non-operating, ritual mutilators or trephiners, we deal, as in the case of the dissectors who were unable to learn anatomy, with a particular brand of "ignorance", an ignorance not of technical means, but existing in spite of technical means through different orientation, interests, and values. We must realize that such behavior is primarily dictated by

200 E.g., Abyssinia, Janus, 6: 289, 1902.   201 Rivers, 1923, p. 95.
202 I am indebted to Dr. David Bidney who drew my attention to the fact that lack of surgery in those instances which cannot be accounted for by supernaturalistic fear of mutilation can be explained on the basis of my hypothesis of a general supernaturalistic orientation of primitives in medicine (see chapter VIII of this volume, p. 135).
203 One of the many ritual mutilators reluctant to adopt medical amputation are the Cheyenne (Grinnell, 1923, II, p. 147). I am obliged to Dr. E. A. Hoebel for drawing my attention to the fact that, nevertheless, one case of medical amputation among the Cheyenne is on record (Llewellyn and Hoebel, 1941, pp. 122/123).

magico-religious ideas and is not merely "irrational". (In some respects, it is even very logical.) Irrational behavior is a general psychological mechanism in humans like, for example, suggestibility, and modern empiricist surgeons can be subject to it as well as primitive trephiners,[204] while the supernaturalistic approach has been almost entirely eliminated from modern scientific surgery.

204 Leriche, 1944.

ON THE COLLECTING OF DATA*

When Europeans started the observation of "savages" on a larger scale in the 16th and 17th centuries, medicine was among those traits in primitive cultures which interested them most and which they recorded best. Often this interest was even government-sponsored, as in the case of Francisco Hernández and Willem Piso.[1] The approach of these early observers was in general "matter of fact" and little influenced by theories or prejudices. Their main purpose was to learn the "tricks" of their native colleagues and competitors. The feeling that the medicine of these savages was different in principle from their own could hardly develop in men whose own medicine was theoretically still full of overt magico-religious elements, and in therapeutics depended on practically the same procedures (blood-letting, purging, emetics, drugs taken from the animal and vegetable kingdoms, exorcism, etc.) as did savage medicine.

The interest in, and the recording of primitive medicine declined in proportion to the increase of scientific elements and in proportion to the evergrowing use of chemicals and later of synthetic drugs in Western medicine. The recording of primitive medicine probably reached its lowest ebb towards the end of the 19th century, paradoxically enough just when the emerging scientific ethnography was to a very large extent in the hands of trained medical men (A. Bastian, P. Ehrenreich, D. Livingstone, F. v. Luschan, W. Matthews, K. von den Steinen, J. Crévaux, etc.). But it is quite possible that it was just because of their professional preparation that these men were more prejudiced against the medical customs of primitives than against any other field of their activities, and were therefore least willing to record "medical" practices which seemed to act preponderantly through suggestion.

The recording of medical data from primitive societies has improved somewhat during the last twenty-five years.[2] Ethnographic techniques in general have greatly advanced. As far as the active rôle of suggestion not only in primitive but in our own scientific medicine is

---

* This article was published first as "On the Collecting of Data Concerning Primitive Medicine" in the *American Anthropologist* 47, 427–432 (1945).

1 Moll, 1944, pp. 42, 179.

2 It is impossible to list here all the valuable contributions made during the last twenty-five years, but it should at least be mentioned that in this field the past years have brought us books of unprecedented quality such as Field, 1937, and Harley, 1941.

concerned, I think many of us have gained insight which has made us sadder but wiser men. Our own society is becoming positively obsessed with the problem of disease, especially mental disease.[3] "Health consciousness" has acquired an almost religious character, and it is surprising that this general attitude of our culture has not had even stronger repercussions in the field of ethnography. As it is, the results of the new trends in ethnography have been rather encouraging. The preoccupation of anthropologists with psychiatric problems during the last ten years has resulted in some very important contributions of anthropologists in the field of general psychopathology.[4]

In spite of the fact that a very large amount of primitive "literature" is of a "medical" character (spells, etc.), and in spite of the fact that primitive ethnobotany probably still contains unknown drugs of a potency at least not inferior to our synthetic products, medicine has remained amongst the least studied phenomena in primitive society. It has never won the loving attention devoted to purely material, purely spiritual, or purely social phenomena – perhaps because it has always transgressed the boundaries of these simple categories.

It is understandable, though perhaps not justified, that modern ethnographers, overwhelmed by the complexity of modern medicine and the taboo set in our own society upon the study of specialties by outsiders, are very often afraid of publishing observations and descriptions of purely pathological or therapeutical facts. It seems to have escaped the attention of the modern ethnographer that there is a host of sociological and psychological data in the field of primitive medicine which he is not only perfectly able to record and analyze, but which he is particularly well qualified to do on the basis of his professional education.

There is a great variety of ways of handling a sick person, ranging from abandonment and contempt to extreme devotion and awe.[5] These attitudes, which are extremely revealing as to the general philosophy of a society, can be quite competently observed without the acquisition of a diploma from a medical school. The economic problems which diseases and their treatment impose upon any society can be faced from the standpoint of organization and psychology in very different ways.

---

3 See above, p. 57.
4 For a convenient summary of this work see the excellent article of C. Kluckhohn, 1944, pp. 589 ff.
5 Sigerist, 1932, pp. 75 ff.

A study of these problems is again not the monopoly of medical men, and will give valuable insight into the economic "theory" and practice of the respective tribes. The sick man himself develops a very definite reaction towards his disease, which considerably influences the outcome of the disease itself. This reaction gives important clues as to the consistency of personal behavior with the official ideology of the tribe.[6]

Perusal of the very conscientious compilation of John Koty on the treatment of the old and the sick in primitive societies[7] reveals that up to this very day we suffer from an almost total absence of reliable information concerning all the above-mentioned phenomena in primitive society.[8] It would be an overstatement to pretend that in our own society all the social and psychological aspects of disease have been adequately and completely dealt with. But at least as compared to the deplorable state of affairs in ethnography the important groundwork is done.[9] There is no doubt that a relatively small systematic effort of a number of field-workers could fill the corresponding gap in our knowledge concerning social and psychological aspects of disease in primitive society. I take therefore the liberty to submit as an appendix to this note a questionnaire concerning these problems, which I hope may prove useful to field-workers.[10]

In recording the facts discussed above, I am convinced that anthropologists could record very essential parts of primitive medicine. They would make an important contribution to modern medicine and be quite consistent with its most recent trends. Just about a hundred years ago a 27-year-old man who was to become the "pope" of modern biological medicine for the following fifty years, Rudolf Virchow,[11] stated that "medicine is a social science", a statement which characteristically enough he never retracted.[12] The fundamental truth of Virchow's thesis was for a while obscured by the great biological discoveries of the second half of the 19th century, but during recent decades it has imposed itself most vehemently upon our minds in a

6 Kluckhohn, 1943, pp. 214, 226.   7 Koty, 1934.
8 The only promising attempts in this direction we know of are: Leighton, 1932, and Joseph, 1942, p. 1.
9 See Committee on the Costs of Medical Care, 1928–1932; Robinson, 1939, etc.
10 I would like to express here my gratitude to Dr. M. J. Herskovits to whom I am indebted for the suggestion to write such a questionnaire and for advice in the course of its preparation.
11 On the relations between Rudolf Virchow and Franz Boas see the highly enlightening study of Kroeber, 1943, pp. 10, 22.
12 Ackerknecht, 1932, p. 87.

society which is suffering from numerous diseases not because of biological, but because of sociological ignorance. Virchow's principle is no longer denied even by those sections of the medical profession which do not agree with certain applications of the principle. In so far as psychological factors of disease are concerned we have just entered the stage of *psychosomatic medicine* and are rediscovering with a great display of terminological acrobatics what most great doctors of all times have more or less known: that there is no such thing as a purely somatic disease without psychological factors being involved in its production and evolution, and, on the other hand, there is no psychic disease which does not involve somatic elements.

I am equally convinced that anthropology would benefit from such studies beyond the immediate gain in understanding certain psychological, economical, and other aspects of a given primitive society. There is little doubt that "the significant unit is not the institution but the cultural configuration".[13] But it would be a mistake to shy away entirely from institutional studies on the force of such statements. It is true that ultimately the parts (institutions) can only be understood by a knowledge of the whole (configuration). But how is the whole to be known without a knowledge of the parts? Just as in psychology we sometimes obtain surprising insight into the whole by testing one trait (e.g., handwriting), we may apply the same procedure for the study of societies. And disease and its treatment are not just more or less incidental traits; they are essential problems in the functioning of every society, in the life of every individual. General historians have lately taken up on a large scale the study of the history of disease and medicine from this angle and with quite satisfactory results.[14] I am certain that anthropologists will not be disappointed in following similar paths.

APPENDIX

Suggested topics for field-workers concerned with the sociopsychological situation of the sick

1. Is the sick man neglected or well treated?
2. Is he regarded primarily with pity, with fear, with awe, with contempt or with anger?
3. Is the tendency to keep the sick man's daily life as much as possible in the rhythm and routine of the life of the community or to isolate him and create a special routine for him?

13 Benedict, 1934, p. 244.   14 Shryock, 1937, p. 887.

4. Who bears the economic burden resulting from his illness?
5. Is this burden accepted or resented?
6. Is this problem recognized as such or overlooked because of other aspects of the disease?
7. Does disease represent an appreciable economic loss?
8. What are the differences of age and sex in this respect?
9. What is the main burden: cost of treatment or loss of the productive forces of the sick?
10. Is treatment applied under all conditions or is it omitted in hopeless cases?
11. Does the idea exist: "It is to the common interest to get the sick well again"?
12. Does he develop a feeling of insecurity and guilt because of the economic consequences of his disease?
13. Is the sick man conscious of the economic losses he causes, and what are his reactions towards the problem?
14. Is he indifferent toward this problem either because it is objectively solved in a satisfactory way or because, subjectively, other aspects of his disease preoccupy him more?
15. Is he mentally any different from the healthy members of his society?
16. Does he feel isolated?
17. Does he indulge in self-pity, analyzing his pains and symptoms?
18. Is he preoccupied with the problem of his possible death, its supernatural or natural aspect, and what is his affective reaction?
19. Has he a feeling of inferiority (being physically invalid, being supernaturally weak)?
20. Has he a feeling of guilt (regarding the disease as a supernatural sanction)?
21. Has he a feeling of hatred (regarding, with or without reason, the disease as being produced by somebody else, by his social situation, etc.)?
22. Has he a feeling of satisfaction (being more interesting and better cared for than usual)?
23. Does he have a feeling of superiority (undergoing a privileged experience)?
24. Does the sick man regard the attitude of his fellows as just or unjust, as adequate or inadequate?
25. Does the sick man believe in the treatment applied or does he ask for the trial of several treatments?
26. Does he believe in the healer rather than in the treatment?
27. Are the reactions of the sick man towards his disease proportional to the gravity of his case in our sense, or are they exaggerated or subnormal?
28. Has the fact of having been sick far-reaching economical (e.g., debts) or psychological consequences after convalescence?
29. What is done to deal with such consequences?
30. Is there one generally accepted "theory" of disease (e.g., "disease is caused by sorcery" or "by taboo violation," or "disease is the work of spirits" or a "sanction of angry gods")?
31. If several of these theories are found simultaneously is there one which is used more generally than the others?
32. Is there consistency in the attribution of a certain disease theory to certain

clinical symptoms, or are the same clinical symptoms explained by different disease theories in subsequent cases?

33. How far does the theory of disease influence the "diagnostic methods" (divination)?

34. How far does the theory of disease influence the therapeutic measures?

35. How far does the theory of disease influence the attitude of the sick toward their own disease, or of their fellows toward them?

SOME PROBLEMS*

Lacking a better expression, we call "primitive medicine" the medicine of the so-called "savage" or "uncivilized" people. We wish by no means to indicate by this expression that this medicine gives us a simple picture of the first stages of medicine. Although the medicine of these tribes is the main and almost the only source at our disposal for the study of these first stages, conclusions have to be drawn with extreme caution. These tribes and their culture have their own history, sometimes as complex and as tortuous as our own. From all that we know today, evolution followed not one, but multiple lines.

Although primitive medicine covers an enormous field in time and space, it has been studied to a surprisingly small degree by both medical historians and anthropologists. The approach taken especially by medical historians was not always a very happy one. Students either decided that certain primitives have no medicine at all, because their medicine fits so badly into our pattern of medicine, or they regarded it only as a mere immature or degenerate variety of our medicine. But our medicine is not *the medicine* nor our religion *the religion*, and there is not one medicine but numerous and quite different medicines in the different parts of the world and in the past, present and future.[1] Measuring everything with our everyday standards, we will never understand either the past or the future. Primitive medicine is not a queer collection of errors and superstitions, but a number of living units in living cultural patterns, quite able to function through the centuries in spite of their fundamental differences from our pattern. This method of seeking in primitive medicine only for what it has in common with ours and of projecting into primitive medicine our categories leads to somewhat strange results. Demonology was put in the same class with bacteriology. Primitive medicine was studied by putting aside consciously every magic and religious element[2] and served even as a model of logical and causal thinking.[3] There developed a myth of primitive "empiricism". A great handicap also was the clinging of medical historians to outmoded anthropological theories (Tylor, Spencer) and the permanent confusion with folk medicine. Folk medicine seems still to complicate the problem by its strange mixture of true primitive traits with degenerate high cultural elements.

* This article was published first as "Problems of Primitive Medicine" in the *Bull. Hist. Med. 11*, 503–521 (1942).

1 Ackerknecht, 1932, p. 158.

2 Hofschlaeger, R., 1910, p. 103.

3 Nieuwenhuis, A. W., 1924, p. 44.

The strong difference made by Lévy-Bruhl between irrational primitive mentality and rational modern mentality may be discussed, although Lévy-Bruhl's real thought is much more sensible than his critics imply.[4] This pragmatic approach to the question proved to be more laborious, of course, but also much more fertile than any other method. But there can be no doubt that there is such an opposition between modern medicine based essentially on rationalism in spite of its magical elements and between primitive medicine based essentially on supernaturalism in spite of its rational elements. A short study of the most salient features of primitive medicine will show us that primitive medicine is essentially magic medicine.[5]

PRIMITIVE MEDICINE IS MAGIC MEDICINE

The expression "magic" is used here in a very broad sense as is sometimes done by anthropological authors.[6] "Magico-religious" should perhaps be more correct for the complex which concerns us. In the relatively little differentiated societies we are studying, magic and religion like their representatives have generally not yet differentiated from their common background.[7] The attempt of Rivers to classify the medical rites into the religious with respect to their more personal, propitious and ideal character, and into the magic with respect to their more coercitive, impersonal and utilitarian character has proved somewhat arbitrary and seems not to advance very much our understanding of the question.

Illness, like death or an accident, is generally not regarded by the primitive as a natural event. It is the consequence of supernatural actions or forces. Even a cold may be explained by such causes.[8] Mystical object-intrusion, loss of the soul or one of the souls, spirit-intrusion, breach of the taboo, or witchcraft are the most common causes of illness. Very often not only one but several of them are accepted in one tribe.[9] The witchcraft theory, which is distributed all over the world,

4 Lévy-Bruhl, 1922, p. III.

5 Garrison, F. H., 1929, p. 20.

6 Thurnwald, R., 1937, p. 19; Preuss, K. T., p. 419.

7 See for the theory of this question: Soustelle, J., p. 7189; Marett, R. R., 1920, p. 206; Wright, J., 1927, p. 376; Koty, J., 1934, p. 325; Rivers, W. H. R., 1924, p. 86; Hubert, H., 1902, p. 24.

8 Lévy-Bruhl, L., 1922, p. 19; Spencer, B., and Gillen, F. J., 1899, p. 530.

9 For the distribution and chronology of these conceptions see the valuable study of Clements in *Univ. Cal. Publ. Am. Anthr.*, vol. 32, No. 2, pp. 185–252.

leads especially in Africa to a kind of witch psychosis even more murderous than our own medieval outbreak.[10] The object-intrusion theory is absent only in the Eskimo districts and on the Asiatic continent. The soul-loss conception has its greatest elaboration among the Eskimos in Siberia and on the North Pacific coast. Of course the soul-notion of the primitive is quite different from our soul-notion. Often it is something rather material, like the kidney fat of the Australians, and can be eaten by the captor. The widespread spirit-intrusion, associated with exorcism and transference, seems most elaborated in the regions of higher culture (China, India, Egypt, Mexico). Again the spirit should not be regarded as the true spiritual being. It can be materialized in a snake, bird, etc. Taboo transgression unites a strange blending of medical, juridical, economic elements on a religious background.

The belief in such causes can of course only occur in a world quite different from ours, in a magical world where the natural is supernatural but the supernatural quite natural,[11] where causality in our sense does not exist, but things, animals and plants are tied together by mystical participations and moved by occult forces. Primitive causality is not afraid of contradictions and looks for the cause of a material effect in another supernatural dimension or vice versa,[12] because it sees no limits between the two realms.[13] That makes Mr. Evans-Pritchard say: "Indeed we may ask whether they have any notion that approximates to what we mean when we speak of physical causes."[14] Here is much more than the usual *post hoc-propter hoc* fallacy. It is quite clear that this "logic" can never become more than the mother of pseudo-sciences. The primitive is not merely surprised by the unusual, because in his world everything is possible; but he reacts with intense emotion.[15] The emotion governs his thought and produces new images and delusions which he takes for realities.[16] While our world had become the world of the *homo faber*, his is rather the world of the poet or the dreamer.[17]

Nevertheless among the countless tribes which do not know natural causes for disease[18] there are no doubt tribes which recognize natural

10 Sumner, W. G., and Keller, A. G., 1927, p. 1321.
11 Garrison, F. H., 1929, p. 20.
12 Lévy-Bruhl, 1922, p. 85.
13 Thurnwald, R., p. 307.
14 Evans-Pritchard, E. E., 1937, p. 315.
15 Lévy-Bruhl, L., 1922, p. 45.
16 Thurnwald, R., p. 296.
17 Essertier, D., 1927, p. 104.
18 Rougier, E., 1907, p. 99; Bourlet, A., 1907, p. 620; Cummins, S. L., 1904, p. 156; Schweitzer, A., 1926, p. 51; Kleiweg de Zwaan, J. P. 1913, p. 18; Dieterlen, H., 1930, p. 14.

causes for certain diseases.[19] The overemphasis of this fact created an entirely false picture of primitive medicine. After a closer examination a number of these cases appear as magic.[20] Some appear clearly as a result of European influence.[21] And the rest seem still so well integrated in the magical system that the primitive does not resent any contradiction between these and supernatural causes, does not feel compelled to employ this new system of thought. Instead it seems to be their very frequency that takes these diseases out of the emotional, magical, religious sphere.[22] The famous process of rationalization (Max Weber) is only in its first beginning, and magic has been submitted to ordeals like inquisition[23] and puritanism[24] before going to pieces.

To find out such unusual causes of disease unusual methods of diagnosis are needed and used. Every kind of divination, trance, astrology and dreams are the current methods. Among the Cherokees the latter method even produces the disease names.[25] Our experience stops at the frontiers of the natural. The most important part of the primitive's experience is on the other side of this frontier in his contact with the dead, the spirits, and the mystic ancestors. What for us is a mere hallucination is for him a privileged experience.[26]

The primitive's treatment is deeply embedded in the whole magico-religious system, hence his extreme traditionalism, conservatism and conformity. Everything new is resented as highly dangerous, and fear, the kernel of primitive man's faith, makes him cling so closely to rules and customs. This traditionalism on the other hand makes him so surprisingly insensible to experience. Dreams again reveal very often the best ways of healing. Counter-magic with ist different manual and vocal rites and dances, soul-hunts, exorcism, and purification are the most common irrational methods of healing. Of course they often contain measures which we now employ rationally as blood-letting, massage, baths and drugs. But they are employed in a magical sense. Amulets serve as magical preventive methods. The primitive treatment centers around symbolical actions, for the symbol is of enormous im-

19 Harley, G. W., 1941, p. 197; Marett, R. R., 1920, p. 210; Roscoe, J., 1907, p. 103; Hrdlicka, A., 1908, p. 220; Lindblom, G., 1920, p. 269; Benedict, R., 1934, p. 122.

20 Harley, G. W., 1941, pp. 51, 54, 57, 58, 64, 66; McKenzie, D., 1927, p. 67; Rivers, W. H. R., 1924, p. 41; Nieuwenhuis, A. W., 1925, p. 46.

21 Rivers, W. H. R., 1924, 45; Spix, J. B. von, and Martius C. F. P. von, 1931, p. 1257.

22 Rivers, W. H. R., 1924, p. 42; Harley, G. W., 1941, p. 21.

23 Hubert, H., 1924.

24 Weber, M., 1934, p. 513.

25 Mooney, 1891, p. 337.

26 Lévy-Bruhl, 1938, pp. 8, 23.

portance in primitive thought. But while our symbol dematerializes, the primitive symbol remains concrete and material, and permits action by mystical participation upon invisible forces which it cannot attain otherwise.

The mechanism of these participations becomes quite obvious in the much decried *couvade*.[27] The primitive father does not lie down as a result of laziness, but to protect his child. He takes the child's medicine[28] or the whole family confesses[29] or keeps a diet,[30] when one member is ill. The borderlines of primitive man's individuality are located differently from ours. As his treatment is magical and miraculous, it has to be strong and short.[31] He distrusts the long treatment of the white man.[32] His magico-religious ideas make the primitive sometimes not only flee the ill person,[33] but even kill him,[34] as he kills twins and monsters.[35] If we finally remember that time and space are qualitative in primitive man's thought, that his classifications separate what we unite and unite what we separate (men, plants, animals), that his medical thought is full of the conception of a mysterious power (mana, orenda, mori, ngye, etc.), we can only wonder about the identification of his "causality" and his "logic" with ours by some of the best students of this problem[36]

IS THE MEDICINE MAN THE ANCESTOR OF THE MODERN PHYSICIAN?

Since Spencer, it has become a kind of axiom that the medicine man is the forefather of the modern physician. This strange personality is very often the first and only professional man in primitive society. His magic tries to produce prosperity in every field for his tribe and to fight its foes by magic. Very often the medicine man is not only magician, priest and sorcerer, but also chief and king, an almost superhuman being. His calling is generally inherited from the father or the maternal uncle. But being cured of a severe illness, being a twin, or becoming possessed may equally qualify him. A strange and widespread custom is his wearing of

27 McKenzie, D., 1927, p. 342.
28 Moffat, R., 1846, p. 591; Lévy-Bruhl, L., 1927, p. 486.
29 Turner, G., 1884, p. 124; Lévy-Bruhl, L., 1934, p. 351.
30 Roth, W. E., 1908, p. 352; Karsten, R., 1923, p. 12; Lévy-Bruhl, 1927, p. 96.
31 Sumner, W. G., and Keller, A. G., 1927, p. 1408.

32 Lévy-Bruhl, L., 1922, p. 468.
33 Bartels, M., 1893, p. 249.
34 Koty, J., 1934, p. 42.
35 Dewey, J., 1925, p. 102.
36 Rivers, W. H. R., 1924, p. 51; Saintyves, P., 1920, p. 98; Nieuwenhuis, A. W., 1924, p. 44.

women's clothes.[37] He undergoes a very severe initiation and is surrounded by strong taboos, which isolate him from society. His costume, food, dwelling, customs (he does not work and sleeps during the day, being awake at night), name and language are different from the ordinary. He has his special drums and rattles, his magical stick and medicine bag. Sometimes he kills his own son to get more magical power. To fail is often very dangerous for him; the killing of the inefficient (or too successful[38]) medicine man is reported all over the world. Different even in death, he goes to another heaven than that of his fellow tribesmen.[39]

A careful analysis of both medicine man and modern physician reveal them rather as antagonists than as colleagues. All that they have in common is that both take care of diseases; everything else is different. The conservative medicine man plays his rôle as the most irrational man in an irrational pattern. The critical modern doctor[40] gains social leadership[41] by expressing the rational tendencies in society, rationalizing even the irrational as for instance the psychoanalyst, and invading in this way the oldest domain of the priest. The medicine man is rather the ancestor of the priest, the antagonist of the physician for centuries.[42] If there is any ancestor or colleague of the modern physician in primitive society, it is the lay healer, usually a woman, the midwife.[43] This female lay healer is not to be confused with the female "medicine man", the priestess.[44]Though she is relatively nearer to empiricism, common sense or rationalism, it should not be forgotten that she also is entirely penetrated by the magic faith.[45]

We are fully aware that with the preceding short description of magic medicine, taking our examples from quite different cultures we sometimes oversimplified and built up one of those anthropological monsters which Ruth Benedict so wittily describes.[46] There is not one kind of primitive medicine; there are many. In Liberia it is the mystical

37 Leiris, M., 1934, p. 129; Bogoras, W., 1901, p. 451; Maddox, J. F., 1923, p. 88; Aichel, O., 1913, p. 165.
38 Benedict, R., 1934, p. 212.
39 Skeat, W. W., and Blagden, C. O., 1906, p. 208.
40 Rosen, G., X., No. 1, p. 13.
41 Haggard, H. W., 1933, p. V.
42 Mooney, J., 1891, p. 980; Marett, R. R., 1920, p. 215.
43 Hrdlicka, A., 1908, p. 224; Thomas, W. I., 1909, p. 288; Sigerist, H. E., 1941, p. 717; Rivers, W. H. R., 1924, p. 68; Harley, G. W., 1941, p. 38; Neuburger, M., 1910, p. 8.
44 Hewat, M. L., 1906, p. 27; MacDonald, XXII JAI, p. 105; Maddox, J. L., 1923, p. 80.
45 Harley, G. W., 1941, p. 203; Lipinska, M., 1900, 35.
46 Benedict, R., 1934, p. 29; Lowie, R. H., 1938, p. 125.

power of the drug that heals; among the Bantu the power of the medicine man; among the Zuñi the medical society.[47] Among the Navahos the greatest part of the religious ceremonial is primarily concerned with disease;[48] elsewhere it is almost free from such purposes. Smallpox may be fled from in panic here and venerated there.[49] Here the medicine man is rich; there he is extremely poor.[50] Here he is priest, sorcerer and magician in one person; there an extreme differentiation takes place.[51]

Here medical practices are genuine; there they are imported and modified[52] etc., etc. The reason is quite obvious: "the significant sociological unit is not the institution but the cultural configuration".[53] Medicine is nowhere independent and following only its own motivations. Its character and dynamism depend on the place it takes in every cultural pattern; they depend on the pattern itself.[54] Therefore in order to reach a better understanding of the whole problem, we described in a special article the different medicines of some primitive tribes in relation to their different cultures (see chapter II of this volume).

THE STONE OF THE MEDICINE MAN

The question whether the medicine man is a deceiver or believes in his own practices seems to us of the greatest importance. It is obvious that our whole attitude toward primitive medicine will depend on this question. Among people less acquainted with the subject, the former assumption prevails. It is highly interesting that among specialists only Sir J. G. Frazer defends this point of view.[55] It is also expressed by A. B. Ellis, Cator, Leonard and Read, but by the latter two with many limitations.[56] Still more limited are the accusations of Hrdlicka and Evans-Pritchard.[57] On the other hand Maddox reaches some conclusions, based on the writings of Kingsley, Sieroszewski, Hoffman, Laflesche, Roth, Nansen, about the proportion of quacks and frauds among primitive medicine men to those who are honest and sincere: "Investigation indicates the fact that the ratio of the false to the true

47 Benedict, R., 1934, p. 104; Harley,
   G. W., 1941, p. 13.
48 Leighton, A. H. and D. C., IV, p. 517.
49 Gurdon, R., 1907, p. 108.
50 Dundas, K. R., 1913.
51 Hewat, M. L., 1906, p. 27.
52 Rivers, 1924, p. 110.
53 Benedict, 1934, p. 244.

54 Dewey, 1909, pp. 175, 184.
55 Frazer, J. G., 1924, p. 46.
56 Ellis, A. B., 1887, p. 128; Cator, D.,
   1905, p. 189; Leonard, A. G., 1906;
   Read, C., 1920, p. 214.
57 Hrdlicka, A., 1908, p. 223; Evans-
   Pritchard, E. E., 1932, p. 81; Evans-
   Pritchard, E. E., 1933, p. 320.

among the uncivilized is practically the same as among the civilized."[58]
May we mention further positive testimonials in favor of the subjective
honesty of the medicine man by Boas, Rivers, Lowie, Harley, von
Martius, Hill-Tout, Jerome Dowd, Howitt, B. Gutmann, Driberg, Hofstra, J. W. Hauer, Wright, Hubert-Mauss, Sumner-Keller, Stone, and
Marett.[59] And it may be said that the majority of these men are not
"armchair anthropologists" but field-workers.

There is no other practice that arouses as much suspicion about the
treachery of the medicine man as his sucking out a stone (hidden before
in his mouth) from the body of the patient. It seems to be just the same
humbug as the stone of the medieval stonecutter, at least as long as we
see things from our own medical standpoint and not from the point of
view of the primitive. But as Im Thurn[60] states: "This foreign substance, at least among the Indians of Guiana is often, if not always,
regarded not as simply a natural body but as the materialized form of a
hostile spirit." The conclusion is rather obvious: "Given the true point
of view which is not empirical but transcendental the procedure is
perfectly sincere and in its way rational. An invisible force is dealt with
visibly by means that are meant and understood to be symbolic. An evil
magician must have projected a crystal in the patient that is invisible. It
becomes now necessary to provide a therapeutic in the form of a manual rite."[61] Or as Lévy-Bruhl[62] points out: "To destroy the misunderstanding it is sufficient to know that the extraction of the stone, insect,
etc., in short, of the materialized disease, is by no means a sleight of
hand. The doctor prefigures the intended expulsion of the evil influence. In the same way the Nagas in order to get a rich harvest, come
down the slope where they planted the rice with their bodies bent
forward as if the weight of the future harvest lay already on their
shoulders." Similar conclusions are reached by H. Meyer[63] and F. E.
Williams.[64] The patients know about the substitution. We should not
forget that in some Indian tribes, for instance among the Dakotas,[65] the

58 Maddox, J. L., 1923, p. 109.
59 Boas, F., 1890, p. 594; Rivers, W. H. R., 1924, p. 50; Lowie, R. H., 1934, p. 315;
    Harley, G. W., 1941, p. 122; Martius, K. F. P. von, 1867, p. 177, 419; Hill-Tout, C.,
    1907; Dowd, J., 1907; Howitt, A. W., 1904, p. 355; Gutmann, B., 1909, p. 159;
    Driberg, I. H., 1923, p. 236; Hofstra, S., 1933, p. 115; Hauer, J. W., 1923, p. 395;
    Wright, J., 1924–1938, p. 25; Hubert, H., and Mauss, M., 1902, p. 186; Sumner
    W. G., and Keller, A. G., 1927, p. 1359; Marett, R. R., 1920, p. 203.
60 Im Thurn, F., 1883, p. 333.   63 Meyer, H., 1933, p. 43.
61 Marett, R. R., 1920, p. 208.   64 Williams, F. E., 1936, p. 354.
62 Lévy-Bruhl, L., 1938, p. 277.   65 Bartels, M., 1893, pp. 24, 184.

same characteristic stone is always used for the procedure, and consequently it is almost impossible for the patient and the public not to know the real fact. But this side of the question is not important for them. They still believe in the act because they believe in its symbolic effect. Besides, why should it be impossible for us to understand this mechanism, since the central rite of our religion, the eating of the savior's body and the drinking of his blood, is still based on a very similar symbolism?

THE REASONS FOR THE SUCCESS OF PRIMITIVE MEDICINE

Why primitive medicine and primitive mentality took this strange course, is still a riddle. We know of no biological difference between the savage and us which necessitated this course. But one thing seems to be certain: in its strange ways primitive medicine nevertheless fulfills its rôle.[66] In looking for the reasons for its effectiveness we may perhaps come nearer to an understanding of the whole problem.

There is no doubt that primitive medicine contains a sufficiently large number of objectively effective factors which we employ in a rational way: massage, bloodletting, dry cupping, baths, cauterization, surgery from appropriate fracture treatment to trephining; even inoculation against smallpox or snake bite are found among the uncivilized. But we should never forget that this, as well as isolating the sick or hiding the excrements or keeping a diet, is not done in a rational sense, but in an entirely magical sense accompanied by spells or prayers or manual rites or dances! The same holds true for native drugs which we find even among the most primitive tribes (Andamanese,[67] Australians,[68] Kubus,[69] Tasmanians[70]). The "spirit" of the herb fights against the disease "spirit".[71] It is amazing what an enormous number of effective drugs is known to the primitives. From twenty-five to fifty per cent of their pharmacopoeia is often found to be objectively active.[72] Our knowledge of opium, hashish, hemp, coca, cinchona, eucalyptus, sarsaparilla, acacia, kousso, copaiba, guaiac, jalap, podophyllin, quassia and many others is taken from the primitive.[73]

There is little doubt that further inquiries in the field of primitive

66 Harley, G. W., 1941, p. 250.
67 Nieuwenhuis, A, W. 1925, p. 299.
68 Palmer, E., 1884, p. 321.
69 Forbes, H. O., 1885, p. 125.
70 Bonwick, J., 1898, p. 285.
71 Kingsley, M. H., 1899, p. 153.

72 Smith, E. W., and Dale, A. M., 1920; Harley, G. W., 1941, p. 192; Mooney, J., 1891, p. 323.
73 Bourke, J. G., 1892, p. 471; Garrison, F. H., 1929, p. 26; McKenzie, D., 1927, p. 184.

plant lore, unfortunately wholly neglected by our too proud "synthetic" chemists, would still give very important results.

Even in the best textbooks of medical history the knowledge of these drugs by the primitive is generally derived from "empiricism", "observation", the "process of trial and error" (Castiglioni, Meyer-Steineg and Sudhoff, Neuburger, Diepgen, Pagel); only Cumston speaks of the instinctive state of medicine. But the strange fact is that such primitive empiricism was never observed. Besides it is a rather grotesque picture to imagine that the primitive should have taken the thousands of herbs and plants and tried one after the other until he had found out the few dozen effective drugs. We may like it or not; we may call it superstition or even stupidity like Preuss, Briffault, Ch. Richet; we may judge it a necessary way for the development of human thought;[74] in any case the first human thought we know and we observe is magical. Under the enormous pressure of his terrifying surroundings man starts to think; but he does not think rationally, in a "plain" and "natural" way with "common sense" about his tools, for instance, which he continues to handle in a rather instinctive way. He first creates supernatural causes and forces.

On the other hand it is not very likely that magical thought could find or invent the effective drugs. As magical thought could gather them only by chance, and as they are otherwise too numerous to have been found only in this way, we have to look elsewhere for the sources of this drug knowledge. It is the merit of Artelt to have formulated and first proved the probable solution: "Neither empiricism nor magic are the beginning of the inner application of drugs by men, but the animal function of instinct."[75] Just as the ill man and the ill animal still instinctively choose their food, just as the ill animal eats herbs and performs other reflex-like healing measures (rubbing, scratching, licking, sucking, blowing, extracting foreign bodies) in the same way man or pre-man chooses his herbs. If what we call instinct were finer or differently developed sense organs, "natural-somnambulic perceptions of primitive sense organs" as the school of Uexküll formulates it,[76] if there were specially endowed individuals leaving their knowledge to their heirs, we do not yet know it. In any case magic replaced to a certain degree "useful instinct-actions by unuseful actions of thought" (Preuss).[77] It counteracted surgery by mystical fears, perhaps introduced cannibal-

74 Lévy-Bruhl, L., 1938, p. 95.
75 Artelt, W., 1937, p. 7.
76 Fritsche, H., 1941, p. 228.
77 Preuss, K. T., 1923, p. 12.

129

ism,[78] paralyzed growing empiricism by its traditionalism, entangled the materially effective measures in an enormous body of materially useless acts and beliefs. Then only empiricism slowly grew up. The birth of scientific thought in the middle of the eighteenth century is just such a revolutionary act against every magical-religious influence that it first throws away everything with a magical past, the effective (opium, quinine, iodine, mercury) as well as the ineffective.[79]

"Although remedies acting through the mind were probably the earliest to be employed by man, the knowledge that the remedies act in this way is one of the most important recent acquisitions of medicine."[80] It is only since we have been applying psychotherapy consciously ourselves that we understand one of the main conditions of the medicine man's success. There are too many well testified cases in primitive tribes where magic kills by suggestion for the fact to be doubted.[81] Why should the power that kills not be able to heal?[82] The medicine man is a soul doctor and his fellow primitive whom we know as an emotionalist needs him badly. He gives peace by confessing his patient. His rigid system, which ignores doubt, dispels fear, restores confidence, and inspires hope. And as Charcot said: the best inspirer of hope is the best physician. The primitive patient "comes into complete harmony with the infinite and as such must of course be free of all ills and evils".[83] In a certain sense the primitive psychotherapist uses more and stronger weapons than the modern psychotherapist. He works not only with the strength of his own personality. His rite is part of the common faith of the whole community which not seldom assists *in corpore* at his healing act or even participates in singing and dancing. The whole weight of the tribe's religion, myths, history, and community spirit enters into the treatment. Inside and outside the patient he can mobilize strong psychic energies no longer available in modern society.

He unchains hypobulical mechanisms, and thinking with his whole body (Janet) he makes his patient think with his whole body. Here lies

78 Koty, J., 1934, p. 254.

79 Maddox, J.L., 1923, p. 253; McKenzie, 1927, pp. 163, 169.

80 Rivers, 1924, p. 122.

81 Howitt, A. W.,p. 42; Howitt, A. W., 1904, p.769; Frazer, J. G.,1924, pp.321 ff.; Marett, R.R., 1920, p. 218; Sumner, W.G., and Keller, A.G., 1927, p. 1326; Nieuwenhuis, A. W., 1924, p. 178. G.H. Pitt-Rivers (Pitt-Rivers, G.H.L.F., 1927, p. 145) derives even the sterility of Polynesian women from psychological depression.

82 Dundas, K.R., 1913, p. 533.   83 Leighton, A.H. and D.C., IV., 521.

even one of the strongest points of primitive medicine. In spite of all that has been said and written about the soul-body problem, our thought is still dualistic. We still know illnesses of the body and of the soul. We differentiate between objective physical treatment and psychotherapy; and in my description, unable to employ other categories than those of my time, I too did so; but the primitive does not. He is no dualist. He knows only one kind of disease and one kind of therapy. When Rivers called primitive medicine "even more rational than ours, because its modes of diagnosis and treatment followed more directly from their ideas concerning the causation of disease" [84] the conclusion was grotesque, but the statement was correct. He may even have continued: and their ideas about disease are more closely connected with their general thinking and feeling. We differentiate between the magical and the rational in their thought and behavior, because we do it in our own. But they do not do the same. This unity of medical lore, this unity of the whole life and thought, makes primitive medicine so strong in a certain sense.

Primitive medicine is but a part of the magical system. This system is a pure creation of society. No special natural perception or association, these qualities being common in all races and cultures, builds this strange system. Society creates these collective representations; society conserves them *and they conserve society*. The strength of the magician and his own belief in himself is the consequence of the belief of the community. Magic is not built on experience; sensual experience never furnished the proofs of a magical judgment. "The general character and the apriorism of the magical judgments seems to indicate their collective origin." [85] Development of social organization, prior to technical development, is based on magical belief, and strange as it seems, magic forms an excellent cement for primitive society. It maintains public order without coercion.[86] If the chief is not the magician or medicine man himself, there is the closest cooperation between them.[87] Or in rather democratic forms of primitive government, he strengthens the influence of the old men's council which rules the tribe. "The social function of the sorcerer is therefore to preserve inviolate the power of

---

84 Rivers, W. H. R., 1924, p. 52.   85 Hubert, H., and Mauss, M., 1902, p. 126.
86 Pitt-Rivers, G. H. L. F., 1927, p. 201; Maddox, J. L., 1923, p. 287; Wright, J., 1917, p. 15; Read, C., 1920, p. XIII; Spencer, H., 1904, p. III, 141.
87 Malinowski, B., 1922, p. 75; Herscovits, M. J., 1940, p. 403.

the chief (who may or may not be a sorcerer himself), to suppress any anarchical or disorderly tendency, to give the community a sense of security in the face of known and unknown danger, to effect cures; to combat epidemics, to inflict injuries on the enemies of the clan, to counter the evil magic of the sorcerers of hostile tribes, to punish those who have offended the chief or the communal susceptibilities of the clan, and, in short, to hold the pulse of the tribe and sustain all those subtle influences that go to form the social cement that marks the difference between a community and a horde of men."[88] In a social formation where primitive mentality dominates, the medicine man is a vital organ. It is no wonder that we find him everywhere.[89] It is no wonder that he is generally a strong personality, the man who was strong enough to undergo the initiation, who is strong enough to live isolated from his very community-minded fellows. He thinks for his people. He knows them quite well and uses that knowledge when, in the ordeal, he detects the culprits. He has an aura of secular and eternal power. And that, no doubt, helps him a great deal in healing.

Besides its materially useful and psychotherapeutical characteristics, besides its social inter-relations, magic medicine seems to have another essential element of success. Magic medicine satisfies, much more than our medicine, a basic craving in humanity, a certain metaphysical need. We are generally very suspicious of such general statements. We have seen too many errors and fallacies in this way; but we cannot on the other hand refuse to recognize a general rule when facts seem to impose it.

"Man has among his most powerful instincts a kind of need for the ideal, a kind of deep and irresistible appetite for dreams, for the unreal. This tendency manifests itself imperiously and exteriorized in the primitive, restrained and perfected in the civilized, but quite precise in all epochs of history" (Hesnard).[90]

"Man is more proud of his metaphysical tendencies than of his scientific conquests; we have seen it already and we will see it without interruption when studying human history" (Le Dantec).[91]

"Every individual has a representation of the reality where he lives and acts, corresponding to the structure of his group. Here the spirits

88 Pitt-Rivers, G. H. L. F., 1927, p. 209.
89 Bartels, M., 1893, p. 47; Lévy-Bruhl, L., 1938, p. 31.
90 Hesnard, A., 1924, p. 167.
91 Le Dantec, F., 1911, p. 54.

are attached to other things than to the objective relations on which practical activity and industry are based" (Lévy-Bruhl).[92]

"In the middle of the ruins of the old moral world stays still intact the triumphant column of religious need" (Michels).[93]

If they state it as a matter of fact or if they state it with deep anger like the old super-materialist Le Dantec, if they call it ideal, religious, or metaphysical – they could still find other more or less precise names like emotional, irrational, etc. – all of them: psychologists, biologists, sociologists state the fact of this metaphysical need. Whether we like it or not, man has this irrational tendency,[94] his behavior responds to this symbolical appeal to his unconscious.[95] "Throughout man's history it has been the mechanistic theory that he has found phantastic, not the animistic one."[96]

This need is still strong because in its fulfillment man finds a satisfaction never reached elsewhere. "Compared with ignorance, at least conscious ignorance – knowledge undoubtedly means a possession of its object; but compared with the participation which prelogical mentality realizes, this possession is never anything but imperfect, incomplete, and as it were external. It is the very essence of participation that all duality is effaced. Now the need of participation assuredly remains something more imperious and more intense even among people like ourselves than the thirst of knowledge and the desire of conformity with the claims of reason."[97]

Because magic gives this mystical unity which we feel so important, this deep satisfaction by metaphysical participation, it could be repressed, condemned to a hidden and almost unconscious existence (like ratio lives in primitive mentality) but it could not die, it still lives and acts.[98] As the primitive esteems his medicine man more than his lay-healer independently of their mutual effectiveness,[99] during centuries civilized men placed the physician higher than the surgeon even though the usefulness of the latter may have been much greater than the usefulness of the former. It is not by chance that Lewis Carroll's "Alice in Wonderland", the spirit of which is so near to primitive mentality,[100] became one of the most influential books in English litera-

92 Lévy-Bruhl, L., 1922, p. 93.
93 Michels, R., 1914, p. 47.
94 Lynd, R.S., 1939, p. 234; Essertier, D., 1927, p. 344.
95 Rivers, W.H.R., 1923, p. 51.
96 Benedict, R., 1938, p. 636.
97 Lévy-Bruhl, L., 1910, p. 384.
98 Keith, A., 1926, p. 349; Robinson, V., 1931, p. 10; Frazer, J.G., 1924, p. 56; Lévy-Bruhl, L., 1931, p. 26.
99 Maddox, J.L., 1923, p. 118.
100 Keith, A., 1926, p. 347.

ture. Since Sighele's discovery of the relationship between the mentality of sects and primitive mentality, we have been more attentive to these questions. In a small, but very intelligent book, *Hidden Religions*, C. C. Bry describes the magical character in such movements as Esperanto, Sex-Reform, Christian Science, Anti-Alcoholism, Anti-Semitism, Occultism. We are witnesses of a strange hunger for idols in the masses (dictators, film stars, etc.). We observe the mystical transformations that scientific discoveries undergo in popular thought (vitamins, microbes etc.). Some thirty years ago W. G. Sumner announced another outburst of magical thinking and feeling in our society. Unfortunately it seems that he was not mistaken.

To understand primitive medicine, we had to go very far from our standards and concepts. But these apparently very remote studies are by no means unrelated to our time. Besides presenting their problems to us, they led us back to some of our own problems and thus appear as a legitimate branch of real social sciences.

APPENDIX

This essay, my first published on the subject, contains a number of formulations which I would not use today, and I have hesitated before republishing it. Yet I have not changed my fundamental position, and misunderstandings are cleared up in other articles. As the chapter deals with certain sociological and psychological aspects of the medicine man, and with the "metaphysic need", which I have not had an opportunity to discuss elsewhere, I felt that it still retains its usefulness.

I would like to emphasize again that in the sucking procedure the "fraudulous" production of foreign body is of very secondary importance. The symbolical character of the rite is clearly illustrated by the fact that in several societies it is performed *without the extraction of any material substance whatsoever*. For competent discussions of the rite see also Fortune 1932, p. 298, and Opler 1936, p. 1377.

134

NATURALISTIC AND SUPERNATURALISTIC
DIAGNOSES AND TREATMENTS*

We know that our own rational scientific medicine is not entirely free from supernaturalistic tendencies and notions. For a long time it was thought that in primitive societies ideas concerning causation and treatment of disease were exclusively magico-religious. The discovery that among primitives diseases might have natural causes too and be subjected to rational[1] treatment produced in some quarters the rather premature conclusion that there was no difference at all between modern scientific and primitive medicine, both being just a mixture of magic and science. Yet the question is not one of absolute qualities and potentialities, but one of relative quantities, of gradation and integration. A thorough study of primitive medicine reveals several very significant differences with our medicine. Primitive medicine plays a social rôle[2] and has a holistic or unitarian[3] character which medicine has lost in our society. As far as the proportions between rational and supernaturalistic concepts and methods are concerned, it seems that *primitive medicine is primarily magico-religious, utilizing a few rational elements, while our medicine is predominantly rational and scientific, employing a few magic elements.*[4]

For a better understanding of the latter statement, it seems useful to examine in more detail the data on natural diseases and rational methods, particularly those data that were assembled during the last four decades. Ethnographic methods have greatly improved during this period, and while relevant facts concerning this special problem might have easily been overlooked by earlier ethnographers, the fact that it

---

* Originally published as "Natural Diseases and Rational Treatment in Primitive Medicine" in the *Bull. Hist. Med. 19*, 467–497 (1946).

1 The term "rational" in this context is far from being satisfactory. Primarily it is a mere equivalent for "logical" and, therefore, not opposed to magic which is logical in its way too. But "rational" has been used so widely in the literature on our subject with the meaning of "logical on the basis of empirical premises" that continuing its use in this latter sense here seems less confusing than the introduction of another, more correct term. – I would like to take this occasion to thank Dr. David Bidney and Dr. Francis L. K. Hsu, who, in the preparation of this paper, have helped me through stimulating conversations to clarify my ideas for which, of course, they bear no responsibility.

2 For more details see above, p. 19, 131; chapter X of this volume, p. 167; Spencer, 1941, p. 71.

3 See above, p. 25, 130; Kluckhohn, 1943, p. 226.

4 See above, p. 21, 121.

has been controversial since about 1910 makes such shortcomings less likely as far as more recent field data are concerned.

NATURAL DISEASE CAUSES

Though it seems now established that a majority of tribes recognizes at least a few diseases or accidents as being not caused by supernatural forces, at the present state of our knowledge the possibility cannot be ruled out that some tribes ignore the concept of natural diseases or accidents altogether. We cannot simply discard it as irrelevant when Africanists of the experience and insight of an Albert Schweitzer[5] or B. Gutmann[6] tell us that in their field of observation natural disease causes do not exist at all, or when H. Meyer and G. Tessmann state that for the Barundi[7] and Bafia[8] all diseases are caused by sorcery.

When I started an extensive survey of the medical practices of the South American Indian,[10] I was almost certain that the facts would not corroborate Koch-Gruenberg's sweeping statement that for the Tauli-pang and *all* South American tribes disease is caused either by a spirit or a sorcerer. As a matter of fact, I found natural disease causes mentioned only for the Jibaros and Kamarokoto.[11] Fejos reports that among the Yagua, only violent deaths and diseases such as toothache are held to be natural.[12] A similar survey of Eskimo material[13] did not yield a single clue to natural disease causes. The following data from Oceania cannot be entirely disregarded either:

All disease, sickness, or ailment, however serious or slight, among the Bontoc-Igorot is caused by an a-ni-to (spirit).[13a]

The spirits are believed to be the cause of all sickness and of all deaths resulting from sickness. (Andaman Islands).[14]

All ailments of every kind, from the simplest to the most serious, are without exception attributed to the malign influence of an enemy in either human or spirit shape. (Central Australia).[15]

Diseases are generally attributed to witchcraft of some kind or other, even if the actual cause is known as exposure to rain, long living, carrying loads, etc. (Duke of York people).[16]

It might be fitting to close this little excursion into the field of the

5 Schweitzer, 1922, p. 35.
6 Gutmann, 1909, p. 157.
7 Meyer, 1916, p. 140.
8 Tessman, 1934, p. 221.
10 Handbook of the South American Indian, Smithsonian Institution, vol. V, pp. 621–643, Washington (1949).

11 See Métraux, 1944, p. 157.
12 Fejos, 1943, pp. 89/90.
13 Ackerknecht, 1948.
13a Jenks, 1905, p. 71.
14 Radcliffe-Brown, 1922, p. 139.
15 Spencer and Gillen, 1899, p. 530.
16 Brown, G., 1910, p. 183.

exclusively supernaturalistic explanations of disease by quoting a more qualifying statement of one of the foremost Africanists and contemporary students of primitive magic and medicine.

Azande attribute sickness, whatever its nature, to witchcraft and sorcery. This does not mean that they entirely disregard secondary causes, but in so far as they recognize these, they generally think of them as associated with witchcraft and magic. Nor does their reference of sickness to supernatural causes lead them to neglect treatment any more than their reference to death on the horns of a buffalo to witchcraft causes them to await its onslaught. On the contrary they possess an enormous pharmocopoeia, and in ordinary circumstances they trust drugs to cure their ailments and only take steps to remove the primary and supernatural causes when the disease is of a serious nature or takes an alarming turn. Nevertheless, we must remember in describing the Zande classification of diseases and their treatment that the notion of witchcraft as a participant in their origin may always be expressed, and that if Azande do not always and immediately consult their oracles to find out the witch that is responsible it is because they consider the sickness to be of a minor character and not worth the trouble and expense of oracle consultations.[17]

To attribute every deviation from normal well-being to supernatural causes seems an extreme, even among primitives. In his survey of Southwestern Indian pathology and medicine, Hrdlicka[18] states that the Indian recognizes that disease might be caused by exposure and old age. Yet the same symptoms might be interpreted as due to supernatural agencies, and all serious and protracted illness is referred to such. Opler, who has more recently given much attention to the medicine of the Chiricahua Apache, also states that if a disease will not yield to herbal remedies or decoctions ritually administered, it is thought to be caused by animal spirits or sorcery.[19] On natural disease causes he says:[20]

Though it is true that most of the ceremonies deal with ill health, it does not necessarily follow that all sickness must be treated ceremonially. An individual may become sick through surfeit or through want; he may weaken himself by overexertion; he may suffer injury because of carelessness or needless daring. Advancing years bring their infirmities; old age "can kill you". There are severe ailments you can get by not taking care of yourself, by foolishness—such things as tuberculosis and venereal disease. Of course, in any particular case the reasoning may be reversed, and a malevolent person or force may be blamed finally for the trouble.

Foster lists as natural diseases among the Yuki broken bones, wounds, and rheumatism. The rest are due to 5 different supernatural

17 Evans-Pritchard, 1937, p. 479.   19 Opler, 1941, p. 224.
18 Hrdlicka, 1908, p. 220.   20 *Id.*, p. 216.

agencies.[21] Among the Thompson Indians, disease is caused by natural factors, neglect of certain rites, and the influence of the dead.[21a] Olbrechts mentions the occasional occurrence of natural diseases among the Cherokee, but emphasizes the unpredictability of the notion. The same kind of accidents might be referred to supernatural causation.[22]

Roscoe gives in his book on the Bakitara a very suggestive description of the rôle of natural diseases in African native medicine. In the beginning of the disease, no supernatural danger is felt and home remedies are given. Only when these fail is the whole complicated supernatural machinery, involving augurs, exorcists and scapegoats, put into motion.[22a] Substantially the same pattern is observed by other Africans such as the Bagesu, Basabei, Busorga, Bambwa, Bakyiya, and Batuse.[23] The Banyankole[24] seldom assigned any natural cause to illness except in the cases of old age, food poisoning, and sunstroke. Lindblom gives for the Akamba three causes of disease: spirits, sorcery, and natural causes. "This last cause, however, seems to be regarded as the least usual."[25] The Ba-Ila recognize 6 supernatural disease causes. A natural explanation is given in the case of insolation.[26] The Ubena views slight complaints, such as colds and coughs, headache and mild fever as normal occurrences, but serious illness and intractable diseases are different and are attributed to sorcery, ancestor spirits, and taboo violation.[27] Most diseases among the Baja (such as sleeping disease, smallpox, epilepsy, elephantiasis, gonorrhea, migraine, toothache, etc.) are caused by sorcery. Mild fevers, diarrhea, rheumatism are punishments inflicted by good spirits. Skin diseases and accidents "come by themselves". A fourth category is diseases imported by the whites.[28] The Pangwes know diseases produced by sorcery, cult gods, and natural causes.[29] The Hottentots differentiate between two kinds of disease: "sickness", treated by massage, and "death", ceremonially treated.[31] Among the Manos of Liberia, studied very carefully by Dr. G. Harley, natural causes are only one of the 6 categories of disease causation, the rest being supernatural.[32] Yet the Manos seem to explain more diseases on natural grounds than most other primitives. Harley

21 Foster, 1944, p. 213.
21a Teit, 1900, p. 368.
22 Olbrechts, 1932, p. 17.
22a Roscoe, 1923, pp. 285 ff.
23 Id., 1924, pp. 36, 82, 127, 153, 179, 197.
24 Id., 1923, p. 134.
25 Lindblom, 1920, p. 269.

26 Smith and Dale, 1920, I, p. 244.
27 Culwick, 1935, p. 393.
28 Tessmann, 1937, I, pp. 100 ff.
29 Tessmann, 1913, II, p. 73.
31 Schapera, 1930, p. 406.
32 Harley, 1941, p. 35.

lists as naturally caused the ubiquitous yaws, sore toes caused by jiggers, urticaria caused by plants, bee stings, snake and scorpion bites, smallpox, colic from eating too much rice, common colds, measles, toothache.[33] The peak of rationalism seems to be reached by the Masai, who derive diseases rarely from sorcery, never from bad spirits.[34] Long before Ronald Ross, they seem to have understood the connection between malaria and mosquitoes. Yet elephantiasis scroti is a punishment by God for incest. They use amulets, and the bite of scorpions is treated with the spittle of mothers of twins.

We might close our survey with some data from Oceania. Already Codrington reported from Melanesia:

Any sickness that is serious is believed to be brought about by ghosts and spirits; common complaints such as fever and ague are taken as coming in the course of nature.[35]

Boils, cuts, colds, scabies are natural with the Fijians. But even a headache or toothache may be caused by ancestor spirits or sorcery.[36] The Kiwai Papuans recognize natural disease causes as well as sorcery and spirits.[37] Among the Manua of Samoa, elephantiasis, and the consequences of eating rotten fish or of exposure are regarded as natural. Dr. Mead feels unable to decide whether this attitude was introduced by white contact or not. The Bukana of New Guinea derive diseases not only from spirits and sorcery, but from "imprudence".[39] Malinowski, after making a strong plea for the scientific in primitive cultures, writes concerning the Trobriand Islands: "But besides these natural causes there is the enormous domain of sorcery and by far the most cases of illness and death are ascribed to this."[40] At Ontong Java, the spirits of the dead bring about nearly all illness and disease. The main exception is malaria, which was introduced 60 years ago.[41] At Malekula all diseases, except wounds and those resulting from old age, are due to sorcery or the revenge of ghosts.[42] "The Kwoma believe that all *serious* sickness is caused by sorcery"[43] (not only malaria, filariasis, tuberculosis, but accidents also). According to Warner, the interpretation of sickness and death among the Australian Murngins by anything other than black magic is very rare.[44]

33 *Id.*, p. 21.
34 Merker, 1910, p. 179.
35 Codrington, 1891, p. 194.
36 Spencer, 1941, p. 20.
37 Landtman, 1927, p. 220.
38 Mead, 1930, p. 98.

39 Lehner in Neuhauss, 1911, III, p. 462.
40 Malinowski, 1926, p. 33.
41 Hogbin, 1930/31, p. 150.
42 Layard, 1942, p. 630.
43 Whiting, 1941, p. 136.
44 Warner, 1937, p. 193.

Simmons has recently drawn attention again to the fact that many primitives deny altogether the possibility of natural death. Among 49 tribes examined, he found no less than 17 entertaining this belief.[45] To this list could be added, e.g., the Dobuans[46] and the Kitimat.[47] His much shorter list of tribes believing wholly in natural death in old age (four) could be extended, e.g., by the Ba-Venda,[47a] the people of Lesu,[48] of Malekula,[49] or of Fiji.[49a] The disbelief in natural death is only a variant of the exclusively supernaturalistic concept of disease, and death being even more mysterious and dramatic than disease, it is small wonder that naturalistic ideas are rarer in this particular situation.

When we examine the diseases mentioned above as being regarded as natural by primitives, three groups seem to stand out: the very slight diseases (colds); the very common diseases (old age, tuberculosis, venereal diseases, malaria, filariasis, yaws, food poisoning, sun-stroke, skin diseases); and the diseases imported by the Whites (Jibaro,[50] Baja, Ontong Java). To group 2 (the very common diseases) we may add children's diseases: the only two diseases in Zande not attributed to witchcraft are very frequent children diseases.[51] "The Manus regard the death of infants with considerable equanimity."[52] Diseases imported by the Whites are also excepted from supernatural causation by the Hill Dama[53] and by the Dobuans.[54] For the latter attitude two explanations are possible: the savages are too polite or timid to accuse the Whites of sorcery in their presence; or the traditional medical magic system has become so rigid that it is simply unable to assimilate new phenomena. Partly, too, the imported diseases have become so frequent that they have to be explained together with group 2 (the very common diseases). As far as these are concerned, their very commonness undoubtedly makes for greater familiarity and, correspondingly, for less mysteriousness and smaller necessity of supernatural interpretation.

There is still another possible explanation why at least some of them

45 Simmons, 1945, pp. 218 ff.
46 Fortune, 1932, p. 81.
47 Lopatin, 1945, p. 73.
47a Stayt, 1931, p. 280.
48 Powdermaker, 1933, p. 293.
49 Layard, 1942, p. 536.
49a Spencer, 1941, p. 74.
50 The differentiation between "witchcraft" (headaches, colic, rheumatism) and imported "disease" (dysentery, smallpox, other fevers imported by the Whites) was first reported by Spix and Martius and recently confirmed by Karsten (1923, p. 9) and Stirling (1938, p. 116).
51 Evans-Pritchard, 1937, p. 478.
52 Fortune, 1935, p. 74; see also Forde, 1930/31, p. 185.
53 Lebzelter, 1928, p. 299.
54 Fortune, 1932, p. 138.

are not regarded as being of supernatural origin: *they have ceased altogether to be diseases*. This idea is less paradoxical than it might appear at first sight. It is suggested by data from the field. Intestinal worms, for instance, are so common among the Thonga that they think them to be necessary for digestion.[55] Primary and secondary yaws are so ubiquitous among the Manos that they say: "Oh that is no sickness, everybody has that." [56] For more examples of this kind we need by no means go to savage Africa. Research on the history of malaria in the Mississippi Valley, for instance, has shown that at the peak of its endemicity during the 19th century, malaria was no longer regarded by many there as a disease either.[57] We should not forget that *what is mental, and even bodily disease is primarily defined not by nature but by society*.[58] E. Biocca (*Arch. Biol. [Sao Paulo] 29,* 712, 1945) has published recently a very graphic example of this fact. Pinta (dyschronic spirochetosis) is so common among North-Amazonian Indians that the anatomically sick and disfigured are regarded as normal, while the few normals in the biological sense are regarded as pathological to the point of being excluded from marriage.

METHODS OF RATIONAL TREATMENT

Most data on treatment in general ethnographic monographs consist of a list of drugs or other techniques used, of a list of the diseases in which they are applied, and of statements as to the possible objective effect that such measures have. It is obvious that such descriptions, valuable as they are, omit just the points needed for our special inquiry: what are the ideas underlying these therapeutic acts, and under what circumstances (with or without ritual) are they performed? It may be said at this point that the knowledge of these facts is of more than purely theoretical interest. An efficient drug, or therapeutic measure, used without rational indication, can easily be replaced by an inefficient one, just as an efficient drug or therapeutic measure, given without rational indication, can very easily be misused. Drugs or therapeutic measures based on rational grounds have other developmental potentialities than those based on supernaturalistic ideas. A clear view concerning the existence of rational therapeutic measures among primitives is obscured through white influences. Among the Creek, for instance, white contact undoubtedly produced a shift from religious rites

55 Junod, 1927, II, p. 474.
56 Harley, 1941, p. 21.
57 Ackerknecht, 1945, p. 5.
58 See above, p. 54, 63.

to pure drug application.[59] The Maoris had no internal remedies whatsoever, but adopted the idea very easily, and started concocting strange herbal remedies themselves.[60] Another stumbling block are terminological difficulties:

Some of their medicines are pure magic, with no other function than to protect them from disease or from calamity in general. Others are thought to have power to bring them good luck. They call these all by the same name "medicine" or nye. There is a distinct tendency for them to limit the term to rational measures for curing disease, but they still extend it in a loose way to include poisons, fetiches, charms and even black magic. Anything with a hidden power under a control of the user is "nye" or "medicine."[61]

We will later come across numerous examples of magic methods being misinterpreted as rational. But the opposite may occur just as well (and this misunderstanding is current in other fields, e.g. in the evaluation of 17th century medicine): a fundamentally rational therapeutic method may be misunderstood because of its magic, semantic cloak.

As in the case of natural disease causes, we are faced in the case of rational treatment, though probably to a lesser extent, with statements of modern and well informed observers that purely rational methods of treatment are entirely absent in a given tribe, or that there do not exist any therapeutic measures which are not interpreted subjectively in supernaturalistic terms. In Southern Nigeria medicine is effective only when combined with an incantation.[62]

Neither the doctor nor his patient believes that the remedy prescribed will cure as the result of its physiological action: both are convinced that it owes its efficacy rather to the supernatural power which it contains (Ubena).[63]

In spite of these empirical elements in Zande treatment of minor ailments, my own experience has been that Zande remedies are of an almost completely magical order.[64]

Then where, it is sometimes asked, is the dividing line between a medicine man's use of herbs and the matter-of-fact action of a Ga mother who goes and gathers a handful of nyanya leaves for her child's stomach ache? Where do you leave off using the herb in a simple physiological manner like food and begin to use it to help the supernatural action of an invisible being? The answer is very certain. There is no such thing in Ga dogma as the purely physiological action of foods and drugs.[65]

59 Swanton, 1928, p. 622.
60 Best, 1924, II, p. 202.
61 Harley, 1941, p. 7.
62 Talbot, 1926, II, p. 159.
63 Culwick, 1935, p. 393.
64 Evans-Pritchard, 1937, p. 499.
65 Field, 1937, p. 115.

Almost identical quotations could be given from other regions.[66]

Although some of the simples used are undeniably of officinal value this would seem in the majority of cases to be a mere matter of accident rather than evidence of conscious experiment or even of fortunate experience. The rule underlying the choice of a certain plant as an antidote against a given ailment is of a mythological and occult rather than of a natural nature.[66a]

The disbelief in natural causes undoubtedly favors the absence of rational treatment. The Yagua have no materia medica.[67] The Bontoc Igorot make very few attempts at treatment.[68] The Dama have a very limited drug knowledge because of their supernaturalistic ideas concerning disease causation.[69] On the other hand, savages are not necessarily more consistent than we are. In Mafulu (New Guinea) most illnesses are believed to be of supernatural origin, but there is little supernaturalistic treatment.[70]

In a parallel field, sorcery, which is a kind of negative medicine, we come across similar problems. While sorcery may be nothing but a pseudonym for actual poisoning,[71] sorcerers might be entirely ignorant of poisonous substances.[72]

The total absence of remedies which are used without supernaturalistic implications seems, nevertheless, characteristic only for a minority of primitive tribes.

Hrdlicka, e.g., gives an exhaustive list of household remedies of the Southwest Indians.[73] Opler mentions as non-ceremonial a number of drugs and the following treatments: blood letting in the case of fatigue, pitch and grease for frostbite, massage for "displaced internal organs", buckskin truss for hernia, heat for rheumatism and toothache.[74] The Zuñis[75] and Acoma[76] have matter-of-fact treatments, etc., etc.

Harley, in his excellent book on the medicine of the Liberian Manos, describes the progress of treatment (see also the quotation from Roscoe in the foregoing chapter). First, rational home remedies are applied either by the patient's family or neighbors. Then a woman doctor (midwife – "priestess") is called. Then a Zo (medicine man).

66 See e.g. Tantaquidgeon, 1942, p. X;
   Bolinder, 1925, p. 132.
66a Olbrechts, 1932, p. 53.
67 Fejos, 1943, p. 89.
68 Jenks, 1905, p. 71.
69 Vedder, 1923, I, p. 87.
70 Williamson, 1912, p. 240.

71 E.g. Harley, 1941, p. 22; Gutmann,
   1909, p. 165; Talbot, 1926, II, p. 162;
   Kingsley, 1899, p. 185.
72 E.g. Seligman, 1910, p. 289.
73 Hrdlicka, 1908, p. 231.
74 Opler, 1941, p. 217.
75 Stevenson, 1904, p. 384.
76 Corlett, 1935, p. 152.

Both use rational and supernatural methods. Only in the last instance a diviner is called to find the guilty witch.[77] Harley gives a long chapter on rational methods and, tabulating the results, states that out of 99 pathological conditions, 32 receive purely rational treatments, 13 only purely supernaturalistic.[78] The diseases treated most rationally are the ones with visible pathology. Those treated most magically are either serious and chronic conditions or those appearing with startling suddenness.

The Tanala call the medicine man only in serious cases. In every village are old people of both sexes who treat minor ailments without any pretension to magic. They use mostly herbal remedies.[79] We already know the Masai as a most rational people in medical matters. Merker gives a list of 500 plant remedies[80] which supplement their prayers and sacrifices in case of disease.[81]

The Sinaugolo of New Guinea consult the sorcerers only when ordinary treatment has been found of no avail.[82] Even the magic-ridden Dobuans have rational bleeding and non-magic abortifacients.[83] Leaves and roots, belonging ordinarily to magic rituals, may be used alone for treatment in Lesu.[84] In Orokaiva "common-sense treatments" exist besides the magic expulsive and placatory treatments, though they are not very efficient and not very often used.[85] In the d'Entrecasteaux Islands there are certain simples, though in general the natives have recourse to magic.[86] At Ontong Java, boils, contusion, ringworm, malaria and sprains are exempt from ceremonial treatment.[87] The Manua have supernatural and ordinary medicines.[88]

The tradition-bound attitude of primitive medicine is in general unfavorable to the use of trial and error methods. But occasionally the trying and discarding of ineffective drugs is reported (Evans-Pritchard, 1937, p. 495; Grinnell, 1923, II, p. 167). Even charms may be handled this way (Linton, 1933, p. 202). Medicines with the Manos are in gener-

---

77 Harley, 1941, p. 16.

78 *Id.*, p. 192.

79 Linton, 1933, p. 225.

80 Merker, 1910, pp. 352 ff. The Masai are also one of the very few primitive tribes which have developed an extensive rational surgery. Data on surgery are omitted from this article as they will be dealt with in detail in a forthcoming article on "Primitive Surgery".

81 *Id.*, p. 200.

82 Seligman, 1902, p. 300.

83 Fortune, 1932, pp. 98, 240.

84 Powdermaker, 1933, p. 206.

85 Williams, 1930, p. 295.

86 Jenness, 1920, p. 137.

87 Hogbin, 1930/31, p. 151.

88 Mead, 1930, p. 98.

al handed down from father to son. But a new one is occasionally acquired by a dream, and only the effective ones are retained; this would also be a kind of trial-and-error method (Harley, 1941, p. 37).

THE RATIONAL AND THE HABITUAL IN PRIMITIVE MEDICINE

Our material seems to show that natural explanation of disease and rational treatment are most likely to be found when the primitive deals with a slight ailment and uses domestic remedies. In such cases the pattern is very similar to the one encountered in our society when we suffer from what we often call only an indisposition. The fundamental difference is that when the indisposition becomes a disease, the primitives summon the magically orientated medicine man, while we call the scientific doctor. Already Rivers has raised the question whether the term "natural" is the most appropriate in such cases:

Because certain cases of disease are not ascribed to direct human or spiritual agency, we must not conclude that they therefore fall within the domain of what we should call "natural" causation. It would seem that these diseases attract little attention, and do not afford material for speculation.[89]

I have repeatedly drawn attention to the fact that there are forms of medical behavior which are neither supernaturalistic nor, properly speaking, rational, calling them instinctive, automatic, etc.[90] So far the best description, analysis, and denomination, *"habitual"*, for this fact has been given by Dr. F.L.K. Hsu [91] in his work on magic and cholera in Yunnan. In the rare cases where ethnographers have recorded their observations on non-supernatural diseases and treatment in purely descriptive terms, the terminology used points in the same direction: we meet rather negative definitions. Things are *not* supernaturalistic; treatments make "no pretension to magic".[91a] In the case of colds the Manam "do not trouble about cause".[92] Diseases "come of themselves".[93] It is perhaps less a consequence of insufficient observation than of lack of articulate formulation by the native in the non-supernatural field that ethnographers give considerably fewer details on the latter than on supernaturalistic medical beliefs and practices.

In Tonga there is a great amount of highly developed and skillful massage, but people do not know, how they do it.[94] "On the cause of

89 Rivers, 1924, p. 41.
90 See, e.g., p. 22 of this volume.
91 Hsu, 1943.
91a Linton, 1933, p. 225.

92 Wedgwood, 1934/35, p. 65.
93 F. A. Müller, 1907, p. 73; Rivers, 1924, p. 41.
94 Collocott, 1923, p. 137.

145

many phenomena the Cree are just silent. They do not know and have no explanations, scientific or magical or mythical. In this category would fall, for instance, comets, eclipses, rain, foetal inclusions, twins." [95] It seems legitimate to interpret a number of medical beliefs and practices, often called natural and rational, along these lines. *They are actually habitual. Tradition determines certain almost automatic acts in certain situations, which together are not important enough to theorize about.* If an explanation would be given, it is more likely that it would be a magic one according to the general philosophy of the tribe (see quotation from Evans-Pritchard in the chapter on natural disease causes, and same author p. 509-510). But the main fact is that none whatsoever is given. *To call such attitudes "naturalistic" or "rational" seems to inject into the data contents they actually do not have. People in this case operate below the threshold of full consciousness.*

Such an approach might also throw some light on the much decried "increase in magic" among horticultural peoples as compared to pre-horticultural peoples, [96] which parallels the progressive and simultaneous increase of both magic and scientific lore during the Middle Ages and Renaissance, emphasized again and again by Thorndike. Part of this increase in magic, in both primitive and medieval societies, is clearly due to the decline of religion and acculturational difficulties. [97] *But partly we deal simply with an increase of formulated and articulate knowledge and opinion in general,* an increase which is most spectacular in the field of magic, because magic has a broader basis from which to start than has rational thought. Actually we do not seem to go from much rational and little magic thought to little rational and much magic thought, but from little magic and almost no formulated rational thought to more rational and still more magic thought until, at a certain late stage of the civilizing process, the rational element becomes scientific and strong enough to replace and drive back the magic.

The attempt to oppose the exoteric, essentially rational thought of the "common man" to the esoteric, essentially magical lore of the medicine man, who eventually succeeds in putting over his devilish invention, made for the sake of political power, on the gullible savage John Doe, does not seem to be corroborated by the existing data. In a way, both attitudes, the rational and the magic, are esoteric and sometimes the medicine man may prefer a natural explanation when the

---

95 Cooper, 1935, p. 362. 97 See above, p. 79, 88.
96 *Id.*, p. 371; Thurnwald, 1937, p. 52.

patient thinks of a supernatural cause.[98] The medicine man, esoteric specialist in the supernatural, knows, of course, more about magic than the layman. The medicine man can complicate and elaborate existing concepts, but he cannot introduce a new fundamental attitude. He can only develop trends which are already present in the general culture.[99] The examination of primitive societies which have no medicine man, where everybody is conversant with some medical lore,[100] or where every family has its own healer does not reveal a fundamentally more rational orientation in medical matters than that of societies with medicine men.

It is often supposed that the herbalist or lay-healer, existing in many tribes with the medical magician, is in general fundamentally different from the latter insofar as his power and practices have nothing to do with the supernatural. A brief survey will show that this is an oversimplification of the actual situation and that, even where such divisions among healers exist, a tendency towards such a cleavage is noticeable in only a small minority of cases. Such a division seems to exist among the Chorti, where diviners and curers work by supernatural power, while the midwives, massagers, herbalists, and surgeons, who lack this power "merely cure with their hands".[101] A similar situation exists among the Yuma, who do have herbal remedies, but their doctors don't use them. The Assiniboines and Dakotas have "root doctors" and "holy men" as healers.[102] Concerning the Crows, the same author states:[103]

There were physicians who worked without higher sanctions. There were household remedies and techniques, and sometimes it is not easy to draw the line between the two kinds of doctoring, for an herb or mechanical process may be ultimately traced to a vision. Again, a medicine-man may combat a natural cause of illness by his revealed power of smoking out an obtrusive object.

Hrdlicka declared the medicine women of the Southwest were rational. "They serve in quite the same manner as do corresponding practitioners among the less civilized whites."[104] If that is the case, I would, on the basis of my knowledge of these white "wise women", be somewhat reluctant to call their Indian equivalents "rational". Both classes of doctors among the Delaware, the herbalists and the "sweat-

98 Kootz-Kretschmer, 1926, p. 237.   99 Boas, 1940, p. 312 ff.
100 E.g. every Manam Islander knows some simples, nursing, massage, and spells, used together with the latter. Wedgwood, 1934/35, p. 285.
101 Wisdom, 1940, p. 343.   103 Lowie, 1935, p. 62.
102 Lowie, 1910, p. 42.   104 Hrdlicka, 1908, p. 224.

house doctors" are clearly supernaturalistic.[105] The same holds good for the Yuki[106] and Chippewa,[107] and the four classes of Navaho healers (singers, herbalists, curers, diagnosticians).[108] The division, not along the line of herbalist and "shaman", but between diagnosticians and healers, both supernaturalistic, is also known among other tribes.[109]

Among the African Manos, the lowest medical practitioner is a woman "Zo". She is the midwife, the gynecologist, the pediatrician, the general practitioner, the "circumciser" of girls, skilled in the use of poisons, the aborter – and a "priestess".[110] Herb knowledge among the Ga is more extensive and less confused by laymen than by medicine men, but every herb has supernaturalistic meaning.[111] The Thonga have three classes of medicine men, all supernaturalists: exorcisors, magicians, and diviners.[112] Among the Akamba we find medicine men, purification specialists, and "healers". "Even the knowledge of the latter is mixed with magic and superstition."[113] More numerous than the diviners and divining doctors among the Tembu are the herbalists, who practice sorcery.[114] The most numerous, most normal, and most rational type of Tanala medicine man, the ombiasy nkazo, "believe in their charms and divination".[115]

At Nias, both the priest-physician and the herbalist submit their treatment to the rules of lucky and unlucky days.[116] The Fijians have real lay herbalists.[117] Priests and medicine men are differentiated from each other among the Todas, but they use the same formulas.[118]

There is sometimes, though not very often, a real differentiation between magic medicine men and rational herbalists. More often there is one class of healers which is more magic than the others, mainly because it possesses more knowledge in general. But, and this is the crux of the matter, in most cases the other classes of healers are supernaturalists too, though to a lesser extent. It seems that those who want to make a strong case for general medical rationalism among all primitives will have to look for arguments outside of the field of professional specialization and differentiation.[119]

105 Tantaquidgeon, 1942, p. 18.
106 Foster, 1944, p. 212.
107 Densmore, 1928, p. 322.
108 Wyman-Harris, 1941, p. 8.
109 E.g. Creek; Swanton, 1928, p. 615/616.
110 Harley, 1941, p. 38.
111 Field, 1937, p. 130.
112 Junod, 1927, II, p. 413.
113 Lindblom, 1920, p. 319.
114 Laubscher, 1937, p. 34.
115 Linton, 1933, pp. 199 ff.
116 Kleiweg de Zwaan, 1913, p. 36.
117 Spencer, 1941, p. 46.
118 Rivers, 1906, p. 271.

In the magic diagnosis and healing rites, there is embedded an enormous amount of objectively effective attitudes and measures. It is quite impressive to hear from a single African tribe:

Dans le traitement des maladies, les indigènes emploient: les massages locaux, les frictions, les inhalations, les instillations dans les yeux malades, les gargarismes, les masticatoires, les emplâtres et onguents, la sudations, la succion, la scarification, les ventouses, les pointes de feu, les bains de siège, les lavements, les suppositoires, les onctions et lustrations, les infusions, les décoctions, les fumigations.[120]

No less impressive are the drug lists in ethnographic monographs or surveys with their surprisingly high percentages of effective herbs, roots, etc.[121] Unfortunately, uncritical admiration for these effective elements or ethnocentric blindness have produced one of the worst confusions which beset the student of primitive medicine; the magic nature of most of these treatments has been unconsciously[122] overlooked and *the objectively effective has been simply identified with the rational.* Hence the myth of the overwhelmingly rational primitive medicine! This attitude is only equalled by the primitive's custom of projecting his magic into our actions, and by his totally magic interpretation of our scientific medicine. Because actions dictated by supernaturalism are so often inefficient or even detrimental, the somewhat naïve conclusion was that all effective actions are rational and free from supernaturalism. It has been conveniently overlooked how many practical discoveries have been made in the bosom of supernaturalism, *how many effective actions are possible not only without any rational, but even without any conscious thought at all.* After all, even animals have a kind of effective medicine.[123] In order to gain an intelligent insight into the true nature of primitive medicine, we cannot afford to overlook any element of any medical opinion or action; we have to see them as they

119 For other aspects of primitive specialization see above, p. 29, and Rosen, 1944, pp. 5 ff.
120 Vergiat, 1937, p. 165.
121 An excellent survey of African druglore is found in Harley, 1941. Valuable attempts of synthesis for North and South America were made by Stone (1932) and Pardal respectively. No such compilation exists for Oceania where druglore anyway is rather poor. For a general survey see Mackenzie, 1927.
122 E.g. Nieuwenhuis, 1924, p. 189; Hofschlaeger, 1910, p. 103. One might term this attitude the behavioristic fallacy.
123 Neuburger, 1910, p. 1.

are in their totality and we have to assess the relative importance of their elements in the minds of those who produce them.

In some cases where rational insight had been made responsible for objectively effective but basically magic actions, as for example in the hiding of excrement for fear of witchcraft,[124] circumcision, penis envelopes, sexual abstinence during the nursing period,[125] the quarantine of villages in the case of epidemics,[126] the error has become obvious long ago, and has been termed very aptly by Crawley "the fallacy of sanitary intention".[127] Mooney stated: "The Cherokee are able to treat some classes of ailments with some degree of success, although without any intelligent idea of the process involved."

In many cases the non-rational character of the theory or procedure applied is easy to see. Sucking is undoubtedly objectively efficient, but it is the magic therapeutic procedure par excellence. Blood-letting is effective in some diseases although we do not know why and have discarded it, therefore, almost entirely. It may be rational sometimes. In most cases its magico-religious "purificative" character or its objective to drive out disease demons is obvious. The same holds good for emetics, purgatives, baths, and massage. In the latter case, the direction of the supernaturalistic massage (towards the periphery to drive out the spirit, while we massage towards the center) might provide a valuable clue. Food undoubtedly gives strength. But when it is applied as poultices which are thrown away afterwards, because their strength has left them,[128] the rational character of this feeding procedure appears at least doubtful. Certain African[129] and South American[130] tribes have developed a very efficient inoculation against snakebite, but the magic character of the treatment is unequivocal in all existing descriptions. Bones of an old animal are undoubtedly of objective value in some disease, but they are not given for their calcium content but because they contain "vital power".[131] No comments on the "rational" approach described in the following quotation concerning the Konde are necessary. "Illness may be due to natural causes which the natives call

124 E.g. Opler, 1941, p. 44.
125 See Webster, 1942, pp. 69 ff.
126 Bartels, 1893, p. 250.
127 Crawley, 1927, I, p. 170.
128 Wisdom, 1940, p. 351. It is amazing how consistently the protagonists of primitive rationalism disregard the obvious supernaturalistic components of primitive food-lore and food habits.
129 Harley, 1944, p. 213.
130 Corlett, 1935, p. 222.
131 Callaway, 1870, p. 175; Jones, 1942, p. 162.

God. They yield to treatment without any ceremony." (The treatment in this case consists of prayers.)[132]

Sometimes only closer inspection will disclose the disappointing fact that another "rational" idea or procedure was not rational.[133] Leprosy and tuberculosis are regarded by the Thonga as contagious. But this is a different contagiousness from ours as it acts only among relatives.[134] Leprosy is often attributed to "dietetic error".[135] "In most cases where dietetic errors are blamed for disease, it will be found that the supposed dietetic error is really a breach of some food taboo."[136] A "diet" which is imposed upon the whole family also bears the earmarks of the taboo. The Pangwes with great caution prepare a "medicine" which is actually a strong poison. They have old lepers handle it, and they try it on dogs (an experiment!) – but it is effective when buried under the bed of the victim![137] In Eddystone Island, certain treatments lack spells, but the healer has to keep certain taboos during the treatment.[138] Success in a seemingly rational fracture treatment among the Manos depends on what happens to a chicken whose bone had been broken simultaneously.[139] Massage in Vaitupu looks rational until we hear that it is destined to bring a "snake" back into place.[140] The gathering of herbs and their administration is in many cases a clearly magic or religious act.[141] Before declaring a drug purely rational, it might be advisable to look at the conditions which accompany collecting and use of the drug. If it is revealed in a vision or dream,[142] if certain formulas have to be used while it is gathered,[143] if it works as an emetic when held or cut upward, as a purgative when held downward,[144] if it makes at the same time part of a fetish,[145] then scepticism as to its rational use seems legitimate.

A great many so-called rational medical judgments or measures are actually no more rational than the biting of the latrine beam, a medical rite of the Maori,[146] or defecating into one's hands for fear of sorcery in New Ireland.[147] Yet in some cases it is really very difficult to decide

132 Mackenzie, 1925, p. 276.
133 For other examples see Ackerknecht, 1945, p. 30.
134 Junod, 1927, II, p. 434.
135 Warner, 1937, pp. 144, 207.
136 Mackenzie, 1927, p. 67.
137 Tessmann, 1913, p. 145.
138 Hocart, 1925, pp. 252, 254.
139 Harley, 1941, p. 95.
140 Kennedy, 1931, p. 247.
141 E.g. Mackenzie, 1925, p. 273.
142 E.g. Opler, 1941, p. 284; Field, 1937, p. 125.
143 Fletcher-La Flesche, 1911, p. 582.
144 Wisdom, 1940, p. 365; Schapera, 1930, p. 412.
145 Field, 1937, p. 120.
146 Best, 1924, II, p. 43.
147 Brown, 1910, p. 184.

whether we deal with a rational or a supernaturalistic idea or action. Indians attribute the bad healing of wounds of whites to eating salt.[148] Is this observation or an old taboo idea as in the Cherokee disease "when they spit blood"?[149] Is the massaging of the stomach to bring it "back in place" in Tonga rational or not?[150] When the people of Nias do not bathe, is it really fear of ghosts[151] or do they simply fear aggravation of the ubiquitous skin diseases like the d'Entrecasteaux Islanders?[152] On what is the often reported refusal of medicine men to treat hopeless cases[153] actually based?

We need not be surprised about the prevalence of the confusion between the rational and the effective if we find it even with Harley, one of the very best observers of primitive medicine. We have already mentioned above his long chapter on rational treatment among the Manos. But in this chapter we find listed such behavior as the symbolic magic gestures of the midwife, which undoubtedly are objectively useful but most certainly not rational.[154] Similarly, we find clearly magic practices (as, for instance, drinking one's bath water) listed under "rational" on pp. 44, 46, 51, 54, 63, 66, etc. One has the feeling that Harley, like so many others, never defined clearly for himself what exactly he means by rational: the logical, the effective or the empirical. How he comes to list the magic as rational can be easily seen from the following quotation:

There is no assurance that any particular remedy used for the treatment of a particular disease is chosen for its drug content, and not for some fancied resemblance of leaf, seed, flower, or thorn to the lesion or the organ which is the seat of disease. . . . Yet, in spite of this possible admixture of the magical element, there is no doubt that most of the remedies included under the discussion of rational treatment have therapeutic value . . . and continue in use because they are known to work.[155]

The great advantage of Harley's writings is that he gives his material in great enough detail to allow other than his own interpretations, and that his intellectual honesty is such that he does not hide facts like the following which throw a strange light on the "rationalism" of his Manos:

148 Fenton, 1941, p. 511.
149 Olbrechts, 1932, p. 65.
150 Collocott, 1923, p. 141.
151 Kleiweg, 1913, p. 49.
152 Jenness, 1920, p. 138.

153 E.g. Densmore, 1928, p. 323; Sieroszevski, 1902, p. 323.
154 Harley, 1941, p. 63.
155 Id., p. 85.
156 Id., p. 102.

The blindworm (Typhlops) is considered by the natives to be very dangerous. As a matter of fact it is absolutely harmless. But they think one will die unless treatment is carried out.[156]

The fact that Harley, who is in the first line a medical man, (he has done outstanding work, e.g. on yaws, and was first exclusively interested in drugs) had to allow so much space and weight to magic in his study of Mano medicine, is in itself a strong argument in favor of the primarily magic character of primitive medicine.

In some of our examples it was already obvious that primitives, in using effective drugs or poisons, do not differentiate between them and the ineffective ones. "It must not be supposed that where part of a treatment is of therapeutic value it is necessarily the part which Azande stress as vital to the cure."[157] The Kwoma employ the same word to describe putrifying meat or fruit and to describe food which they believe is "poisoned" by sorcery.[158] The Indonesians make no difference between pure magic and pure poison.[159] The South American Yekuana use an effective poison in their countermagic, but it is thought to act magically through the air.[160] The Kpelle identify actual poisoning with strophanthus and magic poisoning by waving strophanthus in the direction of the enemy.[161] As the following examples show, this situation has brought a great number of authors, who might otherwise differ very widely in their approach, to almost identical conclusions:

Since Azande speak of, and use, medicines which really are poisonous in the same way as medicines which are harmless, I conclude that they do not distinguish between them.[162]

To the Mano man the medical and the religious elements of nye (medicine) are never completely separated and a certain degree of magic runs through all of them.[163]

The Wabena consider the art of the occult as a whole: curing and preventing disease is only one aspect of that art, and they make no attempt to classify their practices except on moral grounds.[164]

Any division of secular and religious treatement of disease is arbitrary.[165]

The magic implications of apparently rational drugs become obvious in the numerous cases where mere knowledge of a plant is insufficient for its successful use; to obtain this result, the knowledge or application has to be paid for.[166] The same holds good when the effec-

157 Evans-Pritchard, 1937, p. 502.
158 Whiting, 1941, p. 208.
159 Rivers, 1924, p. 66.
160 Koch-Grünberg, 1923, III, p. 372.
161 Westermann, 1921, p. 207.
162 Evans-Pritchard, 1937, p. 316.

163 Harley, 1941, p. 14.
164 Culwick, 1935, p. 285.
165 Opler, 1941, p. 218.
166 E.g. Rivers, 1924, p. 44; Harley, 1941, p. 37; Evans-Pritchard, 1937, p. 234; Vergiat, 1937, p. 159.

tive drug is taken by the medicine man or the family.[167] The indiscriminate use of medicines, reported from several quarters,[168] rather excludes rationality. Monica Hunter, in her book on the Pondo, rightly states that it is primarily a matter of affect, not of reasoning, whether a particular case of disease is referred to natural or supernatural causes.[169] It might also be a question of social rank.[170]

It has always been to me a matter of keen surprise to see how little primitives actually know about those diseases and treatments which might be regarded as natural and rational, and how little such isolated technical advances influence the rest of their medical beliefs. This might be due partly to the fact that the latter are upheld by the strength of society and have important social, if not medical, functions. "The most striking and far reaching characteristic of all the Indians visited, even from the medical standpoint, is their improvidence and seemingly a decided inability to take advantage of some of the lessons of experience. This keeps them disarmed against all accidents and diseases."[172] This tradition-bound attitude,[173] this lack of curiosity[174] and inaccessibility to experience are most probably carry-overs from magic, which, "as its action transcends experience, cannot easily be contradicted by experience".[175]

Scepticism towards particular medicine men or particular charms is reported from many primitive tribes. But it never goes beyond these limits. It is always combined with the firm and unshaken belief in magic medicine as such, and in other medicines and medicine men.[176]

One of the most striking features of primitive medicine is the apparent *inconsistency* in the use of rational and supernaturalistic elements. We have already given data from Opler, Olbrechts, and Warner concerning the fact that the same disease may be interpreted rationally or supernaturally,[176a] and quoted Evans-Pritchard for the fact that a *supernatural disease might be treated rationally*. Harley gives numerous examples for the same phenomenon.[177]

167 Swanton, 1942, p. 220; Moffat, 1844, p. 591.
168 Collocott, 1923, p. 137; Henry, 1941, p. 83; Landtmann, 1927, p. 224.
169 Hunter, 1936, p. 274.   170 Codrington, 1891, p. 194.
172 Hrdlicka, 1908, p. 31. A case in point is the Indians' persistent refusal of vaccination in spite of their terrible sufferings from smallpox and the observable value of enforced vaccination.
173 Harley, 1941, p. 104.   174 Fejos, 1943, p. 109.   175 Evans-Pritchard, 1937, p. 475.
176 E.g. Spier, 1928, p. 280; Opler, 1941, p. 313; Olbrechts, 1932, p. 106; Evans-Pritchard, 1937, p. 475; Culwick, 1935, p. 392; Jenness, 1920, p. 140.
176a Forde, 1930/31, p. 185.

Examples of the opposite case, that a natural disease is treated supernaturally, are equally numerous.[178] Eventually both "inconsistencies" can be observed in the same culture. At Manam Island sorcery is sometimes treated by practical methods, and natural disease by spells.[179] The same inconsistency is eventually observed in the so-called mixed treatments where rational and magic elements are used simultaneously. Many of the inconsistencies might be due historically to the blending of elements of different origins. There might actually exist mixed treatments.[180] The essential fact is that to the native they do not appear either mixed or inconsistent.

In this method of curing framboeasia we notice a mingling of the "magical" with the practical, and indeed we often find this in Manam medicine. The people themselves do not, I think, recognize any such distinction.[181]

The use of material medicines is not inconsistent in Carib thought with the theory that disease is due to spiritual causes. It is believed that the application of medicine to a wound for instance is so unpleasant to the spirit which has caused the wound that is ceases its interference.[182]

What appears inconsistent or mixed to us, seems actually in many cases to be nothing but well integrated magic.

It is impossible to consider the intimately associated subjects of medicine and magic except in conjunction with each other. Although a few of the purely medicinal and herbal treatments are of real therapeutic value, nearly all depend for their efficiency upon the inclusion of a magical element. Magico-medical seems to me the most appropriate term to describe the twofold art which is founded on one fundamental concept, the belief that every object, animate or inanimate, possesses a kinetic power for good or evil.[183]

The particular power of integration, characteristic of magic, has been commented upon often.[184] In primitive medicine, we deal with a situation in which in general no notion of the "natural" as different from and opposed to the "supernatural" has yet developed.

The idea that natural ideas and rational acts may be integrated into a magic system is in contradiction to Malinowski's theory of magic, a theory so incongruent with his otherwise integrative and synthetic functional thought. According to Malinowski, magic ideas and actions appear only where knowledge and technical control are absent, and the

177 Harley, p. 186, 35; see also Driberg, 1929, p. 54.
178 Opler, 1941, p. 222; Williams, 1930, p. 289; Rivers, 1924, 41.
179 Wedgwood, 1934/35, p. 280.
180 See Harley, 1941, p. 31; Grinnell, 1923, II, p. 127.
181 Wedgwood, 1934/35, p. 289.
182 Gillin, 1936, p. 176.
183 Stayt, 1931, p. 263.
184 E.g. Hubert-Mauss, 1902, p. 15; Rivers, 1924, p. 94.

presence of the latter crowds out the former.[185] We have already quoted evidence from Hsu, Brown, Evans-Pritchard to the contrary. Evans-Pritchard has given a particularly good description of the true interrelationship of the different elements of the disease situation,[186] a description which should be read by all who are interested in the subject.

To those whose main category of the causation of disease is human agency there is a firmly rooted belief in this mode of production, not only where causation would otherwise be mysterious and unknown, but also in those cases, where the cause would seem even to the most uninstructed lay mind in our own community to lie within the province we call natural.[187]

The habitual is, of course, outside the realm of magic theory, but for that matter outside the realm of any theory. Neither the not too numerous rational elements in primitive medicine, nor the many effective ones, produce any contradiction but they are all absorbed into a system which to us appears as supernaturalistic.

The question of the origin of the objectively effective elements in primitive medicine may eventually be raised. Though every answer to this question is necessarily speculative, I would like to submit a few suggestions concerning this problem.

Almost everywhere where we observe primitive medicine, we encounter the habitual, the magic, and a few rational elements, all containing in different degrees the objectively effective. It seems unlikely that this stage was preceded by a period of more extended rationalism or even experimentation, followed by "degeneration" into magic.[188] I side with those who think that the first therapeutic measures were dictated by "instinct"[189] – the expression is old-fashioned, but its meaning in this connection clear – and *the majority of effective measures seem to have been inherited from this period.* The first elaborate thought seems to have evolved as magic, which incorporates many effective methods. Others survive in the domain of the habitual. A few become independent from both fields as rational. Rational elements increase slowly and at a certain moment profit greatly from certain methods of systematic thought developed by magic. History shows that

185 Malinowski, 1922, pp. 420 ff.   187 Rivers, 1924, p. 10.
186 Evans-Pritchard, 1937, pp. 507 ff.   188 Ackerknecht, 1942, p. 513.
189 E.g. Sigerist, H. E., *Man and Medicine*, New York, 1932, p. 243; Koty, J., *Die Behandlung der Alten und Kranken unter den Naturvölkern*, Stuttgart, 1934, p. 239; van]Andel, M. A., *Materia Medica of Tropical America*, *Janus*, 1928, p. 21; Lewin, L., *Pfeilgifte*, Leipzig, 1923, p. 1; Robinson, V., *The Story of Medicine*, New York, 1931, p. 1; Artelt, W., *Heilmittel und Gift*, Leipzig, 1937, p. 7, etc.

magic as such has never produced anything but pseudo-sciences, but that science has greatly profited from certain developments in magic. The fusion of rational elements and advanced methods allows the replacement of magic by science, an event that lies rather beyond the limits of primitive society.

RATIONAL OR SCIENTIFIC ELEMENTS OF PRIMITIVE MEDICINE

A number of authors have adopted the custom of calling "scientific" the rational elements in primitive medicine. This point of view has been most forcefully expressed by Malinowski.[190] In the same symposium, a few pages later on, Charles Singer, the eminent historian of science, states:

Science is the purposeful search for such general laws that can be used to link together the observed phenomena. The savage has none of this faith, this aspiration. If he had, he would cast off his magic and cease to be a savage. This faith, we have said, is a thing consciously held. It is something moreover which is by no means necessarily implied when the savage resorts, as he often does, to reason. While many modern anthropologists are disposed to deny the existence of a prelogical stage of human development, they must, we believe, admit a prescientific stage.[191]

Singer, in a footnote, calls his differences with Malinowski "almost entirely verbal". In this respect, I cannot agree with Singer. Malinowski's approach expresses and helps increase a growing misunderstanding of the history and essence of science which is bound to be fatal for a culture which, for better or worse, is based on science.

Science is not the mere knowledge of facts. According to George Sarton, the outstanding contemporary historian of science:

Science is more than an accumulation of facts: systematized knowledge, not un-guided analysis and haphazard empiricism, but synthesis; not passive recording but constructive activity.[192]

Practical behavior is not yet science. A butcher is no scientist. Science, full of a disinterested curiosity, aims primarily at truth, not at practical success or psychic relaxation.

Science is not even merely laws. Magic is full of "laws", but purely subjective ones, based on supernaturalistic premises, and even "natural magic", the medieval reform movement in magic, did not succeed in changing this situation.[193]

Science is unthinkable without the experiment, almost completely lacking among primitives. In the whole literature, we have encountered

190 Malinowski, 1926, p. 35. 192 Sarton, I, 1931, p. 8.
191 Singer, 1926, p. 89. 193 Essertier, 1927, p. 181.

157

only four cases of true animal or human experimentation – and all lay in the field of pure magic![194]

Science presupposes a quality of scepticism and an amount of individualism not found in primitive societies. The primitive specialist is trained for preservation of existing lore, not for new discoveries.[195]

Science is nothing "natural". It is a late invention of humanity.[196] "Throughout man's history it has been the mechanistic theory that he has found phantastic, not the animistic one."[197]

The supposed clear separation between the "sacred" and the "profane", the "magic" and the "scientific" among primitives, which is at the basis of Malinowski's claim, does not exist in primitive medicine.

The fact that changes from primitive to modern medicine are more far-reaching than changes in the field of government, art or religion, is often disregarded, and medical phenomena on both levels are too often identified without sufficient justification through evidence. The labeling of the rational, and at best prescientific elements in primitive medicine, as "scientific" is one more case in point.

RATIONAL METHODS AND LOGICAL THOUGHT IN PRIMITIVE MEDICINE

Rivers regarded as an important result of his studies on primitive medicine the discovery that the primitives acted medically with perfect logic, though on the basis of false, supernaturalistic premises.[198] When we add Boas' statement that superstition exists also among us,[199] then we are in possession of two perfectly true theses which, nevertheless, help us very little in an understanding of the real character of primitive medicine.

The differences in the proportion of animistic thought in primitive and civilized communities is so striking that every student of comparative ethnology feels it necessary to comment upon it. It is possible to demonstrate the lack of an essential difference between the mind of primitive man, whose thought is prevailingly animistic in character, and that of civilized man, from whose thought animism has been largely eliminated. But after the advocate of the lack of qualitative difference between primitive man and civilized man has documented his point with instances of civilized animism and primitive natural science, the actual facts remain the same. Primitive man undoubtedly can think as we do; in practice he does very little of such thinking. A great part of his behavior is very differently orientated.[200]

194 Tessmann, 1913, p. 145; Field, 1937, p. 114; Malinowski, 1922, p. 74.
195 Lowie, 1940, p. 337.
196 Linton, 1945, p. 218; Friedmann, 1901, p. 221.
197 Benedict, 1938, p. 636.
198 Rivers, 1924, p. 52.
199 Boas, 1938, p. 135.
200 Mead, 1928, p. 72.

In this situation, paradoxically enough – but such paradoxes are by no means rare in the history of human thought – the late Lucien Lévy-Bruhl, whose fundamental thesis of the prelogical thought of primitives was wrong, has been able to illuminate many more of the problems of primitive medicine than those whose statements were correct but meaningless. Lévy-Bruhl, whatever his conclusions, sensed at least the one thing which is so essential for the understanding of primitive medicine: the *different* approach on both levels of civilization. As I have always freely acknowledged my indebtedness to my late teacher, this might induce somebody to transform an otherwise very desirable and useful discussion on primitive medicine into a discussion of Lévy-Bruhl. This would be very much beside the point, mainly for two reasons:

1. In his central thesis on prelogical thought, Lévy-Bruhl was wrong. I almost entirely agree with Radin's fair criticism of Lévy-Bruhl's theories.[201] *I am fully aware of the fact that the essential differences between primitive and scientific thought lie not in the logical mechanism, but in the difference of the premises, the interests, the values, which are differences in degree not in kind.* One could even argue that one of the traits which often separate primitive from modern mentality is an exaggeration of logic in the primitive; an obsession to find a cause everywhere; the absence of the concept of "accident".

On the other hand I believe that Lévy-Bruhl's point of view has been "quite extensively misunderstood".[202] In spite of his central error, he made an enormous number of very valuable observations. Authors like Thurnwald,[203] Junod,[204] Evans-Pritchard,[205] Birket-Smith,[206] the Leightons,[207] and Kluckhohn[208] have uttered ideas very similar to those of Lévy-Bruhl. But as they have avoided his error and his nomenclature, as they enjoy the label of "field workers" instead of "armchair anthropologists", and as they have never committed the crime of teaching philosophy, and have not been "excommunicated" by F.Boas (Boas, by the way, was quite innocent of the docility of other people), they have never aroused similar feelings and criticism.

2. I am dealing with primitive medicine, not with "primitive mentality" in general. Even if I would accept J.M.Cooper's somewhat bold statement that primitive culture is 95 to 98 per cent purely rational and

---

201 Radin, 1933, pp. 13 ff.
202 Dubois, 1937, p. 253.
203 Thurnwald, 1937, p. 55.
204 Junod, 1927, II, p. 279.

205 Evans-Pritchard, 1937, p. 315.
206 Birket-Smith, 1936.
207 Leighton, A. and D., 1942.
208 Kluckhohn, 1943, p. 226.

scientific,[209] I would still place the bulk of primitive medicine among the remaining 2 to 5 per cent. The reason why, I have tried to prove by a rather intensive study and collection of facts. It seems to me that only other and better data can invalidate my thesis.

That primitive medicine is logical, is true. But it is not the central problem in connection with primitive medicine. The central problem lies in the differences between primitive and modern medicine. One of the essential aspects of this problem is how numerous rational (in the sense of empirical) elements are in primitive medicine and what rôle they play. The statement that primitive medicine is logical does not answer in any way this question.

THE RATIONAL IN PRIMITIVE AND THE SUPERNATURAL IN MODERN MEDICINE

Even when we prefer to regard much of the so-called rational in primitive medicine as habitual, even when we find many practices described as rational to be actually misunderstood supernaturalism, because neither being logical nor being effective necessarily makes a therapeutic method rational, even when we deny the scientific character of primitive rational practices, there remains a hard core of rational and naturalistic elements which we have found again and again in the course of this survey. Certainly my purpose has not been to "interpret" these elements out of existence. But it was necessary to establish the true proportions and nature of the rational elements as compared to the supernaturalistic ones in the medical thought of primitives. The rational elements seem mostly well integrated into a magic system, on the character of which they have no fundamental influence.

That there is some amount of supernaturalism even in modern medicine, especially as far as the attitude of the patient is concerned, cannot be denied, and a qualitative study of it would be quite interesting. A quantitative study, whether its frequency is in any way comparable to the occurrence of supernaturalistic elements in primitive medicine, seems, in view of the matter presented above, rather superfluous with anybody who has even the slightest inkling of modern disease theories and methods of diagnosis and treatment. It seems unnecessary to elaborate upon the fact that medicine in our culture is one thing, and quite another in cultures where even linguistically medicine and magic are still comprised in the same term, a fact which is well known to

209 Cooper, 1935, p. 370.

laymen as regards the American Indian, but which is also found among other primitives.[210] Ignorance and faulty explanation of medical facts are widespread in our society no less than in primitive societies. But except for very backward rural areas and very special strata of our city population, this is with us *"naturalistic"* and not *"supernaturalistic" ignorance.* Explanations may be absent or faulty but if given, they are usually along the line of natural causes and methods, and not along the lines of spiritual intervention or magic powers. Confusion arises from the fact that certain *psychological mechanisms* are the same in primitive and modern medicine. For instance, certain forms of unreasonable conservatism are by no means the exclusive privilege of primitive medicine. Suggestion is one of the major implements of the shaman and of the M.D. But while in the same situation the shaman and his patients believe in the action of spirits and powers, the modern doctor consciously uses suggestion, or at least labors under the rational delusion that vitamine B or the discovery of a childhood trauma brought about an improvement. *Ideational contents and psychological mechanisms are not the same phenomena,* and the former are by no means unessential, mere epiphenomena which can be disregarded in analyzing a situation. We have dealt above with the importance of knowing the basic ideology of purely physical treatments and mechanisms. The same holds good for psychological mechanisms. Medicine has progressed so rapidly in the direction of the rational during the last 30 years that these changes have perhaps not yet been fully realized in all quarters. The differences between modern and primitive medicine are only differences in degree. So, for that matter, are the differences, for example, in colors. This will hardly deter anybody, except those suffering from color blindness, from differentiating colors, a process which, in the case of the red and green light, is even rather useful.

210 E.g. Culwick, 1935, p. 385; Smith and Dale, 1920, I, p. 222; Harley, 1941, etc.

INCUBATOR AND TABOO*

It seems that as far as the problem of premature children is concerned, medical science from the time of Hippocrates down to the eighteenth century limited its efforts to discussions of the viability of seventh versus eighth month births. Christianity had brought about a new theoretical attitude toward child and fetus, and outlawed abortion and infanticide, but exerted no practical influence in this domain. The fatalistic attitude of John Hunter that nothing can be done for ill children is symptomatic of the state of things up to the eighteenth century. Though incubators for the eggs of fowl had been known already to the Egyptians, it appears that the systematic use of incubators for the conservation of the premature child started only in the middle of the nineteenth century (Dauncé of Bordeaux, 1857).

In view of the indifference shown and the difficulties encountered even by high civilizations in the upbringing of premature children, it is not surprising to see that primitives in general have developed no medical techniques in this field. Therefore, it is all the more remarkable that two primitive populations, the Eskimos and the South African Thongas, did invent contrivances for the care of premature children. Bogoras[1] describes the technique of the Asiatic Eskimos as follows:

A baby born prematurely is put into the soft skin of a big sea-bird. This skin, taken off whole and turned, has the feathers inside. Then it is tied up very securely, and hung over a big lamp in which a small flame is kept constantly burning. Of course, in doing this, they take care that the child's head shall be in a proper position. In this position the babe is kept for from a week to four weeks, during which time it is fed with small quantities of oil, as well as with mother's milk drawn from her breasts. Little by little the portion of milk is increased, and at last the babe is allowed to suckle.

H. S. Junod[2] reports from the Thongas:

When a child is born prematurely and is very small and delicate, it is wrapped in the leaves of the castor-oil plant and put into a big pot, which is then exposed to the heat of the sun. This is a true incubator, and the treatment is said to be attended with success.

These facts are interesting enough in themselves to be worthy of emphasis. So far they seem to have escaped any special attention from the readers of the two classic monographs. Still more exciting is the question why, among the hundreds of primitive populations observed

* Reprinted from *Journal of the History of Medicine and Allied Sciences, 1,* 144–148 (1946).

1 Bogoras, W., 1904–09, p. 514.   2 Junod, H. A., 1913, I, p. 40.

by modern ethnographers, should these two, so different in culture, race, and geographical location, have made so momentous a discovery. Both populations are gifted in the field of techniques, but not more so than many others. As both have a high birth rate and as the Eskimos even practise infanticide, there seems to exist no special biological incentive for making such an invention. Climatic conditions cannot be instrumental in view of the great differences in the respective environments of both people. The only common denominator which can be found between them, and which is most likely to be a causative factor in the elaboration of this medical technique, lies in a quite unexpected field – in the field of taboo.

It is a well known fact that all over the world the sexual and reproductive functions of women are heavily tabooed because of their mysterious, awesome, and disgust- or fear-inspiring character. It ist not improbable that this primitive attitude toward the female sex function is instrumental in the discrimination against women in cults and various other activities in primitive societies, all the more as such discrimination usually ceases when women have passed the menopause and become sexually neutral. Of almost universal distribution and surviving in a rationalized form in our society are the *taboos against menstruating women*.[3] Less common but still very widespread are the taboos against *pregnant women, women in childbirth and in childbed*.[4] *Yet only in a very few regions is miscarriage regarded as a parcticularly dangerous and, therefore, heavily tabooed event*. This specialization and elaboration of the usual birth taboos has been described only among the Eskimos, the South African Thongas and their neighbors, the Maoris, and the Bri-Bri Indians of Costa Rica. Boas[5] records of the Baffin Land Eskimos:

Cases of premature birth require particularly careful treatment. The event must be

---

3 For a list of such taboos see H. Webster, 1942, pp. 82 ff., or D. McKenzie, 1927, pp. 281 ff. There are nevertheless tribes which are indifferent toward menstruation: Trobriands (Malinowski, B., *The Father in Primitive Psychology*, New York 1927, p. 27); Veddas (Seligman, C.G. and B.F., *The Veddas*, Cambridge 1911, p. 94); Hopi (Titiev, M., *Old Oraibi*, Cambridge, Mass., 1944, p. 16). Or even such where menstrual blood is regarded as containing curative powers: Ten'a Indians (Jetté, *Anthropos.*, 1911, 6: 699); Ainu (Pilsudski, B., *Anthropos.*, 1910, 5: 774); Arapesh (Mead, M., *Anth. Publ. Am. Mus. Nat. Hist.*, 37: 345); Apache (Opler, M.E., *An Apache Life Way*, Chicago 1941, p. 98); Akamba (Lindblom, G., *Akamba*, Uppsala 1920, p. 40).

4 See Webster, *l.c.*, pp. 51 ff.; pp. 54 ff.

5 Boas, F., *Bull. Am. Mus. Nat. Hist.*, *15*, 125.

announced publicly, else dire results will follow. If a woman should conceal from other people that she has had a premature birth, they might come near her, or even eat in her hut of the seals procured by her husband. The vapor arising from her would thus affect them and they would be avoided by the seals.

Rasmussen gives a two-page list of restrictions which the unhappy Polar Eskimo woman has to observe for one year after a miscarriage.[6] Among the Polar Eskimos, as among the Baffin Land Eskimos, concealment of miscarriage and avoidance of taboo restrictions are said to produce famine.

If a woman keeps her miscarriage secret to avoid the severe penance entailed, she may either fall ill herself or she may plunge her compatriots into misfortune through failure of the fishery, or some assault of the forces of nature.[7]

The same ideas were expressed by the South African Thonga medicine man Maukhelu, who told Junod:[8]

When a woman has had a miscarriage, when she has let her blood flow secretly and has buried the abortive child in an unknown place, it is enough to make the burning winds blow, and to dry up all the land: the rain can no longer fall, because the country is no longer right. Rain fears that spot. It must stop at that very place and can go no further. This woman has been very guilty. She has spoilt the country of the chief, because she has hidden blood which had not yet properly united to make a human being. That blood is taboo! What she has done is taboo. It causes starvation.

Other tribes of the same region, such as the Ama Xosa,[9] the Ba Venda[10] and the Ba Ila,[11] entertain similar beliefs in the supernatural damage caused by miscarriage which has not been properly atoned for by all kinds of taboo restrictions and purification rites.[11a]

Elsdon Best (The Maori, Wellington 1924, vol.II, p.5) reports the following attitude for the aborigines of New Zealand:

Cases of premature birth were supposed to have been brought about by the mother having infringed some law of tapu . . . An immature birth is always a danger for the community, for its nairua (spirit) may develop into a atua kahu, a malignant demon delighting in harassing man . . . A rite to lay the demon spirit was some-times performed over the spot whereat the foetus had been buried.

6 Rasmussen, K., 1908, p. 120.

7 *Ibid.*, p. 128. For other Eskimo taboos on miscarriage, see Weyer, E. M., *The Eskimos*, New Haven 1932, p. 377.

8 Junod, *l.c.*, II, p. 317.

9 Soga, J. H., *The Ama-Xosa*, Lovedale 1931, p. 300.

10 Stayt, H. A., *The Ba Venda*, Oxford 1931, p. 90.

11 Smith, E. W., and Dale, A. M., *The Ila speaking tribes of Northern Rhodesia*, London 1920, II, p. 6.

11a A very similar combination of miscarriage fears and bringing up of premature children in clay pots is reported from the neighboring Akamba (Lindblom, *l. c.*, pp. 32, 34, 283).

Among the Bri-Bri Indians of Costa Rica, a woman who has had a miscarriage is not only secluded, but is considered so dangerous that all contact with things she has used is avoided, and her food is passed to her on the end of a long stick.[12]

These are the only relatively well documented cases of belief in the particular dangers of miscarriage. Apparently similar notions exist or have existed, especially in South America, which we ignore only because of the incompleteness of our records. It is controversial whether the South American Mojos killed women who had a miscarriage.[13] Tapuya women are reported to devour miscarriages. Burial of miscarriages in special vessels in ancient Troja instead of the usual cremation is equally suggestive of special taboos.[14]

It is not difficult to understand that people who are so much in fear of a miscarriage would be interested in avoiding it, at least in some of the cases, by attempting to bring up the premature child. And, as a matter of fact, in two out of the four known cases of such belief, an appropriate method for nursing premature children was invented. As far as the Bri-Bri Indians are concerned, our records tell nothing of such a method; but the records are so extremely scanty that this by no means constitutes positive proof that the Bri-Bri had not worked out some similar idea.

Why the Eskimos, Thongas, Maori, and Bri-Bri taboo just miscarriage so severely is as unknown as the reason for most taboos. That these tribes have centered their fears around abortion is rather surprising in view of the fact that abortion is one of the very few pathological phenomena which to most primitives has no supernatural implications.[15] The practice of artificial abortion is almost universal among primitives, forbidden by many, but actually punished only by very few (Ama Xosa, Battak).[16] As in certain cases of infant mortality[17] or venereal disease,[18] it is perhaps the very commonness of the phenomenon which deprives it of its supernatural character.

The sociological and economic importance of taboos has been increasingly recognized by ethnographers. "The natives understand how

12 Pittier de Fabrega, H., *Sitzgsber. phil. hist. Classe Kais. Ak.* Wien, *138*, 20, 1898.

13 Métraux, A., *Native Tribes of Eastern Bolivia and Western Matto Grosso*, Washington 1942, p. 70.

14 Ploss, H., and Bartels, M., 1908, I, p. 839.

15 McKenzie, *l.c.*, p. 316. See also Fortune, R. F., *The Sorcerers of Dobu*, New York 1932, p. 240.

16 Ploss-Bartels, *l.c.*, I, pp. 843 ff.

17 Fortune, R. F., 1935, p. 74; Evans-Pritchard, E. D., 1937, p. 478.

18 Opler, *l.c.*, p. 227.

our own legal system is imposed with the help of rifles perfectly. They say typically 'You have your rifles – we have taboo, witchcraft and sorcery our weapons'."[19] In health matters taboos are sometimes so useful that they have been regarded wrongly as conscious health measures, "the fallacy of sanitary intention" as Crawley called it, such as the taboo against sexual intercourse during the nursing period, the hiding of excrement for fear of magic, etc. But in general they are, at best, physically indifferent. Often taboos are directly detrimental to the bodily well being, like the mourning taboos of Eskimos which produce famine in time of scarcity, the tabooing of the colostrum among many primitives, taboos against bathing at Nias, etc. In any case, taboos in general are by their very nature obstacles in the way of inventions. This is particularly striking in the field of primitive surgery which is so poor not because primitives lack technical skill, but because of their supernatural beliefs. In our case, paradoxically enough, a taboo seems to have provoked a technical invention in the medical field. This observation seems to complement my earlier analysis of primitive autopsies[20] where I showed that primitives in spite of dissecting continuously gain no anatomical knowledge because of their mental unpreparedness.

These minor examples from the field of primitive medicine emphasize that medical discoveries often owe their existence to "ideologies" rather than to mere experience.[21]

19 Fortune, 1932, p. 157. 21 Galdston, I., 1939, 729 ff.
20 See chapter IV of this volume, p. 91.

PRIMITIVE MEDICINE'S SOCIAL FUNCTION*

The medicine of primitives shows occasionally amazing accomplishments. Some of our most effective drugs like strophantine, emetine, picrotoxine, cocaine, quinine, reserpine stem from primitive pharmacopoeias, not to speak of their innumerable effective emetics, purgatives, expectorants, or diuretics. Many primitives master all methods of physiotherapy. In some areas (East Africa and Polynesia) surgery has reached a relatively high level. (I am not including Peru here, as Peruvian civilization most certainly cannot be classified as primitive.) Primitives have performed successfully such difficult operations as trepanation and Cesarian section. But these interesting and admirable phenomena, rather difficult to explain in the small communities in which they were observed, are neither the most characteristic, nor the essential aspects of primitive medicine. The most characteristic feature of primitive medicine is that we deal here with a functioning system of medicine based almost completely on magico-religious or "supernaturalistic" representations, a situation unique in the history of mankind.

As soon as the biological disorder rises above the level of habitual behavior[1], as soon as it is recognized by society as a disease (what is disease, is in the last instance not a biological fact, but a decision of society – what is regarded in one culture as disease, might not be so in another one)[2] it is dealt with in magico-religious terms. Magico-religious are the causal explanations of disease in most cases in most primitive societies. It is of secondary importance in this context whether the powers who send disease are spirits, gods, or ghosts, whether they are provoked by a sin of the patient, or whether he rationalizes his bad conscience as aggression by a sorcerer, whether they act through foreign body intrusion, spirit intrusion or soul abduction[3]. Having once explained disease in magico-religious terms, and being all too logical[4], primitives will have to resort for diagnosis not to mere observation,

---

* This article was published in: Miscellanea Paul Rivet, México, 1958.
1 For habitual behavior in primitive medicine see: Hsu, F.L.K., 1943; Ackerknecht, E.H., this volume p. 145.
2 See above, p. 54, 63, 141.   3 Clements, C.E., 1932.
4 Lucien Lévy-Bruhl was certainly superior to many of his critics in sensing the difference between primitive and modern thought; yet he was most unfortunate in characterizing this difference as "prelogical". Actually primitives are rather super-logical, lacking the concept of accident, and obsessed by the urge to casually explain everything they are often, like all overdeterminists, forced into absurd conclusions.

but again to magico-religious practices like trance, dreams, crystal gazing, bone throwing, etc. For the same reason treatment consists primarily of incantations, spells, or prayers. With these might be combined the use of drugs and physiotherapy. We might differentiate these elements of the healing ritual. Primitives do not. To them they are all of one magico-religious kind.

It is obvious that from our present-day biological point of view most of these practices are meaningless. (While our impersonal biological point of view makes disease meaningless as an individual experience.) The only meaning and function which is easily sensed by the present day western observer is of a psychotherapeutic nature. The successes of primitive medicine are primarily due to effective, though unconscious psychotherapy. We recognize readily the abundant use of suggestion and confession, techniques still practiced in our society. We realize that in making the disease meaningful, in substituting psychologically the medicine man for the patient, anxiety is dispelled, faith is established, and psychological and physiological relief is obtained. We are less aware of the fact that the same ideas which dispell anxieties often create new anxieties (fear of ghosts, etc.)[5].

In this analysis one more meaning of primitive medicine, perhaps the most important one, is often overlooked: that is primitive medicine's social meaning. And yet the message of primitive ideologies concerning disease is easily spelled out: "Be peaceful, and disease will spare you and your family, or go away[6]." And having acquired social meaning, it so happens that primitive medicine is also acquiring a very important social function, far beyond counteracting the disruptive effects of disease on society. Disease becomes the most important sanction against asocial behavior in primitive societies, providing at little expense the services that in our society are rendered by courts, policemen, newspapers, teachers, priests and soldiers. The medical practitioner holds the keys to social control. Witch diagnosis usually confirms public opinion. Medical diagnosis becomes thus a kind of "social justice[7]."

Primitive medicine obviously owes its ability to perform this interesting and important social function to the accident that it is expressed in religious or "supernaturalistic" terms[8], that it belongs to the

5 Hallowell, A. I., 1938.
6 Ackerknecht, E. H., this volume p. 19;
   Opler, M. E., 1941, p. 245.

7 Harley, G. W., 1941.; Hallowell, A. I.,
   1941.

sphere of the sacred. Primitive man, anxiety-ridden and under terrific pressure from all sides in a hostile and unpredictable world, has to give some sense to it. He finds relief in explaining the world in terms symbolizing his primary reality, in creating religion, the sacred. It comes as a kind of surprise to us when analysing primitive religion that it is not nature, but apparently social and family relations which impress man first and most profoundly. Yet this is grounded in man's unique position in the animal kingdom. He alone has an inordinately prolonged infancy where his survival primarily does not depend on nature but on society. The helpless infant does not live directly on nature, but through the intermediary of his family. His earliest menaces are not wild animals either, but his fellow men. (It is, of course, this prolonged infancy which allows man to base his life not on innate instincts, but on culture, a non-biological, learned and ever expanding inheritance[9].) Even later, society is man's main support. Man's early thought thus explains the universe by projecting social situations in it, and symbolizing them, not nature, in his religion. The elements of reality we find in primitive religion are primarily not such of nature, but such of social reality[10].

This is quite obvious when we analyse magico-religious explanations of disease, which seem to either symbolize the behavior of punishing parents, or of aggressive age-mates. Disease concepts reflect social conflicts rather than events in nature[11]. The contrast to our own concepts is quite obvious. We do not think in terms of friendly or hostile bacteria, glands, vitamins, neither did our fore-fathers associate such traits with the famous four humors. The same personal traits are exhibited in magico-religious treatment, the success of which depends on the personal intervention of gods, medicine men, herb spirits, and

8 "Supernaturalistic", though often used by the best authorities, is quite obviously a misnomer for these primitive representations, as it presupposes the notion of the predictable natural which primitives characteristically do not have. This notion of natural is a much later invention. So is the transformation of religion into an escapist, non-practical, "other world" affair. Primitive religion is meant to be eminently practical and of this world. See also Soustelle, J., "L'Homme et le Surnaturel", 1936.

9 Although insight into the role of man's prolonged infancy is regarded by many contemporary anthropologists as a new and brilliant discovery, it was not rare at all with French early 19th century physiologists. See e.g. Bérard, F.J., Paris, 1826, pp. V, IX; Virey, J.J., 1824, p. 73 ff.; James, L.M., 1825, vol. I, p. 76; vol. II, p. 253.

10 All the justified detail criticisms directed against Durkheim's "Les formes élémentaires de la vie réligieuse" seem not to invalidate the soundness of his basic approach to regard primitive religion as a symbolisation of social relations.

11 Gilbert, W.H., 1943, p. 296.

on impersonal mechanisms. From the above it becomes also clearer why natural causes are so rare among primitive disease theories. In primitive medicine the magico-religious element is even stronger than in other fields like ship-building, agriculture, weaving, tanning, etc. This is probably because disease poses other problems than the above named activities, dealing with humans, not with objects, and is thus even more unpredictable than these techniques[12]. Obsessed with fear, unable to wait for natural explanations, primitive man has to give these religious answers to what at his level are unanswerable questions. In using religious symbolizations of society as medical ideologies, he transforms these medical ideologies into a social force, guaranteeing social cohesion. This, perhaps more than therapeutic successes, explains the survival of primitive medicine, even when faced by more successful western competitors.

But disease becomes in the course of history gradually an answerable question, and to the extent that it does, medicine becomes secularized or rationalized, to use the notion of Max Weber. As a matter of fact it has now become secularized to such a degree that it has moved much farther from the sacred to the secular than many other fields of human interest like politics, art or law. It has become extremely successful in controlling the natural phenomena of disease. It has therewith acquired an important objective influence on society, producing demographic changes, stabilizing economy, etc. But by the same token it has lost its "sacred" character, its social control function, its subjective influence on society, its meaning in moral terms. From a factor conditioning social behavior, it has become a mere function of society. While it once taught society what is right or wrong, society now has to tell it what is right or wrong.

12 Malinowski's postulate of a separate existence of "science" and magic in primitive societies is quite unreal (Malinowski, B., in Needham, J., Science, Religion and Reality, London, 1926, p. 35). To begin with, "primitive science" as claimed by Frazer and Malinowski does not exist. Science is, as rightly emphasized by R. Linton (1945, p. 218), a late invention of humanity. Furthermore empiricism (Malinowski's "Science") and magico-religious behavior are mixed in a complex fashion which has been excellently illustrated by Ruth Benedict (1938, p. 642), "It is an attitude that is familiar in our behavior even today. We know the physical things that must be done for our children. We must feed and clothe them and provide them with the necessary wherewithal. But it is repulsive to us to stop there, and parents who do so, we think, are running a great risk of failure. For children are people, and we must not treat them only as things. As persons, for successful handling, they call for love and consideration and praise. It is just the attitude of primitive man toward the external world."

BIBLIOGRAPHY*

ACKERKNECHT, E. H.: Beiträge zur Geschichte der Medizinalreform 1848. Sudhoffs Arch. Gesch. Med. Naturwiss. *25*, 61–183 (1932).
- Problems of Primitive Medicine. BHM *11*, 503–521 (1942), chapter VII of this volume.
- Primitive Medicine and Culture Pattern. BHM *12*, 545–574 (1942), chapter II of this volume.
- Primitive Autopsies and the History of Anatomy. BHM *13*, 334–339 (1943), chapter IV of this volume.
- Psychopathology, Primitive Medicine and Primitive Culture, BHM *14*, 30–67 (1943), chapter III of this volume.
- White Indians. BHM *15*, 15–36 (1944).
- Origin and Distribution of Skull Cults, Ciba Symposia *5*, 1654–1661 (1944).
- Malaria in the Upper Mississippi Valley, 1760–1900, Baltimore (1945).
- Primitive Medicine, Trans. N.Y. Ac. Sci., Ser. II, *8*, 26–37 (1945), chapter I of this volume.
- Incubator and Taboo, J. Hist. M. *1*, 144–148 (1946).
- Natural Diseases and Rational Treatment in Primitive Medicine. BHM *19*, 467–497 (1946), chapter VIII of this volume.
- Medical Practices of the South American Indian, Hdb. of the South Am. Indian, Smiths. Inst., vol. 5, 621–643, Washington (1949).
- "Mesmerism" in Primitive Societies. Ciba Symposia, *9*, 826–831 (1948).
- Medicine and Disease among, Eskimos, Ciba Symposia *10*, 916–921 (1948).
AICHEL, O.: Die Heilkunde der Ureinwohner Chiles. Arch. f. Gesch. d. Med. *6*, 161–204 (1913).
AITKEN, B.: Temperament in Native American Religion. JAI *40*, 363–387 (1930).
AITKEN, R. T.: Ethnology of Tubnai, Honolulu (1930).
AKIGA: Akiga's Story, London (1939).
ALAJOUANINE, TH., and THURE, R.: Perte de substance oranienne consécutive à un traumatisme fermé. Revue Neurologique *77*, 71–77 (1945).
ALVAREZ, W. C.: From Folkways to Modern Medicine, in March of Medicine IV, p. 3 ff., New York (1940).
ANDRES, F.: Die Himmelsreise der caraibischen Medizinmänner. ZE *70*, 331 ff. (1939).

* *Abbreviations*
    A – Anthropos
    AA – American Anthropologist
    AMH – Anuals of Medical History
    BAE-B – Bureau of American Ethnology Bulletin
    BAE-R – Bureau of American Ethnology Report
    BHM – Bulletin of the History of Medicine
    J – Janus
    JAI – Journal of the Royal Anthropological Institute
    JASP – Journal of Abnormal and Social Psychology
    UCPAAE – University of California Publications in American Archeology and Ethnology
    ZE – Zeitschrift für Ethnologie

ANDREWS, E.: The Aboriginal Physicians of Michigan. V. C. Vaughan Mem. Vol., Ann Arbor, 1903, p. 42 ff.

ANDROS, F.: Medical Knowledge of the Indian, in: Schoolcraft, The Indian Tribes of the U.S., Part III, Philadelphia (1853).

ANGUS, H. C.: A Year in Azimba. JAI 27, 324 ff. (1897/98).

ANKERMANN, B.: Kulturkreise und Kulturschichten in Afrika. ZE vol. 37 (1905).

APTEKAR, H.: Anjea. Infanticide etc. in savage societies, New York (1931).

ARCOS, G.: La Medicina entro nuestros aborigines (Ecuador). Rev. Soc. Jur. Let. 1932, 81–110.

ARNOTT, G.: La magica y el curanderismo entro los Toba-Pilaga. Rev. Jeogr. Americana 2, 135 ff. (1934).

ARTELT, W.: Studien zur Geschichte der Begriffe "Heilmittel" und "Gift", Leipzig (1937).

ASHTON, E. H.: Medicine, Magic, and Sorcery among the Southern Sotho, Capetown (1943).

BALK, N.: Die Medizin der Lappen (1934).

BANDELIER, A. L.: Aboriginal Trephining in Bolivia. AA 6, 440 ff. (1904).

BANSFIELD, W., and SLATIN PASCHA: The native methods of treatment in Kassala. 3. Rep. Wellcome Res. Lab., p. 273 ff., Khartoum (1908).

BARBER, B.: Acculturation and Messianic Movements, Amer. Soc. Rev. 6, 663 ff. (1941).

BARRETT, S. A.: Pomo Bear Doctors. UCPAAE 12, 443–465 (1917).

BARTELS, M.: Die Medizin der Naturvölker. Leipzig (1893).

BARTON, J.: Notes on the Kipsikis of Kenya. JAI 53, 42–78 (1923).

BARUCH, BERNARD: Foreword to MACKAY: Extraordinary Popular Delusions and the Madness of Crowds. Boston (1932).

BASTIAN, A.: Der Mensch in der Geschichte. Berlin (1860).

BAUMANN, E. D.: Medisch-historische Studien. Arnheim (1934).

BAUMANN, H.: Likundu. ZE, pp. 73–85 (1929).

BEAGLEHOLE, E.: Culture and Psychosis in Hawaii, in Some Modern Hawaiians, Honolulu, pp. 156–171 (1939).

BEAUGRAND-CHAMPAGE, A.: Les maladies et médecins des anciens Iroquois. Cahiers des 10, 227–242 (1944).

BELL, R.: The Medicine Man (1886).

BELLO, E.: El original tratamiento con orina de la heridas tradicional entre los Indios Peruanos. Ref. Med. 25, 6–10 (1940).

BELTRAN, J. R.: La Medicina de los pueblos primitives. Prens. Med. Arg. 25, 668 ff. (1938).

BENEDICT, RUTH: Anthropology and the Abnormal. J. of Gen. Psychol. 10, 59–82 (1934).

– Patterns of Culture. Boston (1934).

– Religion, in BOAS, F.: General Anthropology. New York (1938).

– Magic, in Encycl. Soc. Sc., vol. X, p. 41.

BÉRARD, F. J.: Discours sur les améliorations progressives de la santé publique par l'influence de la civilisation. Paris (1926).

BERTONI, M. S.: Civilización Guarani. Medicina e Higiena, Puerto Bertoni (1927).

BEST, E.: Maori Medical Lore. J. Polyn. Soc. 13, 219 ff. (1904).

– The Maori, 2 vol. Wellington (1924).

BETH, K.: Medizin und Religion bei den Naturvölkern. Wien, Med. Wschr. (1914).

BIRKET-SMITH, K.: The Eskimos. London (1936).

BISWAS, P.: Concepts of Disease among the Primitive Peoples of India. Un. of Calcutta J. of the Dept. of Letters, 1934, 25.

BLONDEL, CH.: La conscience morbide. Paris (1913).

BOAS, F.: Race, Language and Culture. New York (1940).

– The Mind of Primitive Man. New York (1938).

– The Doctrine of Souls and of Disease among the Chinook. J. Am. Folkl. 6 (1893).

– The Central Eskimo. BAE-R VI, Washington (1890).

BODDING, P.O.: The Santals and Disease. Mem. As. Soc. Bengal, X; 1, Calcutta 1925, X, 2 (1927).

BOGORAS, W.: The Shamanistic Call in North Asia and North America. Proc. 23. Int. Congr. Americ., p. 441 ff. New York (1930).

– The Chukchee. Leiden-New York (1904–1909).

BOLINDER, G.: Die Indianer der tropischen Schneegebirge. Stuttgart (1925).

BONWICK, J.: Tasmanians. London (1898).

BOSTOCK, J.: Insanity among Australian Aborigines. M. J. Austr., Suppl. 2, pp. 459–464 (1932).

BOUCHINET, A.: Des états primitifs de la médicine. Paris (1891).

BOURKE, J.G.: The Medicine Men of the Apache. BAE-R 9 (1892).

– Popular med. Customs of the Rio Grande. J. Am. Folkl. 7, 119 ff. (1894).

– Scatologic Rites of all Nations, Washington (1891).

BOURLET, A.: Les Thay. A 2 (1907).

BRACHWITZ, G.P.: 30 Jahre Geisteskrankenbehandlung in Ostafrika. Allg. Zschr. Psych. 102, 362 ff. (1934).

BRÉVIÉ, J.: Islamisme contre Naturisme au Soudan Français. Paris (1923).

BRILL, A.: Piblokto. J. Nerv. Ment. Dis. 40, 514 (1913).

BRINTON: Nervous Dis. among Lower Races. Science, vol. XX.

BROCA, P.: Sur la perforation congénitale des deux pariétaux. Bull. Soc. d'Anthr. Paris, 1875, p. 192 ff.

BRODSKY, Is.: The Trephiners of Blama Bay. Brit. J. Surg., 1938, p. 1 ff.

BROOKS, H.: The Contribution of the Primitive American to Medicine, in: Medicine and Mankind, p. 79 ff. New York (1936).

BROUGH-SMYTH, R.: The Aborigines of Victoria. London, Melbourne (1878).

BROWN, G.: Melanesians and Polynesians. London (1910).

BROWNE, C.A.: The Chemical Industries of the American Aborigines. Isis (1935), XXIII, 406–424.

BROWNLEE, CH.: Reminiscences of Kaffir Life and History. Lovedale (1898).

BRY, C.C.: Verkappte Religionen. Gotha (1924).

BRYANT, A.P.: Zulu medicines and medicine men. Annals Natal Museum 2, 1–103 (1909).

BUEGGE, G.: Das rational-empirische Element der Geburtshilfe bei den Naturvölkern. Freiburg (1927).

BUMKE, O.: Kultur und Entartung. Berlin (1922).

BUSCHAN, G.: Einfluss der Rasse auf Geisteskrankheiten. Allg. Med. Centr. Ztg. 66, 104 ff. (1897).

‒ Über Medizinzauber und Heilkunst im Leben der Völker. Berlin (1941).

CABANÈS, A.: L'histoire éclairée par la clinique. Paris (1920).

CADIÈRE, L.: Sur quelques faits magiques observés pendant une épidémie de choléra à Annam. A 5, 519 ff. (1910).

CALLOWAY, C.: The religious system of the Amazulu, London (1870).

CANHAM, P.: An Ashanti Case History. Africa 17, 35 ff. (1947).

CANNON, W.B.: Voodo death. AA 44, 169 (1942).

CAPITAN, L.: Coutumes de chirurgie nerveuse des peuples sauvages. Paris (1899).

CARNOCHAN, F.J.: The Empire of the Snakes. New York (1935).

CASANOWICZ, I.M.: Shamanism in Siberia. Smith. Inst. Rep., 1924, 415 ff.

CASTAGNE, J.: Magie et exorcisme chez les Kazak-Kirghises. Rev. Et. Islam., 1930, 53 ff.

CATLIN, G.: Illustrations of the Manners, etc. of the North American Indians. London (1876).

CATOR, D.: Among the Headhunters. New York (1905).

CESBRON, H.: Histoire critique de l'hystérie. Paris (1909).

CHAMBERLAIN, A.F.: Kootenay medicine men. J. Am. Folkl. 14, 95 (1901).

‒ Disease and Medicine, in Hastings Encyclop. Rel. Eth. vol. 4.

CHAPPLE, E.D., and COON, C.S.: Principles of Anthropology. N.Y. (1942).

CHINNERY, E.W.P., and HADDON, A.C.: Five New Religious cults in New Guinea. Hibbert J., 1917, 446 ff.

CHOU, YI-LIANG: Tantrism in China. Harv. J. of As. Studies 8, 241–332 (1945).

CLAIR, J.B.: Notes sur la médecine Annamite. A 6, 109 (1911).

CLEMENTS, F.E.: Primitive Concepts of Disease. UCPAAE 12, 185–252 (1932).

CODRINGTON, R.H.: The Melanesians. Oxford (1891).

COLLOCOTT, E.E.V.: Sickness, Ghosts and Medicine in Tonga. Jour. Polyn. Soc. 32, 136 ff. (1923).

COMAS, J.: El maestro y el médico. Am Indigena 5, 318–325 (1945).

Committee on the Costs of Medical Care, Reports, 28 vols. Univ. of Chicago Press (1928–1932).

CONDON, M.A.: Anthropos 6, 377 (1911).

COOPER, J.M.: The Cree Witiko Psychosis. Prim. Man, vol. VI (1933).

‒ Magic and Science. Thought 10, 357 ff. (1935).

‒ Mental Disease Situations in Certain Cultures. JASP 29, 10th (1934).

COOK, A.D.: The Medical History of Uganda. E. Afr. Med. J. 13, 66–110 (1936).

CORIAT, F.H.: Psychoneuroses Among Primitive Tribes. J.Abn. Psych. 10, 201 (1915).

CORLETT, W.T.: The Medicine-man of the American Indian. Springfield (1935).

CRAWLEY, E.: The Mystic Rose. London (1927).

‒ Sexual Taboo. JAI 24, 223.

CRUMP, T.A.: Trephining in the South Seas. JAI 21, 167 (1901).

CULWICK, A.G., & G.M.: Ubena of the Rivers. London (1935).

CUMMINS, S.L.: Sub Tribes of Bahr-el-Ghazal Dinkas. JAI 34 (1904).

CUMSTON, C.F.: History of Medicine. New York (1926).

CZAPLICKA, M.A.: Oboriginal Siberia. Oxford (1914).

DARBY, G.E.: Indian Medicine in British Columbia. Canad. M.A.J., 1933, 433 ff.

DARLINGTON, H.S.: An Instance of Primitive Psychotherapy. Psych. Rev. 25, 205 ff. (1938).

DAVIDSON, S.: Choreomania. A Historical sketch with an account of an epidemic observed in Madagascar. Edinburgh (1867).

DAVIS, K.: Mental Hygiene and the Class Structure. Psychiatry *1*, 55–65 (1938).

DEGRAER, A. M.: L'art de guérir chez les Azande, Congo (1929).

DELOBSOM, D.: Les secrets des sorciers noirs. Paris (1934).

DEMBO, A., and IMBELLONI, J.: Deformaciones intencionales del cuerpo humano de carácter étnico. Buenos Aires, N. d. (? 1938).

DEMERATH, N. J.: Schizophrenia Among Primitives. Am. J. Psych. *98*, 703–707 (1942).

DENIKER, J.: Les races et les peuples de la terre. Paris (1926).

DENSMORE, F.: Uses of Plants by the Chippewa. BAE *44*, 275 ff. (1928).

DEVEREUX, G.: A Sociological Theory of Schizophrenia. Psychoanal. Rev. *26*, 315–342 (1939).

– Mohave Culture and Personality. Char. and Persons *8*, 91–109 (1939/1940).

– Primitive Psychiatry. BHM *7*, 1194 ff. (1940).

– Mental Hygiene of the American Indian. Mental Hygiene *26*, 71 ff. (1942).

DEWEY, J.: Interpretation of the Savage Mind, in THOMAS, W. J.: Sourcebook of Social Origins. Chicago (1909).

D'HARCOURT, R.: La médecine dans l'ancien Pérou. Paris (1939).

DHUNJIBHOY, J. E.: A Brief Resumé of Insanity commonly met with in India, with a full description of Indian Hemp Insanity. J. Ment. Sc. *76*, 254 ff. (1930).

DIETSCHY, H.: Über den Medizinmann zur Inkazeit. Bull. Schweiz. Ges. Anthr. Ethn., 1938/1939, p. 9 ff.

DIETERLEN, H.: La Médecine et les médecins au Lessouto. Paris (1930).

DIJOUR, E.: Les cérémonies d'expulsion des maladies chez les Matakos. J. Soc. Am. Paris N. S. *25*, 211 (1933).

DIXON, R. B.: Some Aspects of the American Shaman, J. Am. Folkl. *21*, 1–12 (1908).

DONNISON, C. P.: Civilization and Disease. London (1937).

DORSEY, G. A.: The Cheyenne. Field Mus. Anthr. Ser. IX, 1–186 (1905).

DOUTSÉ, E.: Magie et religion dans l'Afrique du Nord. Alger (1909).

DOWD, J.: The Negroe Races. New York (1907).

DRIBERG, I. H.: The Lango. Oxford (1923).

DRIBERG, J. H.: The Savage as he really is. London (1929).

– People of the Small Arrow. London (1930).

DUBOIS, C.: Some Anthropological Perspectives on Psychoanalysis. Psychoanal. Rev. 1937, *24*, 246–263.

DUNDAS, K. R.: The Wawanga. JAI *43* (1913).

ECKERT, G.: Prophetentum in Melanesia. ZE, 1937, p. 135 ff.

EHRENREICH, P.: Beiträge zur Völkerkunde Brasiliens. Berlin (1891).

ELLA, S.: Native Medicine in the South Sea Islands. Australiaa Soc. Advanc. Science, 1892, p. 639, or Med. Times & Gazette, London, 1874, *1*, 50.

ELLIS, A. B.: The Tshi-speaking Peoples. London (1887).

– The Yoruba-speaking Tribes of the Slave Coast. London (1894).

ELLIS, E. S.: Primitive Anaesthesia and Allied Conditions. London (1945).

ELLIS, W.: Polynesian Researches. London (1853).

ELLIS, W. G.: Amok. J. Ment. Sc. *39*, 325–338 (1893).

– Latah. J. Ment. Sc. *43*, 32–40 (1897).

EMIN BEY: Reise von Mruli nach der Hauptstadt Unjoros. Petermanns Mitt., 1897, *25*, 179, 220, 388 ff.

EMSHEIMER, E.: Zur Ideologie der lappischen Zaubertrommel. Ethnos, 1944, 141 ff.

ENGELMANN, L.J.: Labor among Primitive Peoples. St.Louis (1883).

ESSERTIER, D.: Les formes inférieures de l'explication. Paris (1927).

EVANS, I.H.N.: Schebesta on the Sacerdo-Therapy of the Semang. JAI, 1930, 115 ff.

EVANS-PRITCHARD, E.D.: Some Collective Expressions of Obscenity in Africa. JAI, 1929, 311 ff.

– Heredity and Gestation as the Zande See Them. Sociologus (Berlin) *8*, 400 ff. (1932).

– The Zande Corporation of Witch-doctors. JAI (1932).

– Witchcraft, Oracles and Magic among the Azandes. Oxford (1937).

FARIS, E.: The Nature of Human Nature. New York (1937).

FARIS, R.E.L.: Some Observations on the Incidence of Schizophrenia in Primitive Societies. JASP *29*, 30 ff. (1934/35).

FEJOS, P.: Ethnography of the Yaguas. New York (1943).

FELKIN, R.W.: Caesarean Section in Uganda. Edinb. Med. Jour. 1884, *29*, 928 ff.

FENTON, W.N.: Masked Medical Societies of the Iroquois. Smith. Inst. Ann. Rep. f., 1940, 397–429 (1941).

– Contacts between Iroquois Herbalism and Colonial Medicine. Smith. Inst. Rep. 1941, 503–526.

FENWICK, N.P.: Notes on some Vandi Remedies. Man. *16*, 83 (1916).

FEUILLOLEY, B.P.: Notes au sujet de quelques phénomènes psychiques observés chez les primitifs du Centre Africain. Bull. Soc. Anthr. *8*, Paris (1930).

FIELD, M.J.: Religion and Medicine of the Ga People, London (1937).

FIRTH, R.: Economic Psychology of the Maori. JAI *55*, 340–362 (1935).

FLETCHER, A., LA FLESCHE, F.: The Omaha. BAE-R *27*, 15–672 (1911).

FLORIANI, LUIS: Materia médica americana en el período pre-Colombiano. Rev. Farm. *83*, 445 (1941).

FORBES, H.O.: On the Kubus of Sumatra. JAI (1885).

FORD, E.: Trephining in Melanesia. M. J. Austr. 1937 II, 471 ff.

FORDE, C.D.: Ethnography of the Yuma. UCPAAE, vol. *38* (1930/31).

FORTUNE, R.F.: Sorcerers of Dobu. London (1932).

– Manus Religion. Philadelphia (1935).

FOSTER, G.M.: A Summary of Yuki Culture. Berkeley (1944).

FRAUCHIGER, E.: Seelische Erkrankungen bei Mensch und Tier. Bern (1945).

FRAZER, J.G.: The Golden Bough, one vol. ed. London (1924).

FREELAND, L.S.: Pomo Doctors and Poisoners. UCPAAE *20*, 57 (1923).

FREEMAN, L.: Surgery of the Ancient Inhabitants of America. Art and Archaeol. 1924, *18*, 21–36.

FRIEDMANN, M.: Über Wahnideen im Völkerleben. Wiesbaden (1901).

FRITSCHE, H.: Der Erstgeborene. Berlin (1941).

FROMM, E.: Escape from Freedom. New York (1941).

FRY, H.K., and PULLEINE, R.H.: The Mentality of the Australian Aborigine. Austr. J. Exp. Biol. and Med. Sc. *8*, 153 ff. (1931).

GALDSTON, I.: The Ideological Basis of Discovery. BHM 7, 729 ff. (1939).

176

GALLINEK, A.: Psychogenic Disorders and the Civilization of the Middle Ages. Am. J. of Psychiatry *99*, 42–54 (1942).

GARBUTT, H.W.: Native Witchcraft in South Africa. JAI *39* (1909).

GARRISON, F.H.: An Introduction to the History of Medicine. Philadelphia, London (1929).

– Quackery and Primitive Medicine. N.Y. Ac. Med. Bull. 1933, 601 ff.

GAUS, A.: Ein Beitrag zur Rassenpsychologie (Java). Münch. Med. Wschr. 1922, II, 1503 ff.

GAYER-ANDERSON, R.: Medical Practices of Kordofan, 3. Rep. Wellcome Trop. Res. Lab., Khartoum (1908).

– Some Tribal Customs in Their Relation to the Medicine and Morals of the Nyam Nyam. V. Rep. Wellcome Trop. Res. Lab., vol. B, pp. 239–278, Khartoum (1911).

GAYTON, A.H.: Yokuts – Mono Chiefs and Shamans. UCPAAE *24*, 1–420 (1930).

GENNEP, A. VAN: De l'emploi du mot shamanisme. Rév. Hist. Rél. (1903).

GILBERT, W.H.: The Eastern Cherokees. BAE-B *133*, 296 (1943).

GILHODES, CH.: Maladies et remèdes chez les Katchins (Birmanie). A *10*, 24 ff. (1915).

GILL, R.C.: White Water and Black Magic. New York (1940).

GILLES DE LA TOURETTE: Latah. Arch. de Neurol. *8*, 68–74, Paris (1884).

GILLIN, J.: The Barima River Caribi. Cambridge, Mass. (1936).

– Personality in Preliterate Societies. Am. Sociol. Rev. *4*, 68–702 (1939).

GIMLETTE, J.D.: Malay Poisons and Charm Cures. London (1923).

– A Dictionary of Malay Medicine. London (1939).

GIRALDOS, P.: Enfermedados y medicamentos de los indigenos de Tonkin. Anthropos *3*, 41 ff. (1908).

GOLD, E.: The Birth Ropes of Manguia. J. Pol. Soc. *54*, 219–222 (1945).

GOLDIE, W.H.: Maori Medical Lore. Proc. N. Zeald. Inst. Auckland (1904).

GRAHAM, G.: An Invocation to Remove Choking. J. Pol. Sci. *55*, 116 ff. (1946).

GRANDIDIER, A. and G.: Histoire physique etc. de Madagascar. Paris (1908).

GREEN, L.C., and BECKWITH, M.W.: Hawaiian Customs and Beliefs Relating to Sickness and Death. A.A.N.S. *28*, 176–208 (1926).

GREENLEE, R.F.: Medical Practices of the Modern Florida Seminoles. A.A.N.S. *46*, 317 ff. (1944).

GREENLESS, DUNCAN: Insanity Among the Natives of South Africa. J. Ment. Sc. (1895).

GRIAULE, M.: Le livre de recettes d'un Dabtara Abyssin. T.M.I.E. *12*, 41 (1930).

– Notes sur la variolisation au Godjain et au Choa. J. Soc. Afr. *12*, 117 (1942).

GRINNELL, J.B.: The Cheyenne Indians. New Haven (1923).

GUERRERO, L.M.: Medicinal Uses of Phillippine Plants. Manila (1922).

GUIARD, E.: La trépanation crânienne chez les néolithiques et chez les primitifs modernes. Paris (1930).

GURDON, R.: Khasis. London (1907).

GUSINDE, M.: Die Feuerland-Indianer. Moedling (1931).

– Plantas medicinales que los indios Araucanos recomandan. A *31*, 555 ff. (1936).

GUTMANN, B.: Dichten und Denken der Dschagganeger. Leipzig (1909).

HADDON, A.C.: Headhunters, Black, White, and Brown. London (1901).

177

HAGAR, S.: MicMac Magic and Science. J. Am. Folkl. *9*, 170 ff.

HAGEN, B.: Unter den Papuas. Wiesbaden (1899).

HAGGARD, H.W.: Mystery, Magic, Medicine. New York (1933).

HALL, CH.F.: Life with the Esquimaux. London (1864).

HALLOWELL, A.I.: Culture and Mental Disorders. JASP *29*, 1–9 (1934).

– Psychic Stresses and Culture Patterns. Am. J. Psychiatry *92*, 91 ff. (1936).

– Shabwan, A Dissocial Indian Girl. Am. J. Orthopsych. *8*, 329–340 (1938).

– Sin, Sex, Sickness in Salteaux Belief. Brit. J. Med. Psych. *18*, 191 ff. (1939).

– The Social Function of Anxiety in Primitive Society. Amer. Sociol. Rev. *6*, 892 (1941).

– The Role of Conjuring in Salteaux Society. Philadelphia (1942).

HAMBLY, W.D.: Origins of Education Among Primitive Peoples. London (1926).

HANDY, E.S.C.: The Native Culture in the Marquesas. Berenice P. Bishop Mus. Bull. *9*, 279.

– Dreaming in Relation to Sickness in Hawaii, in essays in Anthr. pres. to A. L. Kroeh. Berkeley (1936).

HANDY, E.S.C., PUKIN, M.K., LIVERMORE, K.: Outline of Hawaiian Physical Therapeutics. Bern. Bish. Mus. Bull. 126 (1934).

HARLEY, G.W.: Native African Medicine. Cambridge, Mass. (1941).

HARMS, E.: "Mentally Sane and Sick" and Primitive Man. Congr. Intern. Sc. Anthr. Ethn. 1938, p. 207 ff. Copenhagen (1939).

HAUER, J.W.: Die Religionen. Berlin (1923).

HEBERLEIN, H.K.A.: A Shamanistic Performance of the Eastern Salish. AA XX.

HEGER, F.: Aderlassgeräte bei den Indianern und Papuas. Mitt. Anthr. Ges. Wien *23*, 83 ff. (1893).

– Neue Formen von Aderlassgeräten. Festschr. F. Schmidt, Wien 1928, p. 275 ff.

HENRY, J.: Jungle People. New York (1941).

HERNANDEZ, F.: Quatro libros de la natura... de las plantas... de la nueva España. Mexico (1615).

HERSKOVITS, M.J.: Dahomey, New York, 1938, 2nd vol.

– The Economic Life of Primitive Peoples. New York (1940).

HESNARD, A.: Les Psychoses et les Frontières de la Folie. Paris (1924).

HEWAT, M.L.: Bantu Folklore. Cape Town (1906).

HILDBURGH, W.L.: Some Tibetan Amulets and Folk Medicines. JAI *39*.

HILL, W.W.: Navaho Rites for Dispelling Insanity and Delirium. El Palacio *41*, 71–74.

HILL-TOUT, C.: British North America, Toronto (1907).

HILTON-SIMPSON, M.W.: Some Arab and Shawia Remedies and Notes on Trephining in Algeria. JAI *43*, 706 ff. (1913).

HIRSCH, A.: Handb. der histor.-geogr. Path. Stuttgart (1886).

HOBHOUSE, L.T., WHEELER, J.C., GINSBERG, M.: The Material Culture and Social Institution of the Simpler Peoples. London (1930).

HOBLEY, C.W.: Kikuyu Medicine. Man. *6*, 81 (1906).

HOCART, A.M.: Medicine and Witchcraft in Eddystone of the Solomons. JAI 1925, 225–270.

HOERNLE, W.: Magic and Medicine, in SCHAPERA, G.: The Bantu Speaking Tribes of South Africa. London (1937).

HOFFMAN, W.J.: The Midewin or Grand Medicine Society of the Ojibwa. BAE-R 7, 164 (1891).

HOFSCHLAEGER, R.: Die Entstehung der primitiven Heilmethoden. Arch. Gesch. Med. 1910, 81 ff.

HOFSTRA, S.: Differenzierungserscheinungen in einigen afrikanischen Gruppen. Amsterdam (1933).

HOGBIN, H.T.: Spirits and the Healing of the Sick in Ontong, Java. Oceania 1, 146 ff. (1930/31).

HOOPER, D., and MANN, H.H.: Earth-eating in India. Mem. As. Soc. Beng. 1, 12.

HOPKINS, L.C.: The Shaman or Chinese wu. J. Roy. As. Soc. 1945, 3–16.

HOWITT, A.W.: On Australian Medicine-Men. JAI XVI, 29 ff.

– Native Tribes of Southeastern Australia. London (1904).

HRDLICKA, A.: Medicine and Medicine-Men. BAE-B XXX, vol. I, p. 838 (1907).

– Physiological and Medical Observations Among the Indians of the Southwestern United States and Northern Mexico. BAE-B 34 (1908).

– Anthropology and Insanity. J. Ment. Nerv. Dis. 56, 215 ff. (1922).

HSU, F.L.K.: Magic and Science in Western Yunnan. Inst. Pac. Rel., New York (1943).

HUBERT, H., and MAUSS, M.: Esquisse d'une théorie générale de la magie. Année Sociol. VII, 1–146 (1902).

HUBERT, H.: Revue de Thorndike: History of Magic. Année Sociol., Paris 1924, p. 479.

HUNTER, M.: Reaction to Conquest. Oxford (1936).

IDEN-ZELLER, O.: Ethnologische Betrachtungen bei den Tchuktschen. ZE 43, 855 ff. (1911).

IM THURN, F.: Among the Indians of Guiana. London (1883).

IRELAND, W.W.: Psychology of the Crusades. J. Ment. Sc. 53, 322 (1906/07).

IVENS, W.G.: The Melanesians of the S.E. Solomons. London (1927).

JAMES, L.M.: Observations physiologiques et psychologiques sur l'homme. Paris (1826).

JARCHO, J.: Posture and Practice During Labor Among Primitive Peoples. New York (1934).

JENKS, A.E.: The Bontoc-Igorot. Manila (1905).

JENNESS, D.: An Indian Method of Treating Hysteria. Prim. Man 6, 13–20 (1933).

– The People of the Twilight. New York (1938).

– The Carrier Indians of Bulkley River. Their Social and Religious Life. BAE-B 133, pp. 469–586 (Anthr. Papers No. 25), Washington (1943).

JENNESS, D., and BALLANTYNE, A.: The Northern d'Entrecasteaux Islands. Oxford (1920).

JETTE, J.: The Medicine Man of the Ten'a. JAI 37, 157 ff. (1907).

JOCHELSON, W.: The Koryak. Leiden-New York (1907).

JOHNSON, F.: Notes of MicMac Shamans. Prim. Man 6, 53-80 (1943).

JOHNSON, JAMES: Reality Versus Romance in South Central Africa. New York (1893).

JONES, V.H.: Fossil Bones in Medicine. AA 44, 162 (1942).

JOSEPH, ALICE: Physician and Patient. Applied Anthropology 1 (1942).

JUNOD, H.A.: The Life of a South African Tribe. 2 vol. London (1927).

179

KANNER, L.: Mistletoe, Magic and Medicine. BHM *7*, 875 ff. (1939).

KARDINER, A.: The Individual and His Society. New York (1939).

KARSTEN, R.: Blood Revenge, War and Victory Feasts among the Jibaro Indians. BAE-B *79*, Washington (1923).

– The Civilization of the South American Indian. London (1926).

KEESING, F. M.: Modern Samoa. London (1934).

KEITH, A.: What Should Museums Do For Us? Janus, 1926, pp. 344–352.

KELLY, I. T.: Southern Paiute Shamanism. Anthr. Rec. Univ. Cal., vol. 2, No. 4 (1939).

KELTZ, B. F.: Medicine Men of the Southwestern Indians. Univ. of Kansas Rev. 1942, 189 ff.

KEMPF, E. J.: The Probable Origin of Man's Belief in Sympathetic Magic. Med. Jour. and Rec. *33*, 29 ff. (1931).

KENNEDY, A. G.: Field Note on Vaitupu, Ellice Islands. Mem. Polyn. Soc. *9*, New Plymouth (1931).

KERN, H.: Menschenfleisch als Arznei. Int. Arch. Ethn. Leyden, 1896, suppl. IX.

KINGSLEY, M. H.: West African Studies. London (1899).

KLEIWEG, DE ZWAAN, J.P.: De Geneeskund der Minangkabau-Maleiers. Amsterdam (1910).

– Die Heilkunde der Niasser. Haag (1913).

KLEMENTZ, D.: Buriats. Hastings Enc. Rel. Eth. *3*, 15.

KLINEBERG, O.: Social Psychology. New York (1940).

KLUCKHOHN, CLYDE: The Influence of Psychiatry on Anthropology in America During the Past One Hundred Years, in 100 yrs. of Am. Psy., New York, 1944, p. 589 ff.

– Covert Culture and Administrative Problems. AA *45*, 213-227 (1943).

KOCH-GRUENBERG, L.: Zaubersprüche der Taulipang. Arch. Anth. N.S. *13*, 371 ff.

– Vom Roroima zum Orinoko. Stuttgart (1923).

KOHLER, M.: Die Krankengeschichte eines Zulukaffern. A *26*, 585 ff. (1931).

KOOTZ-KRETSCHMER, E.: Die Safwa. Berlin (1926).

KORITSCHONER, H.: An East African Treatment for Phys. Disorders. JAI *66*, 209 (1936).

KOTY, J.: Die Behandlung der Alten und Kranken bei den Naturvölkern. Stuttgart (1934).

KOWALZIG: Ärztliche Beobachtungen unter den Coemba, in BAUMANN, H.: Lunda. Berlin (1935).

KRAEPELIN, E.: Vergleichende Psychiatrie. Clb. Nervkrk. Psych. *27*, 433 ff. (1904).

KRAUSE, F.: In den Wildnissen Brasiliens. Leipzig (1911).

KRAUSS, H.: Volksmedizinische Beobachtungen bei den Küstennegern Deutsch-Ostafrikas. Korrbl. Anthr. Ethn. Urgesch. (1918).

KREEMER, J.: Medicine in Northwest Sumatra. Janus *20* (1915).

KROEBER, A. L.: Observations in Hawaiian Anthropology. Am. Anthr. (1921).

– Handb. of the Ind. of Calif. BAE-B *78* (1925).

– in Bentley: The Problems of Mental Disorder. New York (1934).

– History and Science in Anthropology. Am. Anthr. *37*, 539 ff. (1935).

– Psychosis or Social Sanction. Char. and Personal. *8*, 204 ff. (1939/40).

– Franz Boas: The Man (Franz Boas, 1858–1942). Memoir Series of the Am. Anth. *61*, Menasha (1943).

KRZYWICKI, L.: Primitive Society and its Vital Statistics. London (1934).
KUELZ: Chirurgie und Rassenpsychologie in den Tropen. Med. Klin. 1912, pp. 214 ff.
KYRLE, ROGER MONEY: Superstition and Society. London (1939).
LA BARRE, W.: Some Mechanisms of Primitive Psychotherapy. JASP (1946).
LA FLESCHE, F.: The Omaha Buffalo Medicine Man. J. A. Folkl., vol. III, p. 215 (1890).
LAGERCRANTZ, S.: The Chewing Brush in Africa. Ethnos 2, 63 ff. (1946).
– Fingerverstümmelung in Afrika. ZE 67, 129 ff. (1935).
– Zur Verbreitung der Monorchie. ZE 70, 199 ff. (1938).
LAIDLER, P. W.: The Magic Medicine of the Hottentots. S. Afr. J. Sc. 25, 433–447.
LAMSON, H. D.: Social Pathology in China (1935).
LANDIS, R.: The Personality of the Ojibwa. Char. & Pers. 6, 51 ff. (1937).
– The Abnormal among the Ojibwa. JASP 33, 14–33 (1938).
LANDTMAN, G.: The Kiwai Papuans. London (1927).
LARSEN, N. P.: Medical Art in Ancient Hawaii. 53 Ann. Rep. Haw. Hist. Soc.,
   pp. 27 ff. (1946).
LASTRES, J. B.: Medicina Aborigen Peruana. Rep. Mus. Nao. 12, 61 ff. (1943).
LAUBSCHER, B. J.: Sex, Custom, and Psychopathology. London (1937).
LAUFER, B.: Geophagy. Field Mus. Publ. 280, 101–198 (1930).
LAUFER, G.: Beiträge zur Kenntnis der tibetischen Medizin. Berlin (1900).
LAWRENCE, R. M.: Primitive Psychotherapy and Quackery. Boston (1910).
LAYARD, J.: Shamanism in Malekula. JAI 60, 526–550 (1930).
– Stone Men of Malekula. London (1942).
LEBZELTER, V.: Zur Heilkunde der Bergdama. ZE, 297 ff. (1928)
LE DANTEC, F.: Traité de Biologie. Paris (1911).
LEECHMAN, D.: Trephined Skulls from British Columbia. Trans. Royal Soc.
   Canada, Sec. II, 99–102. (1944)
LEH, L. L.: The Shaman in Aboriginal American Society. Univ. Col. Stud. 20,
   199–203 (1934).
LEHMANN, A.: Aberglaube und Zauberei. Stuttgart (1898).
LEIGHTON, D. C.: El Indio y la Medicina Indigen. a. Am. Indig. 3, 127–133 (1943).
LEIGHTON, A. H., and D. C.: Some Types of Uneasiness and Fear in Navaho Com-
   munity. AA 44, 194–209 (1942).
– Elements of Psychotherapy in Navaho Religion. Psychiatry 1941, 4, 515–523 ff.
LEIRIS, M.: Le culte des Zars à Gondar. Aethiopica t. II, no. 4, Paris (1934).
LEONARD, A. G.: Lower Niger Tribes. London (1906).
LERICHE, R.: La Chirurgie à l'ordre de la vie. Paris (1944).
LÉVY-BRUHL, L.: Les fonctions mentales dans les sociétés inférieures. Paris (1910).
– La mentalité primitive. Paris (1922).
– L'Ame primitive. Paris (1927).
– Le surnaturel et la nature dans la mentalité primitive. Paris (1931).
– H. Spencer lecture. Oxford (1931).
– L'expérience mystique et les symboles chez les primitifs. Paris (1938).
LEWIN, L.: Die Pfeilgifte. Leipzig (1923).
LEWIS, J. H.: The Biology of the Negro. Chicago (1942).
LILLICO, J.: The Use of Enemata by Primitive Peoples. AMH S. III, 3, 55 ff. (1941).
– Primitive Blood-letting. AMH Ser. 3, 2, 133–139 (1940).
LINDBLOM, G.: The Akamba. Uppsala (1920).

181

LINTON, R.: Annual Ceremony of the Pawnee Medicine Men. Field Mus. Leaflet *8* (1923).

- The Tanala. Chicago (1933).
- The Science of Man in the World Crisis. New York (1945).

LIPINSKA, M.: Histoire des femmes médecines. Paris (1900).

LLEWELLYN, K.N., and HOEBEL, E.A.: The Cheyenne Way. Norman, Okla. (1941).

LOEB, E.: Shaman and Seer. AA *31*, 61 ff. (1929).

LOPATIN, J.A.: Social Life and Religion of the Indians in Kitimat, Brit. Col. Los Angeles (1945).

LOPEZ, C.: Ethnographische Betrachtungen zur Schizophrenie. Zschr. ges. Neur. Psych. *142*, 706 (1932).

LOPEZ, L.V.: Apuntes para la historia médico-quirúrgica de los Yungas. An. Soc. Perudna Hist. Med., 1940, 58–63 (1942).

LOWIE, R.H.: The Assiniboine. New York (1910).

- Primitive Religion. London (1925).
- Primitive Society. London (1929).
- The Crow Indians. New York (1935).
- The History of Ethnological Theory. New York (1938).
- An Introduction to Cultural Anthropology. New York (1940).
- American Contributions to Anthropology. Science *100*, 321–327 (1944).

LUBLINSKI, I.: Der Medizinmann bei den Naturvölkern Südamerikas. ZE *52/53*, 234 ff. (1921/22).

LUMHOLTZ, C.: Unknown Mexico. New York (1902).

LYMAN, R.S., MAEKER, V., LIANG, P.: Social Psychological Studies in Neuro-Psychiatry in China. New York (1939).

LYND, R.S.: Knowledge for What? Princeton (1939).

MACCURDY, G.G.: Human Skeletal Remains from the Highlands of Peru. Am. Journ. Phys. Anthr. *6*, 218–329 (1923).

MACDONALD, East Central African Customs. JAI XXII.

MACKAY: Some Notes on Native Medicine. Antanarive Annual *5*, 45 ff. (1893).

MACKENZIE, D.R.: The Spirit-ridden Konde. London (1925).

MACLEISH, R.: Notes on Folk Medicine in the Hopi Village of Moenkopi. J. Am. Folkl. *56*, 62.

MCKEEL, H.S.: Clinic and Culture. JASP *3*, 29 ff. (1935).

MCKENZIE, DAN: The Infancy of Medicine. London (1927).

MADDOX, J.L.: The Medicine Man. New York (1923).

MAJOR, R.C.: Aboriginal American Medicine North of Mexico. AMH (1938),534–549.

MALCOLM, L.W.C.: Prehistoric and Primitive Surgery. Nature, 133, 200 ff. (1934)

MALINOWSKI, B.: Argonauts of the Western Pacific. London (1932).

- The Father in Primitive Psychology. New York (1927).
- Magic, Science, and Religion, in Needham, J.: Science, Religion and Reality. London 19–84. (1926)

MARETT, R.R.: Psychology and Folklore. London (1920).

MARIE, A.: Psychopathologie éthnique, in Traité Intern. de Psychopath. *3*, 469–680. Paris (1912).

MARINER: Account of the Natives of the Tonga Islands. London (1817).

182

MARIOTT, A.: The Ten Grandmothers. Norman (1945).

MARROQUIN, J.: La medicina indigena Punena. An. Soc. Per. Hist. Med. for 1940 pp. 42–57 (1942).

MARSH, L. C.: Group Psychotherapy. J. Ment. Nerv. Dis. *82*, 389 (1935).

MARTIUS, K. FR. PH. V.: Das Naturell, die Krankheiten, das Arzttum und die Heilmittel der Urbewohner Brasiliens. München (1844).

– Beiträge zur Ethnographie und Sprachenkunde Brasiliens. Leipzig (1867).

MASSON, G.: Médecins et sorciers en pays Bamileks. L'Anthrop. *49*, 313 (1938).

MATTEWS, W.: Ethnography of the Hidatsa. Washington (1877).

MEAD, M.: Coming of Age in Samoa. New York (1924).

– A Lapse of Animism among a Primitive People. Psyche, *33*, 72–77. (1928)

– Social Organization of Manua. Honolulu (1930).

– The Changing Culture of an Indian Tribe. New York (1932).

– Sex and Temperament in Three Primitive Cultures. New York (1935).

MEANS, PH. A.: Ancient Civilizations of the Andes. New York (1931).

MEEK, C. K.: Law and Authority in a Nig. Tribe. London (1936).

MEGGERS, B. J.: Recent Trends in American Anthropology. AA *48*, 176–214 (1946).

MEIER, P. J.: Die Zauberei bei den Küstenbewohnern der Gazelle-Halbinsel. Anthr. *8*, 688 (1913).

MEINHOF, C.: Die Religionen der Afrikaner in ihrem Zusammenhang mit dem Wirtschaftsleben. Oslo (1926).

MÉRAB: Médecins et médecine en Ethiopie. Paris (1912).

MERKER, M.: Die Masai. Berlin (1910).

MERTON, R. K.: Science and Technology in the 17th Century England. Osiris *4* 360–630 (1938).

MÉTRAUX, A.: Medecine Men of the Chaco. Nat. Hist. *20*, 6–13 (1942).

– Le shamanisme Araucan. Rev. Inst. Anthr. Tucuman *2*, 319 ff. (1942).

– The Native Tribes of Eastern Bolivia and Western Matto Grosso. BAE-B *134*, Wash. (1942).

– Suicide Among the Matako of the Gran Chaco. Am. Indig. *3*, 199 ff. (1943).

– La Causa y el Tratamiento Mágico de las Enfermedadas entre los Indios de la Región Tropical Sud-Americana. Am. Indig. *4*, 157 ff. (1944).

MEYER, H.: Die Barundi. Leipzig (1916).

– Wunekau. Anthropos (1933).

MICHELS, R.: Les partis politiques. Paris (1914).

MIKLUCHO-MACLAY, N. V.: Bericht über Operationen australischer Eingeborener. ZE *12*, 526 (1882).

MILNE, E.: Home of an Eastern Clan. Oxford (1924).

MOFFAT, R.: Missionary Labors in South Africa. London (1844).

MOLL, A. A.: Aesculapius in Latin America. Philadelphia (1944).

MONARDES, N.: Joyful News Out of the New Found World. Reprint, London (1925).

MONTAGU, M. F., ASHLEY: The Origin of Subincision in Australia. Oceania *8*, 193–207 (1937).

– Coming into Being among the Australian Aborigines. New York (1938).

MOODIE, R. L.: Injuries to the Head Among the Pre-Columbian Peruvians. AMH *9*, 277 ff. (1927).

MOONEY, J.: The Sacred Formulas of the Cherokees. BAE-R *7*, 307–397 (1891).

- The Ghost Dance Religion. BAER XIV, 2 (1893).
- The Mythos of the Cherokees. BAER XIX, 3–548 (1898).
- The Cheyenne Indians. Mem. Am. Anthr. Ass., I, 357–442 (1907).
MOREIRA: Geisteserkrankungen in Brasilien. Zbl. Neur. 53, 782 (1929).
MORGAN, W.: Navaho Treatment of Sickness. AA 33, 390 ff. (1931).
MORICE, A.G.: Dené Surgery. Trans. Canad. Inst. 1900/1901, 15–28.
MUELLER, F.A.: Wahrsagerei bei den Kaffern, 1907, 43–58.
MUELLER, F.: Drogen und Medikamente der Guarani, in: Publ. d'Hommage offerte au P.W. Schmidt, Ed. W. Koppers, Wien (1828).
MUELLER, R.F.G.: Die Krankheitsgottheiten des Lamaismus. A 22, 956 ff. (1927).
MÜLLER-WISMAR, W.: Yap, Hamburg (1917).
MUNIZ, M.A., and McGEE, W.J.: Primitive Trephining in Peru. BAER 16, 11 ff. (1894/95).
MYERS, C.S.: Primitive Medicine, in Hastings Enc. Rel. Ethics.
MZAMANE, G.I.: Some Bantu Medicinal Plants. Fort Hare Papers 1, 29–35 (1945).
NADKARIN, K.M.: The Indian Materia Medica. Bombay (1927).
NEKES: Die Yaunde. Kolon. Rundschau, 134–143, (1913)
NELL, A.: Ceylon Olasor Book on Early Medicines. AMH 10, 293 ff. (1928).
NEUBURGER, M.: History of Medicine. London (1910).
NEUHAUSS, R.: Deutsch-Neu-Guinea, 3 vols. Stuttgart (1911).
NGOI, P.: La grossesse chez les Nkundo. Aequatoria 7, 63 ff. (1944).
NIETZSCHE, F.: Zur Genealogie der Moral. Reclam, Leipzig, n.d.
NICHOLS, L.A.: Neuroses in Native African Troops. J. Ment. Sc. 40, 862 ff. (1945).
NIEUWENHUIS, A.W.: Die medizinischen Verhältnisse unter den Bahan und Kenja Dayak. Janus, 1906, March and April.
- Die Anfänge der Medicin unter den niedrigst entwickelten Völkern. Janus, 1924–1926.
- Principles of Indian Medicine in American Ethnology. Janus 28, 305 ff. (1924).
- Die ursprünglichsten Ansichten über das Geschlechtsleben. Janus pp. 288 ff., (1928)
NIORADZE, G.: Der Schamanismus der sibirischen Völker. Stuttgart (1925).
NOEL, P.: Pratiques médicales au Ksouar. L'Anthrop. 30, 551 (1920).
NOLTE, K.: Krankheiten und Heilmittel der Buschmänner. Deutsch. Kol.-Ztg. 3, 629 (1886).
NOMLAND, G.A.: A Bear River Shaman's Curative Dance. AA 33, 38 (1937).
NORDENSKJÖLD, E.: Recettes magiques au Pérou. J. Soc. Améric. Paris N.S. 4, 153 ff. (1907).
- Medicine among the Cuna of Panama, in Fschr. f. P.W. Schmidt, Wien (1928).
- The Use of Enema Tubes among Indians. Comp. Ethn. Studies 8, 194 ff. Gothenburg (1930).
NOVAKOWSKY, ST.: Arctic Hysteria as a Reflex of Geographic Environment. Ecology 5, 113 ff. (1924).
OESTERREICH, T.K.: Possession, Engl. Transl. London (1930).
OHLMARKS, A.: Studien zum Problem des Schamanismus. Lund. (1939).
OLBRECHTS, F.R., and MOONEY, J.: The Swimmer Manuscript. BAER 99, Washington (1932).
OLIVIER, G., and ANJOULAT, L.: L'obstétrique en pays Younde. Bull. Soc. Et. Cam. 12, 7–71 (1945).

OPLER, M.E.: Some Points of Comparison and Contrast between the Treatment of Functional Disorders by Apache Shamans and in Modern Psychiatric Practice. Am. J. Psychiatry *92*, 137 ff. (1936).

– An Apache Life Way. Chicago (1941)

OVERBECK-WRIGHT, A.W.: Lunacy in India. London (1921).

PACKARD, F.: History of Medicine in the United States. Philadelphia (1901).

PALMER, E.: On Some Australian Tribes. JAI 1884, 310 ff.

PANDLER, F.: Scheitelnarbensitte und Kulturkreislehre. Brünn (1932).

PARDAL, R.: Medicina Aborigen Americana. Buenos Aires, N.D. (1937).

PARHAM, H.B.R.: Fiji Native Plants with their Medicinal and other Uses. Polyn. Soc. Mem. No. *16*, Wellington (1943).

PARK, R.E.: Human Migration and the Marginal Man. Am. J. Soc. *33*, 881 (1928).

PARK, W.Z.: Shamanism in Western North America. Evanston (1938).

– Paviotso Shamanism. AA *36*, 104 ff. (1934).

PARKER, A.C.: The Code of a Seneca Prophet. N.Y. St. Mus. Bull. *163* (1913).

– Indian Medicine and Medicine Men. Archeol. Rep. *36*, Toronto (1927).

PARKINSON, R.: Dreissig Jahre in der Südsee. Stuttgart (1907).

PARSONS, E.C.: Curanderos in Oaxaca. Sc. Mthly *32*, 60 ff. (1931).

PAULITSCHKE, P.: Ethnographie Nordost-Afrikas. Berlin (1896).

PECHUEL-LOSCHE, E.: Volkskunde von Loango. Stuttgart (1907).

PETTAZONI, R.: La confessione degli peccati, 3 vol. Bologna (1929).

PHISTER: The Indian Messiah. Am. Anthr. *4* (1891).

PILSUDSKI, B.: Der Shamanismus bei den Ainu von Sachalin. Globus *95* (1909).

– L'accouchement chez les indigènes de l'île Sakhaline. Anthrop. (1910).

PISO, J.: Historia Naturalis Brasiliae. Lugdunum Batavorum (1648).

PITTARD, E.: A propos de la trépanation préhistorique. Arch. Suisse d'Anthrop. Gén. *11*, 56 ff. (1945).

PITT-RIVERS, G.H.L.F.: The Clash of Culture and the Contact of Races. London (1927).

PLEHN, F.: Die Kamerunküste. Berlin (1898).

PLOSS-BARTELS: Das Weib in der Natur- und Völkerkunde. Leipzig, 2 vols. (1899)

POBÈGUIN, H.: Les plantes médicinales de la Guinée. Paris (1912).

POWDERMAKER, H.: Vital Statistics of New Ireland as revealed in genealogies. Hum. Biol. *3*, 350 ff. (1931).

– Life in Lesu. New York (1933).

PREUSS, K.TH.: Menschenopfer und Selbstverstümmelung in Amerika, in: Festschrift für Adolf Bastian. Berlin (1890).

– Der Ursprung der Religion. Globus LXXXVII.

– Die geistige Kultur der Naturvölker. Leipzig, Berlin (1923).

PROELL, F.: Heilkunde der Lappen. Münch. Med. Wschr. (1936).

QUINIAN, C.: The American Medicine Man and the Sibirian Shaman. AMH (1938) 508 ff.

RACHMATI, G.R.: Zur Heilkunde der Niguren. Sitzber. Preuss. Ak. Wissch., Berlin, Phil. Hist. Kl. XXIV, 1930.

RADBILL, S.X.: Child Hygiene among the American Indians. Texas Rep. on Biol. and Med. *3*, 419–452 (1945).

RADCLIFFE-BROWN, A.R.: The Andaman Islanders. Cambridge (1922).

RADIN, P.: Social Anthropology. New York (1933).

RADLOFF, W.: Aus Sibirien. Leipzig (1884).

RASMUSSEN, K.: The People of the Polar North. London (1908).

RAY, S.H.: The People and Language of Lifu, Loyalty Islands. JAI *47*, 239 ff. (1917).

RAY, V.P.: The Kolaskin Cult. AANS *38* (1936).

READ, C.: The Origin of Man and his Superstitions. Cambridge (1920).

REDFIELD, R., and M.P.: Disease and its Treatment in Dzitas, Yucatan. Carnegie Inst. of Wash. Publ. *523*, 49–81 (1940).

REDFIELD, R.: The Folk Culture of Yucatan. Chicago (1942).

REHSE, H.: Kisiba, Land und Leute. Stuttgart (1910).

REICHARD, G.A.: Navaho Medicine Man. New York (1939).

REITZENSTEIN, F.V.: Der Kausalzusammenhang zwischen Geschlechtsverkehr und Empfängnis im Glauben der Naturvölker. ZE *31*, 644 ff. (1907).

RIJPER, C.: Med. Folklore of the Abantu, Transvaal. Trans. R. Soc. S. Afr. *9*, 217 (1921).

RISOTORCELLI, M.: Le traitement indigène de la trypanosomiase chez les Peuls du Fonta-Djallou. J. Soc. Afr. *9*, 1 ff. (1939).

RITZENTHALER, R.: Ceremonial Destruction of Sickness by the Wisconsin Chippewa. AA *47*, 320 ff. (1945).

Report Cambridge Exp. to the Torres Straits (A.C. Haddon ed.), 1908, V. 362; 266.

REVESZ, B.: Rassen und Geisteskrankheiten. Arch. f. Anthr. *6*, 180 (1907).

RICHET, CH.: L'homme stupide. Paris (1919).

RIVERS, W.H.R.: The Todas. London (1906).

– Essays on the Depopulation of Melanesia. Cambridge (1922).

– Psychology and Politics. London (1923).

– Medicine, Magic, and Religion. London (1924).

– Psychology and Ethnology. London (1926).

ROBERTS, S.H.: Population Problems of the Pacific. London (1922).

ROBINSON, G., CANBY: The Patient as a Person. New York (1939).

ROBINSON, V.: The Story of Medicine. New York (1931).

ROEMER, R.: Abortiva der Malaien auf der Ostküste Sumatras. Janus (1909).

ROGERS, SP.L.: The Healing of Trephine Wounds in Skulls from Precolumbian Peru. A.J. Phys. Anthr. *23*, 321 ff. (1937/38).

– Disease Concepts in North America. AA *46*, 559 ff. (1944).

ROHEIM, G.: Racial Differences in Neuroses and Psychoses. Psychiatry (1939).

ROSCOE, J.: The Bakitara or Banyoro. Cambridge (1903).

– The Bahima. JAI (1907).

– The Baganda. London (1911).

– 25 Years in East Africa. Cambridge (1921).

– The Banyankole. Cambridge (1923).

– The Bagesu. Cambridge (1924).

ROSEN, G.: Disease and Social Criticism. BHM *10*, 5–15 (1941).

– The Specialization of Medicine with Particular Reference to Ophthalmology. New York (1944).

ROSENTHAL, S.P.: Racial Differences in Mental Disease. JASP *28*, 301 ff. (1933).

ROTH, W. E.: Superstition, Magic and Medicine of North Queensland Aborigines. North Queensland Ethn. Bull. *5*, 105 ff.

– The Animism and Folklore of the Guiana Indians. BAER *31*, 103 ff. (1908/09).

ROUGIER, E.: Maladies et médecins à Fiji. A *2*, 69 ff. (1907).

RUSH, B.: An Inquiry into the Natural History of Medicine among the Indians of North America, in Med. Inquiries and Observ., vol. I, pp. 55–91, Philadelphia (1815).

RUSSILON: Un culte chez les Sakalava de Madagascar: le tromba. Paris (1912).

SACHS, W.: Black Hamlet. London (1937).

SAFFORD, W. E.: Narcotic Plants and Stimulants of the Ancient Americans. Ann. Rep. Smiths. Inst. 387–424 (1914).

SAINTYVES, P. (NOURRY, EMILE): Les origines de la médecine. Paris (1920).

SANDSCHEJEW, I.: Schamanismus der Burjaten. A *23*, 976 ff.

SANTESSON, C. G.: Einige Drogen aus dem Kamerungebiet. Ark. Bot. *20 A* (1926).

SAPIR, E.: Cultural Anthropology and Psychiatry. JASP *27*, 235 (1932).

SARTON, G.: Introduction to the History of Science. Baltimore (1931).

SCHALTENBRAND, L.: Psychiatrie in Peking. Zbl. Neur. *137*, 168 ff. (1931).

SCHAPERA, J.: The Khoisan Peoples of South Africa. London (1930).

– The Bantu Speaking Tribes of South Africa. London (1937).

SCHEBESTA, P.: Krankheitsbekämpfung bei den Pygmäen. Ciba-Zschr. *1*, 17–21, Basel (1933).

SCHEUNERT, G.: Kultur und Neurose am Ausgang des 19. Jahrhunderts. Kyklos *3*, 258–272, Leipzig (1930).

SCHILDE, W.: Likundu. ZE *70*, 254 ff. (1938).

SCHNEIDER, Otto: Studien über die empirischen Grundlagen des Zauberglaubens. Leipzig (1937).

SCHOTTKY, J.: Rasse und Krankheit. München (1937).

SCHREIBER, J.: Über Bataksche Volksmittel. Janus 1909, 822 ff.

SCHULTES, R. E.: The Appeal of Peyote as a Medicine. AA ns *40*, 689–715 (1938).

SCHULTZ, A. H.: Notes on Diseases and Healed Fractures in Wild Apes. BHM 7, 571 ff., (1939)

– Age Changes and Variability in Gibbons. Am. J. Phys. Anthr. ns *2*, 1–129., (1944)

SCHWEITZER, A.: On the Edge of the Primeval Forest. London (1922).

– Zwischen Wasser und Urwald. München (1926).

SEIDEL, H.: Krankheit und Tod bei den Togonegern. Globus *72*.

SELIGMAN, C. G.: The Medicine, Surgery and Midwifery of the Sinaugolo. JAI *32*, 297–305 (1902).

– The Melanesians of British New Guinea. Cambridge (1910).

SELIGMAN, C. G. and B.: The Veddas. Cambridge (1911).

SELIGMAN, C. G.: Temperament, Conflict and Psychosis in a stone age Population. Brit. J. Med. Psychol. *9*, 196 (1926).

– Ritual and Medicine, in Besterman, Th.: Inquiry into the Unknown. Methuen (1934).

SELIGMANN, S.: Die magischen Heil- und Schutzmittel. Stuttgart (1927).

SEMICOV, B. V.: Die tibetische Medizin bei den Burjaten. Janus, 1 ff., (1935)

SEYFFERT, C.: Einige Beobachtungen über die Ernährung der Naturvölker. ZE *63*, 53 ff. (1931).

187

SHAPIRO, H. L.: Primitive Surgery. Nat. Hist. 266–269, (1927)

SHELFORD, R.: On two Medicine Baskets from Sarawak. JAI *33*.

SHIROKOGOROFF, S. M.: What is Shamanism? China J. of Sc. of Arts II (1924).

– The Psychomental Complex of the Tungus. London (1935).

SHROPSHIRE, D.: The medical outfit of a Wamanjika Doctor. Man *29*, 62 ff. (1929).

SHRYOCK, R.: The Historian Looks at Medicine. BHM *5* (1937).

SIEROSZEWSKI, W.: The Yakuts. JAI *31*, 65–110 (1901).

– Du Shamanisme d'après les croyances des Yakuts. Rév. Hist. Rél. *46*, 311, (1902)

SIGERIST, H. E.: Die Geburt der Anatomie, in: Essays on the History of Medicine presented to K. Sudhoff. Zurich, pp. 194–200, (1924)

– Psychopathologie und Kulturwissenschaft, Abh. aus der Neurologie Psychiatrie, Psychologie und Grenzgebieten, Heft *61*, pp. 140–146 (1930).

– Man and Medicine. New York (1932).

– Developments and Trends in Gynecology. Am. J. Obst. Gyn. 1941, vol. *42*, pp. 714–722.

SIMMONS, L. W.: The Role of the Aged in Primitive Society. New Haven (1945).

SINGER, CH.: Historical Relations of Religion and Science, in Needham, J.: Science, Religion and Reality. London, 87–148, (1926)

SKEAT, W. W., and BLAGDEN, C. O.: Pagan Races of the Malay Peninsula. London (1906).

SKEAT, W. W.: Malay Magic. London (1900).

SKINNER, A.: Medicine ceremony of Menomini, Iowa and Wahpeton Dakota. Ind. Notes and Monogr. IV, Mus. Am. Ind. New York (1920).

SKLIAR, N., and STARIKOWA, K.: Zur vergleichenden Psychiatrie. Arch. f. Psych. u. Nervenkrankheiten *88*, 554–585 (1929).

SMITH, E. A. R.: The Araucanos. New York (1855).

SMITH, E. W., and DALE, A. M.: The Ila Speaking Tribes of Northern Rhodesia. London (1920).

SMITH, H. H.: Ethnobotany of the Meskwaki. Bull. Publ. Mus. City of Milwaukee *4*, 175–326 (1928).

SMITH, H. T.: Materia Medica of the Bella Coola. Nat. Mus. Canada Ann. Rep. for 1927, 47 ff. (1929).

SMITH, H. I.: Sympathetic magic among the Bella Coola. AA *27*.

SODERSTROM, J.: Die rituellen Fingerverstümmelungen in der Südsee und in Australien. ZE *70*, 24 ff. (1938).

SOGA, J. H.: The Ama-Xasa. Lovedale (1931).

SOUSTELLE, J.: L'homme et le surnaturel, in Rivet, P.: L'espèce humaine. L'Encyclopédie Française, t. VII, Paris (1936).

SPECK, F. G.: Medicine practices of the Northeastern Algonquians. 19th Int. Congr. American. *19*, 303–321 (1915).

– Catawba Herbals and Curative Practices. J. Am. Folkl. *57*, 37 ff. (1944).

SPEISER, F.: Über die Beschneidung in der Südsee. Act. Trop. *1*, 9 ff. (1944).

SPENCE, L.: On Medicine. Hastings Encycl. Rel. Eth., vol. *3*, p. 505.

SPENCER, B., and GILLEN, F. J.: The Native Tribes of Central Australia. London (1899).

SPENCER, D. M.: Disease, Religion and Society in the Fiji Islands. New York (1941).

SPENCER, H.: Principles of Sociology. New York (1904).

188

SPIER, L.: The Sun Dance of the Plains Indians. Anthrop. Papers Am. Mus. Nat. Hist., XIV, pp. 451–527, (1921)
– Havasupai Ethnography. New York (1928).
– The Prophet Dance of the N.W. Gen. Ser. Anthrop. *1* (1935).
SPINDEN, H.J.: The Nez Percé Indians. Lancaster, Pennsylvania (1908).
SPIX, J.B. VON, and MARTIUS, C.F.P. VON: Reise in Brasilien. München (1831).
STAESS, A.: Geistesstörung bei den Jakuten. Zurnal Neuropatholic (Russ) *21*, 541 (1927).
STAHL, G.: Die Geophagie. ZE *63*, 346 (1931).
STAYT, H.A.: The Bavenda. London (1931).
STEFANSSON, V.: Notes on theory and treatment of disease among the MacKenzie River Eskimos. J. Am. Folklore *30*, 43 ff. (1908).
STEGGERDA, M.: Plants of Jamaica used by natives for medical purposes. AA n.s., *31*, 431 ff. (1929).
STEINEN, K. v.: Durch Central-Brasilien. Leipzig (1886).
STEPHAN: Ärztliche Beobachtungen bei einem Naturvolk. Arch. d. Rassen- u. Ges.-Biol. *2* (1905).
STEPHEN-CHAUVET: La médecine chez les peuples primitifs. Paris (1936).
STERN, L.: Kulturkreis und Form der geistigen Erkrankung. Sammlg. zwangl. Abh. Geb. Nerven-Geisteskrankheiten Nr. 10, (1913).
STERNBERG, L.: Divine Election in Primitive Religion, XXI. Congr. Intern. Americanistes, Goteborg, pp. 472–512, (1924).
STEVENSON, M.C.: The Zuni Indians. BAE-R *23*, 1–634 (1904).
STEWARD, J.H.: Lemhi Shoshoni Physical Therapy. BAE-B *119*, 179–181 (1938).
STEWART, T.D.: Did the American Indian use the cautery in bone surgery? Am. J. Phys. Anthro. *13*, 83 ff. (1937).
STEYN, D.J.: The Toxicology of Plants in South Africa. Capetown (1934).
STIRLING, M.W.: Historical and Ethnographical Material on the Jivaro Indians. BAE-B *117*, Washington (1938).
– Snake bites and the Hopi Snake Dance. Ann. Rep. Smiths. Inst., 1941, 551–555. Washington (1942).
STOLL, OTTO: Suggestion und Hypnotismus in der Völkerpsychologie. Leipzig (1904).
STONE, E.: Medicine among the American Indians. New York (1932).
– Medicine among the Iroquois. AMH, n.s., H *6*, 529 ff. (1935).
STONEQUIST, E.V.: The Marginal Man. New York (1937).
STRUCK, B.: Afrikanische Ärzte. Münch. Med. Wschr. (1906).
– Pockenschutzmittel der Gaer (Goldküste). Globus *92*.
STUEBEL, H.: Völkerpsychologie in China. Verh. phys. med. Ges. Würzburg *53*, 155, or Fung Chi *2*, 325 (1926/27).
SUMNER, W.G., and KELLER, A.G.: The Science of Society. New Haven (1927).
SUMNER, W.G., and Coll.: Essays I, ch. IV.
SWANTON, J.R.: Source Material on the History and Ethnology of the Caddo Indians. BAE-B *132*, Washington (1942).
– Religious Beliefs and Medical Practices of the Creek. BAE-R *42*, 473–672, Washington (1928).
TALBOT, D.A.: Woman's Mysteries. London (1915).

189

TALBOT, P.A.: The Peoples of Southern Nigeria. London (1926).

TANTAQUIDGEON, J.: A Study of Delaware Indian Medicine Practice and Folk Beliefs. Harrisburg (1942).

TEIT, J.: The Thompson Indians of British Columbia. New York (1900).

TELLO, J.C.: Prehistoric Trephining among the Yanyos of Peru. Int. Congr. Americanists, London, 1912, pp. 75 ff., London (1913).

TEMKIN, O.: Beiträge zur archaischen Medizin. Kyklos 3, 90–135 (1930).

− The Falling Sickness − A History of Epilepsy from the Greeks to the Beginnings of Modern Neurology. Baltimore (1945).

TESSMANN, G.: Die Pangwe. Berlin (1913).

− Die Bafia. Stuttgart (1937).

− Die Baja, 2 vols. Stuttgart (1937).

THALBITZER, W.: Les magiciens esquimaux. Journ. Soc. Améric. n.s. 22, 73–102, Paris (1936).

THOMAS, W.I.: The Relation of the Medicine Man to the Origin of the Professional Occupation, in Source Book for Social Origins, pp. 281–303, Chicago (1909).

THOMPSON, R.: Disease and medicine. Hasting's Encycl. Rel. Eth., vol. 4.

THURNWALD, R.: Primitives Denken. Eberts Reallexikon d. Vorgeschichte, t. X.

− L'économie primitive. Paris (1937).

− Geistesverfassung der Naturvölker, in PREUSS, K.TH.: Lehrbuch der Völkerkunde, Stuttgart 45 ff., (1937).

TITIEV, M.: Old Oraibi. Cambridge, Mass. (1944).

TOOR, FRANCE: Cures and Medicine Women. Mexican Folklore 1, 17 ff. (1925).

TOPINARD, P.: Science and faith. Chicago (1899).

TORDAY, E., and JOYCE, T.A.: Notes on the Ethnography of the Ba-Yala. JAI 136, 39 ff. (1906).

TOWNSEND, J.L.: Indian Health, Past, Present and Future, in La Farge, O.: The Changing Indian. Norman, Oklahoma (1942).

TREBITSCH, R.: Versuch einer Psychologie der Volksmedizin. Mitt. Anthr. Ges. Wien (1913).

TREMEARNE, A.J.N.: The Ban of the Bori. London (1914).

TROWELL, H.C.: The Medical Training of Africans. East Afr. M.J. 2, 33 ff. (1935).

TSCHUBINOW, G.: Beiträge zum Verständnis des sibirischen Zauberers. Halle (1914).

TURNER, G.: Samoa a Hundred Years Ago. London (1884).

TYLOR, E.B.: Primitive Culture. London (1871).

UNKRIG, W.A.: Zur Gegenwartswertung der lamaistischen Heilkunde. Med. Welt, 1934, No. 4.

VALDIZAN, H., and MALDONALDO, A.: La Medicina Popular Peruana, 3 vols., Lima (1922).

VAN ANDEL: Die Heilkunde der Eingeborenen Brasiliens in Willem Piso, Neuburger Festschrift, pp. 16 ff., (1928)

VAN BRERO, C.J.: Einiges über Geisteskrankheiten des malayischen Archipels. Zschr. Psych. Ger. Med. 53, 25–78 (1896).

VAN DER BURGT, J.M.M.: Dictionnaire Français-Kirundi. Bois-le-Duc (1903).

VAN LOON, F.H.G.: Amok and Lattah. JASP 21, 435 (1926/27).

VAN PANHUYS, J.L.C.: About the trafe superstition in Surinam. Janus 357 ff., (1924)

VAN PATTEN, N.: Medical literature of Mexico and Central America. Papers

Bibliogr. Soc. Amer. vol. *24* (1930).

– The Medical Literature of Guatemala. AMH 9 ff., (1932)

VAN WULFFEN PALTHE, P.M.: Psychopathology, in De Langen, C.D., and Lichtenstein, A.: A clinical textbook of tropical medicine. Batavia, pp. 525–538. (1936)

VEDDER, H.: Die Bergdama. Hamburg (1923).

VERGIAT, A.M.: Mœurs et coutumes des Manias. Paris (1937).

VESME, C. DE: A history of experimental spiritualism. London (1931).

VIERKANDT, A.: Die entwicklungspsychologische Theorie des Zaubers. Arch. f. d. ges. Psychol. *98*, 420–489 (1931).

VIGNATI, M.A.: Restos de Traje Ceremonial de! un "Médico" Patagón. Buenos Aires (1930).

VILLAVERDE, M.: Historia della Medicina en Cuba. Habana (1935).

VILLEGAS, A.: Primitive Medicine in the Philippines. AMH 229–241, (1923).

WAFER, L.: A new Voyage and Description of the Isthmus of America (1680–1688), Reprint, Oxford (1934).

WAGNER, CH.J.: Medical Practices of the Yaquis. Texas Teachers Coll. Bull. (1936).

WALKER, ORSMOND: Tuirai le guérisseur. Bull. Soc. Océan. *10*, 1–35 (1925).

WALLIS, W.D.: Medicine used by the Micmac Indians. AA *24*, 24–30 (1922).

WALTON, G.L.: The Prevailing Conception of Degeneracy. Boston M. Soc. J., N. 3, (1904)

WARNECK, J.: Die Religion der Batak. Göttingen (1909).

WARNER, W. LLOYD: A Black Civilization. New York (1937).

– The Society, the Individual, and his mental disorders. Am. J. Psychiatry *19*, 72–83 (1937).

WATT, J.M., and BRANDWIJK, M.J.: Note on a N. Rhodesian Suicide Plant. Bantu Studies *3*, 395 ff. (1927–1929).

– Basuto Medicines, Bantu Studies *3*, 73 ff. (1927x29).

– Medicines and practice of a Sotho Doctor. Bantu Studies *4*, 47–63 (1930).

WATT, J.M., and BREYER/BRANDWIJK, M.J.: The Medicinal Plants of Southern Africa. Edinburgh (1932).

WEBB, T.T.: Aboriginal Medical Practice in East Arnhem Land. Oceania *4*, 91 (1933/34).

WEBER, M.: Gesammelte Abhandlungen zur Religionssoziologie. Tübingen (1934).

WEBSTER, H.: Taboo. Stanford University (1942).

WECK, W.: Heilkunde und Volkstum auf Bali. Stuttgart (1937).

– Die Einstellung der abendländischen Medizin zur Heilkunde der afrikanischen Eingeborenen. Beitr. z. Kol'forschg. *3*, 15–34 (1943).

WEDGWOOD, C.H.: Sickness and its treatment in Manam Island, New Guinea. Oceania *5*, 64, 280 (1934/35).

WEEKS, J.W.: The Congo medicine man and his black and white magic. Folklore *21* (1910).

WEGROCKI, H.J.: JASP *34* (1939).

WEHRLI, G.A.: Krankheitsdarstellungen in den Winterzeichnungen der Dakotah. Jahresbericht der geogr.-ethnogr. Ges. Zürich (1917/18).

WELLMAN, F.C.: Some medical plants of Angola. Am. Med. XI, 94 ff. (1906).

WESTERMANN, D.: The Shilluk. Philadelphia (1912).

191

- Die Kpelle. Leipzig (1921).
WESTERMARCK, E.: Origin and Development of Moral Ideas. London (1906–1910).
WEYER, E.M.: The Eskimos. New Haven (1932).
WHITACRE, F.E., and BARRERE, B.: War Amenorrhea. J. Am. Med. Ass. *124*, 399 ff. (1944).
WHITE, L.A.: A comparative Study of Keresan Medicine Societies. Proc. 23 Int. Congr. Amer. 1928, pp. 604 ff., New York (1930).
WHITING, J.W.M.: Becoming a Kwoma. New Haven (1941).
WIESCHHOFF, H.A.: Artificial stimulation of lactation in primitive cultures. Bull. Hist. Med. *8*, 1403 ff. (1940).
- Concepts of Abnormality among the Ibo of Nigeria. J. Am. Orient. Soc. *63*, 262 ff. (1943).
WILKEN, J.S.: Het Shamanism bij de Volken van den Indischen Archipel. Amsterdam (1887).
WILLIAMS, F.E.: The Vailala Madness. Terr. of Papua Rep. *4* (1923).
- Orokaiva Society. London (1930).
- Papuans of the Trans-Fly. London (1936).
WILLIAMSON, R.: The Mafulu. London (1912).
WILLIAMSON, TH.: Diseases of Dakota Indians (in 1830's). Reprint in Minnes, Med. 1940, 725 ff.
WINIARZ, W., and WIELAWSKI, J.: Imu – a psychoneurosis occurring among the Ainus. Psychoanal. Rev. *23*, 181 (1936).
WINSTEDT, R.O.: Shaman Saiwa and Sufi. London (1925).
WINSTON, E.: The alleged lack of mental disease among primitive groups. AA *36*, 234 (1934).
WIRZ, P.: Exorzismus und Heilkunde auf Ceylon. Bern (1941).
WISDOM, CHARLES: The Chorti Indians of Guatemala. Chicago (1940).
WISSLER, C.: The American Indian. New York (1922).
WITKOWSKI, G.J.: Histoire des accouchements chez tous les peuples. Paris (1887).
WOELFEL, D.J.: Die Trepanation. A *20*, 1–50 (1925); Ciba-Zschr. (Basel), Jg. 4, Heft 39 (1936).
WOOD, C.A.: Sinhalese ceremonials in the prevention of disease. AMH 1934, 483 ff.
WRENCH, G.T.: The Wheel of Health, A Study of a very healthy people (Hunza of Afghanistan). London (1938).
WRIGHT, J.: The primitive medicine man's virtues. New York Med. J. (1917).
- Primitive Medicine. Medical Life (1924–1938).
WRIGHT, L.W.I.: The "Vele" Magic of the South Salomons. JAI *70*, 103 ff. (1940).
WYMAN, L.C.: Navaho Diagnosticians. AA *38*, 236–246 (1936).
WYMAN, L.C., and HARRIS, S.K.: Navaho Indian Medical Ethnobotany. University New Mexico, Bull. 366 (1941).
WYMAN, L.C., and BAILEY, F.L.: Two examples of Navaho physiotherapy. AA n.s. *46*, 329 ff.
YOUNG, J.H.: Caesarean Section. London (1944).
YOUNG, KIMBALL: Personality and Problems of Adjustment. New York (1940).
YOUNG, T.C.: Three medicine men in Northern Nyassaland. Man 267 (1932)
YOUNGKEN, H.W.: Drugs of the North American Indians. Am. J. Pharmacy *96*, 489 ff.; *97*, 158 ff. (1924/25).

ZILBOORG, G.: Suicide among Civilized and Primitive Races. Am. J. Psychiatry *92*, 1347 ff. (1936).

– Overestimation of Psychopathology. Am. J. of Orthopsych. *9*, 86–94 (1939).

ZUCKER, K.: Psychologie des Schamanisierens. Zschr. ges. Neur., Psych. *150*, 693–714 (1934).

INDEX

194